The Hidden Power of Photoshop Elements 2

The Hidden Power™ of Photoshop® Elements 2

RICHARD LYNCH

SAN FRANCISCO | LONDON

SYBEX®

Associate Publisher: DAN BRODNITZ
Acquisitions Editor: BONNIE BILLS
Developmental Editor: PETE GAUGHAN
Editor: LINDA ORLANDO
Production Editor: DENNIS FITZGERALD
Technical Editor: DOUG NELSON
Production Manager: AMY CHANGAR
Compositors: MAUREEN FORYS, KATE KAMINSKI, HAPPENSTANCE TYPE-O-RAMA
CD Coordinator: DAN MUMMERT
CD Technician: KEVIN LY
Proofreaders: DAVE NASH, LAURIE O'CONNELL, YARIV RABINOVITCH, MONIQUE VAN DEN BERG
Indexer: LYNNZEE ELZE
Interior Design: CARYL GORSKA
Icon Illustrator: TINA HEALEY ILLUSTRATIONS
Cover Design: INGALLS + ASSOCIATES
Cover Photograph: ØIVIND SANDUM

LIBRARY OF CONGRESS CARD NUMBER: 2002112917

ISBN: 0-7821-4178-1

SYBEX and the SYBEX logo are either registered trademarks or trademarks of SYBEX Inc. in the United States and/or other countries.

Savvy is a trademark of SYBEX Inc.

Screen reproductions produced with FullShot 99. FullShot 99 © 1991-1999 Inbit Incorporated. All rights reserved.
FullShot is a trademark of Inbit Incorporated.

The CD interface was created using Macromedia Director, COPYRIGHT 1994, 1997-1999 Macromedia Inc. For more information on Macromedia and Macromedia Director, visit http://www.macromedia.com.

TRADEMARKS: SYBEX has attempted throughout this book to distinguish proprietary trademarks from descriptive terms by following the capitalization style used by the manufacturer.

The author and publisher have made their best efforts to prepare this book, and the content is based upon final release software whenever possible. Portions of the manuscript may be based upon pre-release versions supplied by software manufacturer(s). The author and the publisher make no representation or warranties of any kind with regard to the completeness or accuracy of the contents herein and accept no liability of any kind including but not limited to performance, merchantability, fitness for any particular purpose, or any losses or damages of any kind caused or alleged to be caused directly or indirectly from this book.

MANUFACTURED IN THE UNITED STATES OF AMERICA

10 9 8 7 6 5 4 3 2 1

Dear Reader,

Thank you for choosing *The Hidden Power of Photoshop Elements 2*. This book is part of a new wave of Sybex graphics books, all written by outstanding authors—artists and professional teachers who really know their stuff, and have a clear vision of the audience they're writing for.

At Sybex, we're committed to producing a full line of quality digital imaging books. With each title, we're working hard to set a new standard for the industry. From the paper we print on, to the designers we work with, to the visual examples our authors provide, our goal is to bring you the best graphics and digital photography books available.

I hope you see all that reflected in these pages. I'd be very interested in hearing your feedback on how we're doing. To let us know what you think about this, or any other Sybex book, please visit us at www.sybex.com. Once there, go to the product page, click on Submit a Review, and fill out the questionnaire. Your input is greatly appreciated.

Best regards,

Daniel A. Brodnitz
Associate Publisher—Graphics
Sybex Inc.

To Lisa and Julia
for pretending to
be interested, and
Isabel for enjoying
the color.

Acknowledgments

Thanks to Bonnie Bills for the ability to see what other editors did not and for understanding the concept behind this book. Thanks as well to all the pleasant and enthusiastic staff at Sybex, who proved to me that pain is not an essential element to writing a book, including Pete Gaughan, Linda Orlando, Doug Nelson (also of `retouchpro.com`), Dan Brodnitz, Dennis Fitzgerald, Senoria Bilbo-Brown, and Maureen Forys. ■ Special thanks to Al Ward (`http://actionfx.com`), whose enthusiasm, generously open ear, and patience helped me form ideas, concepts, and tools used in the book. Also, David Bookbinder for feedback and testing. ■ Thanks to Victoria Lohvin at Photosphere (`www.photosphere.com`) for generously providing selected images for use in the book. Thanks to Josh Stender and Maria Hernandez at Aladdin who were great in processing my request for an InstallerMaker license for the tools. ■ Thanks to others who don't expect it: Kevin Harvey, Woiwode, Stephen, Mom, Mitch Waite, and Beth Millett, as sounding boards and for providing opportunity, respectively and irrespectively. Mimi, for posing. The Dumenci's for kites. Those abbreviated: AT, LukeD, SB, FZ, TZ, ARW, and other letters. A nod to others who won't see it: Dom, Dad, and Vinnie.

About the Author

Richard Lynch is the author of *Special Edition Using Photoshop 6* and *Adobe Photoshop 5 How-To*, as well as numerous articles on Photoshop, scanning, digital photography and imaging for various magazines. He is the editor of more than 30 photography and digital imaging how-to books. His Photoshop work has appeared in print and on the Web, in website design, magazines, books, music CDs, trade-show installations, and as logos. He currently teaches Digital Rendering at Daemen College and works for a New York software company as a documentation specialist.

Foreword

Some of the best friendships are often unexpected. A little over a year ago, I posted a note to a Photoshop forum hosted by Richard Lynch. I'd seen his book in stores and appreciated his website, though I'd never run into him at the conventions. Shortly after I sent my e-mail, he contacted me. After a bit of conversing, I realized that not only does this guy know his way around Photoshop, he's a heck of a nice guy to boot. I'm pleased to call Richard not only my peer, but my friend as well. ■ I have to admit I used to be a Photoshop purist. That is to say, I was one of those people who scoffed at the idea of any software being comparable to the Big Daddy. Imagine my disbelief when Richard asked a few months ago if I'd ever 1) looked at Adobe Photoshop Elements and 2) considered using Photoshop Elements for design and as a topic for writing and teaching. I nearly spilled my coffee... good thing keyboards are disposable items these days. ■ After a bit of convincing, I did make the leap and check out Elements. I've never once regretted it. Elements has the functionality needed to create graphics that appear professionally done, with an easier dent on the budget than Photoshop. The potential of Photoshop Elements is not immediately obvious, however. That's why Richard wrote *The Hidden Power of Photoshop Elements 2*—to reveal capabilities you might not know existed in Elements, and to give you power-boosting tools that further shorten the list of things that Photoshop Elements "can't do." ■ If you haven't already, *buy this book*. There is not a person on the face of the planet who knows Elements like Richard Lynch (last time I checked, anyway). In these pages, he performs the equivalent of turning a tricycle into a Harley: He takes Photoshop Elements, a very affordable piece of software, and shows you how to make it perform almost like of its big brother, Photoshop. Other books give you the basics; this one gives you both the tools that will make your images look great and the skills to use those tools. With Richard Lynch leading the way, you will be a pro in no time.

—Al Ward

Certified Photoshop Addict; webmaster, Action FX Photoshop Resources (`www.actionfx.com`); author, *Photoshop Elements 2 Special Effects;* coauthor, *Photoshop Most Wanted: Effects and Design Tips* and *Foundation Photoshop 6;* writer, NAPP's official website (`www.photoshopuser.com`), Planet Photoshop (`www.planetphotoshop.com`), and Photoshop Cafe (`www.photoshopcafe.com`).

CONTENTS AT A GLANCE

Contents

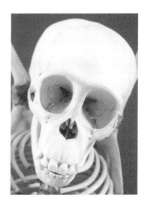

Introduction

I'd been a photography-book editor, digital retoucher, and Photoshop author for ten years, using Photoshop as my primary image-editing tool, when someone asked me to look at Photoshop Elements for the first time. I was a little reluctant, having heard it was nothing but a dumbed-down version of Photoshop, and I expected that I wouldn't find it very interesting and I'd just be wasting my time. From what I understood, the tools I used all the time were missing, including channels, Curves, masking, CMYK tools, and Blend If. I was pretty sure I'd never be able to take the program seriously.

It just goes to show: Never judge a book by how someone else describes the cover.

Instead of being bored with the simplicity of Photoshop Elements, I became fascinated by the possibilities. After toying with Elements for only a few minutes, I found the Recipes palette (now How To) and I was wondering why Photoshop didn't have something where you could reach right into the interface and customize tutorials and how-tos. It piqued my interest. I continued to look around, and within a few days I had discovered ways to either use or imitate every feature I thought I'd miss if I were using Elements. Then I realized that there was a book in it. Elements could do a lot more than most people thought, and more than even the manufacturer let on. It got to the point where I began wondering what Photoshop Elements *couldn't* do, rather than worrying about what the differences were between this program and Photoshop.

Now, I find there are few differences left to conquer.

Since I started working with Elements, one idea became clear to me: tools can actually stand in the way of accomplishing the goal of creating a good image. Some of the tools in Photoshop help you forget about fundamentals entirely, and therefore can isolate you from the process. Ask almost anyone (who hasn't read this book) to make an RGB separation without using channels. This is something that anyone serious about image editing should understand conceptually and be able to do, because it is fundamental to working with and displaying the image. Yet even most experienced image editors wouldn't be able to do it. Knowing how colors separate offers a whole different historical and scientific basis for evaluating, altering, and correcting images and color. It also offers understanding of the way images are created and stored—on film and digitally. It is a better, more fundamental way to look at and understand images from the ground up.

I learned a lot in the process of discovering Elements, and as a result I've gone back to the fundamentals of working with images. *The Hidden Power of Photoshop Elements 2* captures that discovery for the reader, freeing up powerful image properties and tools that help make Elements a serious professional image-editing tool.

What Makes a Good Image?

Photoshop Elements gives you the power to alter any pixel in an image—you can technically do anything. Like a brick-worker building a building, you can get in and create your image one pixel at a time to get exactly what you want. If you know what you like and what you don't, it should be easy to improve on and create images. Just look at the image or canvas and know what you want to see. Once you know—and can trust—what you want to see on screen, all you have to do is make whatever changes are necessary so that your image looks the way you imagine it. The whole thing should be simple, right? Just click a button and fix it, then print and be done with it.

But it isn't always that easy.

The problem starts because of numbers and possibilities. There can be millions of pixels in an image. Each pixel can be one of millions of colors. Every pixel can be altered with numerous tools and options in groups or separately, with changes based on surrounding pixels or considered on a pixel-by-pixel basis. The color and tone of each pixel has to be orchestrated to work together with other pixels adjacent to it to form a recognizable whole. When you are done, that whole has to look as you imagined it. Getting that picture out of your imagination certainly isn't as easy as taking a picture. And building images one pixel at a time overcomplicates the problem of creating what you want to see. Not knowing where to start and what tools to choose just makes the process of working with images that much more difficult.

You have to simplify the approach.

Elements gives you what is potentially a big heavy tool box. Some people blindly fall into a trap, thinking they have to understand and use every tool, filter, and effect, and strap all those tools to their tool belt in order to be able to use the program efficiently or to do anything the 'right' way. There are actually two things wrong with that idea:

- You don't need to know how to use every tool, filter, or effect; you just need the right ones. There are probably many tools (and shortcuts!) that you never use.

- There isn't really a right way and a wrong way; there are harder and easier ways, and ways that are more and less effective.

In Elements there are numerous tools. Not all are essential, some are essentially redundant, some are merely toys, and some are gimmicky, trendy, or unpredictable. While almost all have their place when you get to know them, the ones that are the most powerful, most useful, and most often used—just like the hammer and screwdriver in a carpenter's tool belt—are often not the most spectacular.

A few others have to be coaxed out of hiding, which is part of what the title *The Hidden Power of Elements 2* is all about, and some of what the book will do for you.

Not everything that makes an image look better requires a lot of creativity. There are techniques you can use to make an image look better that require very little thinking at all. In fact much of the initial process of correction should be nearly automatic. If there is a dust speck in a scan, you'll need to remove it; if color correction needs to be done, you'll need to correct it. Although there are a number of different ways to approach making any change, if you've got a few favorite tools and techniques, the process of correction becomes much simpler.

In other words, applying a somewhat limited number of tools and techniques can get you most of the effects you will ever need to improve your images. Using what you have in an image and making the most out of that is often key to getting the best results. Some of the most helpful and powerful information in images is hidden or ignored. This book helps reveal that image content and simplifies the tools you will need to use and apply. With fewer tools (and rules) to remember, you can concentrate on what to do with the images rather than pondering options or quizzing yourself as to how to apply the tools. Using image content to leverage selective changes can help target corrections in ways that freehand work nearly never will. It is a fundamental approach. By using fewer tools, you won't be weighted down by the heavy tool belt. Concentrating on a smaller set of tools and using a structured approach will simplify the corrections you make in any image.

But What Corrections Do You Make?

Say you go to the airport to pick up your cousin who has been in the African jungles for 12 years. No one has seen him in all that time, let alone seen the talking monkeys he was on the trail of. It sounds like a great photo opportunity, so you grab your camera and head out the door.

You meet him at the gate and take some snapshots of him all haggard and weather-beaten from his grueling years living in nature. He looks fresh out of National Geographic.

Later, when you open the images on your computer, they seem to have come out pretty well. But the first thing you probably *won't* do in this situation is add an effect that sets his head on fire. Besides occasionally applying a special effect, the biggest wow you can get from your images will usually be achieved by:

- Taking a good picture that clearly shows an interesting subject

- Using targeted corrections to make those images look the best you can

Most people viewing your picture will want to see the subject of your image, and you can't get that by burying the subject in flames. Special effects have their time and place, but when the subject and image can be good enough on their own, you can do more to improve the look of your photographic images with good corrections. The idea behind this book is to give you a from-the-ground-up method not only for making better images by correction, but also for understanding what makes a better image in the first place. You will find the hidden power not only in Photoshop Elements, but also in your subjects and images. The goal of this book is to make people viewing your images say "wow!" not in response to flames or other effects or magic, but because your images look great.

Much of what used to be my standard process in image correction has been rearranged because of my experience with Photoshop Elements. The result is that my process is now simpler and my images have changed for the better. That was a somewhat shocking thing to have happen after 10 years of experience editing digital images. It was like a carpenter looking at his hammer and suddenly realizing that it actually had two sides and could do more than just bang the nails in. The more shocking thing is that the techniques you'll read about in *The Hidden Power of Photoshop Elements 2* tear down the wall of difference between Photoshop and Elements. I use the same techniques in both programs these days, and—except for a few differences in the interface—I often forget which program I'm in. The most obvious fact is that it doesn't matter, but the hidden fact is that I learned it from Elements, not Photoshop. Using the techniques in this book, you won't often be left using Elements limply and apologetically, as if you were banging in screws with your hammer; you'll be using a regular screwdriver—the proper tool—to fasten your screws.

The Goal of This Book

The goal of *The Hidden Power of Photoshop Elements 2* is to take apart the process of correcting images and the images themselves. You'll learn professional corrections that can be applied with simplicity, and you'll become familiar with the powerful tools you need to know and how they apply to any image. This dissection of process and getting back to fundamentals starts immediately by looking at an essential toolset. The dissection of images starts by looking at tone and separating color into tone before color correction or editing. There can be millions of colors in an image, but there are only 256 grayscale tone levels in a single color component… and that number is much easier to handle. Grayscale tone is the essence of color and content—and creating a better image starts from that simple representation.

This book is for:

- The serious Photoshop Elements user who may feel they are outgrowing or could get more from the program
- Photographers moving into digital imaging who need powerful tools for image correction
- Graphics professionals who thought their only choice for working with digital images was Photoshop
- Anyone who wants to make their images look better

The techniques provided here will help you take your corrections to a professional level without hocus pocus or steps that are impossible to comprehend. It will reveal how to do many things that are generally thought to be impossible using Elements, such as using Curves and Channels, implementing duotones, working in CMYK, and applying image snapshots. —The solutions are used right in Photoshop Elements—with no plug-ins, additional investment, or other programs to learn. You'll see what happens behind the scenes in step-by-step procedures, and you'll be given the tools to move through those steps quickly using customized Hidden Power Tools created just for this book. Though created for this book, the tools will work with any image. These tools empower you to make the most out of Photoshop Elements, and they can be found nowhere else but in this book.

How This Book Is Organized

As you go through the book you will discover a mixture of practical theory, examples of the types of changes you'll make in images, and projects to work on to help you understand the process as well as why it works. Projects are put together so that you don't just complete an exercise or press a button and ogle the result, but so that you see what goes on behind the scenes to help understand what you have done. When you understand, you can apply that understanding to other images predictably—either by using tools provided to drive a process, or by manually applying learned techniques. There are clear goals from the outset of the procedures, and the examples provided assure that you can see the change when they have created the desired result. This understanding will allow you to apply the techniques you learn to other images so that your images can be improved consistently.

You will learn to take apart image color and tone entirely using three-color separation methods, and to isolate image objects and areas in a number of different ways. When you can isolate colors and image areas, this allows you to correct those areas separately from the rest of the image and exchange, move, and replace elements to make better images. After images are corrected and manipulated, you will learn about options for output, including making custom separations to CMYK and duotone. The section on the Web includes everything from how to include your images on a web page to creating animation and rollover effects. Hidden Power Tools are introduced throughout to reveal functionality and simplify procedures.

Chapter 1: Essentials of Images and Image Editing In this chapter you'll learn the basic concepts for simplifying your approach to images and corrections. First you'll learn the basic procedure as a step-by-step process for approaching any image manipulation. Then there is a listing of tools you'll need in different stages of correction and a breakdown of what you want to use them for. You'll also learn all the background you need for understanding the nuts and bolts of your images—not the mathematics and obscure calculations, but the solid theory at the bottom of what you see and how that translates to digital images on your computer.

Chapter 2: Separating Color into Tone This book is not mostly black-and-white by accident. The raw fact is that color in digital images is stored as a tonal representation of color light components. To make good corrections and manipulations, it is best to become an expert in extracting and working with tone. You'll see two ways of splitting color into simpler tonal representations, and we'll look at how black-and-white tone can become color again.

Chapter 3: Manipulating Image Tones Tone is integral to implementing color and making effective color changes. Understanding how to work with tones can make a big difference in the color results. We'll look at doing minor cleanup, evaluating images, and adjusting tone with Levels, Curves, basic sharpening, and advanced masking to isolate image areas.

Chapter 4: Applying Tonal Manipulations to Color Levels and Curves corrections learned in tonal correction in Chapter 3 are applied to color images to show how general corrections of tone and color parallel. You'll see the specific advantages of both tools in color correction and work through specific examples applying each tool.

Chapter 5: Color-Specific Correction Tools Once you've completed general color correction, it is time to get into more selective color corrections. Changes can be initiated by special controls inherent in specific tools, or combined to produce highly targeted and effective results. This chapter introduces Color Range, color-specific masking, History application, duotoning, channel mixing and calculations, CMYK, and controlling printed results.

Chapter 6: Altering Composition Similar to how you can take apart image color, you can extract image elements from an image and then replace, adjust, or remove them. This gives you control over image composition by giving you control of all the objects in an image.

Chapter 7: Shaping and Replacing Image Objects With image elements separated and corrected, you are free to reshape, redesign, and repurpose image parts. Creating new objects is sometimes a good solution for correcting problems, and it brings together many of the techniques you've learned to this point. You'll learn to manipulate tone and color to create object shape and depth and work through an example to create an image object entirely from scratch.

Chapter 8: Vectors Vectors provide another way to control image content, which can be valuable in making resolution-independent, scalable artwork and using printer capabilities to their fullest extent. Do more of the impossible by creating and storing your own custom shapes and applying clipping paths.

Chapter 9: Options for Printing More options exist for printing than just working with your inkjet printer at home. In this chapter, we look at how to get the best results at home, in addition to other options that may be more attractive and less costly than you think. Learn how to print to the edge of the page and get real CMYK prints from your custom separations.

Chapter 10: Creating and Using Web Graphics Web graphics generally follow the same steps for creation as regular images, but some special attributes keep them distinct from images you use in print. Learn to get your images into a web page, but also how to implement a rollover and create image animation.

The Hidden Power Tools

One of the most important parts of this book is the collection of Hidden Power Tools provided on the CD. The tools are meant for readers of this book only, and should not be shared freely. Tools must be installed into Photoshop Elements to be accessible.

To install the tools, first locate the proper Hidden Power installer for your computer system platform on the CD. Installers are supplied for both Macintosh and PC/Windows. Tool installers are available for both Photoshop Elements 1 and Photoshop Elements 2 for each platform. Once you have chosen the installer for your version of Elements and your operating system, initiate the installation by double-clicking the installer. Target the installation by choosing the elements directory when prompted; be sure to read the instructions as they appear on screen carefully. Installing the wrong version of the tools is not recommended, installation may succeed, but the tools will not work, and other functionality may be effected. You'll need a password for the installation, and these are provided below.

Operating System	Photoshop Elements Version	Installer	Password
PC/Windows	Photoshop Elements 1	HpforPE1.exe	hiddenpower1
PC/Windows	Photoshop Elements 2	HpforPE2.exe	hiddenpower2
Macintosh	Photoshop Elements1	Hidden Power for Elements 1	hiddenpower1
Macintosh	Photoshop Elements2	Hidden Power for Elements 2	hiddenpower2

When you've installed the tools, you'll be able to access them from the How To palette (or the Recipes palette in Elements 1). These tools will allow you to access additional tools such as Curves or Color Balance, and they will condense some of the longer step-by-step procedures you'll learn in the book into clicks of the mouse. I expect to expand on these tools even more after the release of this book, but you'll need to have installed the initial tools from the CD in order for additional tools released later to work correctly.

Practice Image Files

All images used as practice files in the book are provided on the accompanying CD so that readers can work along with the exercises. They are Mac- and Windows-compatible and are provided in common formats supported by Photoshop Elements. These images are for educational purposes only, and should not be used freely elsewhere.

Compatible with Windows and Macintosh

Just as Photoshop Elements and the Hidden Power Tools work on both Macintosh and Windows operating systems, the book always gives shortcuts for both so that users on either platform can successfully use the book and techniques. The standard notation for shortcuts gives Mac and Windows keys at the same time: Mac + keystroke/Windows + keystroke. For example, Command+O/Ctrl+O will open an image, that is, use Command+O on a Mac, and Ctrl+O on a PC. The following table of keyboard equivalents will cover almost any situation:

Macintosh	Windows	Example
Shift	Shift	Shift+X
Option	Alt	Option+X/Alt+X
Command	Ctrl	Command+X/Ctrl+X
Control-click	Right-click	Control/right-click

> When following along with the book's step-by-step instructions, use the methods suggested here for accessing the tools, or procedures may not function correctly. For example, opening Levels with the keyboard shortcut (Command+L/Ctrl+L) will open the Levels dialog box but will not produce an Adjustment layer, and this can affect the outcome of a procedure that depends on the Adjustment layer being created.

Going Further with Hidden Power

There are several ways that you can get in contact with me via the Internet. I am interested in your questions and comments as a means to improve the book in the future, to put frequently asked questions to rest, to develop new tools, and to correct any typos or other errors that may have slipped in when I wasn't looking. Use rl@hiddenelements.com to contact me directly. Depending on volume, I'll respond personally to e-mail as often possible, and I look forward to your input. Frequently asked questions will be answered in the *Hidden Power of Photoshop Elements Newsletter*. Additional information can be found on the website for the book or the Sybex website (see the following section).

The Hidden Power Websites

I've set up a website with more information about the book at www.hiddenelements.com. The site includes information for readers, including links to the newsletter, additional tools, tutorials, and a contact page where you can enter comments, questions, and other feedback.

Sybex also strives to keep you supplied with the latest tools and information you need for your work. Please check their website at www.sybex.com for additional content and updates that supplement this book. Enter the book's ISBN, 4178, in the Search box (or search for "lynch"), and click Go to get to the book's update page.

The Hidden Power Newsletter

The *Hidden Power of Photoshop Elements Newsletter* keeps readers up to date on any changes, notifies you of any tools I've made available, and answers frequently asked questions. I send the newsletter to all subscribers several times a month. All you have to do is subscribe to get it. To subscribe to the *Hidden Power of Photoshop Elements Newsletter,* just send a blank e-mail to `hpe-subscribe@yahoogroups.com`. You can also sign up at the newsletter site: `http://www.groups.yahoo.com/group/hpe`. Subscription is free, and the newsletter is available to anyone that wants to join.

Hopefully you see from all this that I don't plan to leave you stranded in deep water. If you have questions, contact me; other people will have those same questions too.

Now let's get on with uncovering the hidden power of Elements.

Part I

Preparation and Concepts for Serious Image Editing

Serious image editing requires serious preparation. Things that can be faked or ignored in your images when you are just starting out become far more important when you look to do serious image editing. You can spend hours correcting something that would have taken moments to fix at the time of capture. The first thing you should do in working with any image is always take the time to capture the best photo you can. In the case of image retouching, you should make the most of a scan and the available information in the image—regardless of how badly it is damaged. The best results require understanding the images themselves and how they retain and display information.

Before getting into image editing, there are some concepts that have to be clear. Understanding these and setting up images correctly can help you bring the right information into Photoshop Elements, optimize image processing, and develop an approach to the processing itself. This part lays the groundwork you'll need for stepping into more advanced concepts.

Chapter 1 **Essentials of Images and Image Editing**

Chapter 1

Essentials of Images and Image Editing

There are really only a few things that can be done with an image, and they all revolve around changing content. To do so, you choose tools and work with tone, color, and composition. That's it. If your process covers color correction, composition changes, and tool selection, you are doing what you should for every image. Following a process and understanding the possibilities gives you a solid foundation to work from. Although the process for each image may be very different, you can use the same set of steps just about every time. The purpose of this chapter is to outline the process for you, and get you set up as you should be. With this foundation, we can then jump into making your images better.

The Image Editing Process

The Tools You'll Need

Basic Concepts of Tone, Contrast, and Color

Understanding and Using Color Management

Resolution

Know Your Equipment

Know Your Images

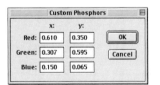

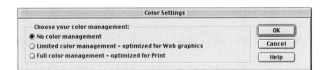

The Image Editing Process

When you go on a vacation, it is often a good idea to make a checklist to help you remember everything you have to do before you go and everything you want to bring along. If you are a seasoned traveler, you can probably do most of your packing and planning without a list. If you are visiting somewhere you've never been before, you might ask someone who's been there what to bring.

When approaching image correction, a checklist can help you ensure that you've covered all the essentials. The list should cover everything you will have to do to an image, and you'll want to do the steps in a particular order until you develop your own preferences and methods.

The following list consists of a procedure I have developed over many years of working with digital images, and it covers all the things you really need to do. For some images you'll skip a step, and for others you might spend hours indulging one step or another. During the process of correction, you will generally want to work from global changes down to smaller and more specific changes. The steps come in three parts:

Preparation Be sure your system and program setup are correct and that you know what you want to do with the image.

Correction Take specific steps to achieve the goal of the image.

Purposing Finalize the image to target it to specific output.

The following sections describe the basic processes of image editing starting with a corrections checklist. However, the most important information you will need cannot be provided by any book; you must know your equipment, and know your images. The final two sections of the chapter show you how to control your own individual circumstances to make your image editing a success.

Image Correction Checklist

Each set of steps in the image editing process is outlined in the following checklist, and this checklist will be the basis for discussion in the rest of the book. Consider this checklist your plan, and consider me your tour guide.

Preparation

1. Store the original image file safely and work with a copy to do all of your image editing. If any step goes awry, you will want to be able to return to the original image to start over, or you may want to repurpose the original in the future.

2. Be sure that your monitor is calibrated and that you have set up your preferences and tested your output. Doing so ensures your best chance of getting the results you intend. (See "Calibrating Your Monitor and Building an ICC Profile," later in this chapter.)

3. Consider resolution and color. Have in mind a target range for the resolution and a color mode for the final image. You may work at different resolutions and in different color modes throughout, but knowing what you need from the outset can help you work smarter, with fewer color conversions (which you generally want to try to avoid). See "Types of Color" and "What Image Resolution to Use", later in this chapter.

4. Evaluate the image. This analysis can include looking at color and tone, determining the image type (high-key, low-key, high contrast), evaluating the extent of work to be done, and considering the composition. The result of the evaluation should be a short list of things you want to improve or change. See "Evaluating Image Tones" in Chapter 3.

Correction

5. Make general color and tonal corrections. Be sure to make a good general correction at this point, but don't spend a lot of time getting it exact. A good general correction will point out some flaws that may otherwise lurk in the image until later in the process. While it isn't bad to double back during the process, it can take your concentration away from progressing through. Overall, doubling back may unnecessarily increase the amount of time you spend on images. See " Redistributing Tone with Levels" and " Snapping and Fading Contrast with Curves" in Chapter 3 and "Levels Correction for Color" and "Curves Correction for Color" in Chapter 4.

6. Make any necessary general damage corrections, such as eliminating dust from scans, fixing cracks and holes in scanned images, and reducing digital noise. See "Do Minor Cleanup First" in Chapter 3 and "Minor Cleanup for Color Images" in Chapter 4.

7. Make more involved color correction. This means do more intensive tonal and color adjustments, but not spot adjustments (using selection). Those corrections will come later. See "Snapping and Fading Contrast with Curves" in Chapter 3 and "Curves Correction for Color" in Chapter 4.

8. Crop and size the image so that you are working with only the image area you really need. See "Cropping as a Tool for Composition" in Chapter 6.

9. Make major specific compositional changes and corrections, including replacing parts of the image with replacement parts you have created. This is the final compositional change. See Chapter 6 and 7.

10. Make targeted color and tonal correction to selected parts of the image. This is really using techniques you've learned throughout to select and mask changes to specific areas of an image. You'll revisit techniques from all chapters 1 through 7 to finish this step. Chapter 5 might hold the most to mine in this step.

11. Make final fine-tuning adjustments to sharpening, contrast, and brightness.

12. Save the layered RGB version of the image. Be sure to give the file a new name, so you do not replace the original.

Purposing

13. Simplify the image as appropriate. This process may include flattening the image or merging layers, altering the color mode, or removing extraneous image information.

Don't delete or merge shape layers that may be important to your output.

14. Make final color and tonal adjustments to optimize the image for output and use. This process can include such changes as setting white and black points and making device-specific color changes.

15. Save the image in output file format.

16. Package the image for output and use.

This checklist may seem involved, but some things you will do naturally and others take just a moment. Practicing correction by following the steps in the list can ensure that nothing gets left behind in making adjustments and corrections and achieving what you intended to do with the image. The tools to use in each of these steps are discussed in the next section.

The Tools You'll Need

In each step of the image editing process, you can usually use a small subset of tools to accomplish your goals. Having these smaller sets in mind will streamline your image processing and keep you on target.

The tool sets listed in Table 1.1 are based on the steps described in the preceding section. These tools are mostly standard ones you already have in Photoshop Elements, along with some of the add-ins you will find on this book's companion CD. These "Hidden Power Tools" can simplify processes or add new functionality to Photoshop Elements.

You may occasionally reach outside these suggested tool sets for a special purpose, but this listing offers a general guideline to simplifying the tools needed to get excellent and consistent results. The choices are based not on which tool is easiest to use, but on which will get the best results.

PROCESS STEP	TOOLS	USE THIS TOOL TO DO WHAT?	LOCATION
1: Store the original image	Save As	Save your image with a specific name and location.	File → Save As
2: Calibrate the monitor	Adobe Gamma	Do free, easy monitor calibration and ICC profile generation in one process.	Your computer's Control Panel, or the Photoshop Elements CD
3: Specify resolution and color settings	New	Set the color, size, and resolution to use for new images.	File → New
	Image Size	Change the size and resolution of an open image.	Image → Resize → Image Size
	Mode	Change the image color mode of an open image.	Image → Mode submenu
4: Evaluate the image	Eyedropper	Sample to check color and tone values in specific image areas.	Eyedropper tool in the toolbox
	Info palette	Display sampled readouts.	Window → Info
	Histograms	View a chart and statistics showing tonal mapping of the image.	Image → Histograms
5: Make general color and tonal corrections	Levels	Adjust tonal levels using simple sliders to effect tonal dynamic range.	Enhance → Adjust Brightness/Contrast → Levels
	Reduce Color Noise	Reduce color noise associated with digital capture	Hidden Power Tools
6: Make general damage corrections	Clone Stamp	Make brush-style corrections via sampling of other image areas.	Clone Stamp tool in the toolbox
	Masking	Customize selections using masking	Hidden Power Tools
	Copy	Copy the selected image area to the clipboard.	Edit → Copy
	Paste	Paste a copied area from the clipboard into a new layer.	Edit → Paste
7: Make advanced color corrections	Separations (Luminosity/ Color and RGB)	Split color into tonal components to simplify and target adjustments.	Hidden Power Tools
	Curves	Adjust tone and contrast with sophisticated, multi-reference point corrections.	Hidden Power Tools
	Hue/Saturation	Adjust color by altering hue, increasing/ decreasing saturation and effecting general lightness and darkness using slider controls.	Layer → New Adjustment Layer → Hue Saturation
	Color Balance	Adjust color by balancing the influence of color opposites.	Hidden Power Tools
8: Crop and size the image	Crop tool	Change the image size by cropping out or adding extra canvas area.	Crop tool in the toolbox
9: Make specific compositional changes	Marquee and Polygonal Lasso	Select regular and irregularly shaped image objects.	Polygonal Lasso tool in the toolbox
	Masking	Customize the transparency of replacement parts and grayscale control of selection.	Hidden Power Tools
	Copy	Copy a selected image area to the clipboard.	Edit → Copy
	Paste	Paste a copied area from the clipboard into a new layer.	Edit → Paste

Table 1.1

Tool Sets

Continues

Continued

Table 1.1

Tool Sets

PROCESS STEP	TOOLS	USE THIS TOOL TO DO WHAT?	LOCATION
9: Make specific compositional changes	Transform	Reshape a pasted object.	Image → Transform submenu
	Guides	Place non-printing edges for alignment.	Hidden Power Tools
	Add Noise	Roughen up tones that are unnaturally smooth.	Filter → Noise → Add Noise
	Gaussian Blur	Smooth out tones that are unnaturally rough.	Filter → Blur → Gaussian Blur
10: Make targeted color and tonal corrections	History Brush	Paint in adjustments from filtered results, such as to target Dodge and Burn.	Hidden Power Tools
	Gradient Map	Influence specific tones and colors using gradients.	Layer → New Adjustment Layer → Gradient Map
	Blend Mask	Influence specific tones and colors using tone and color measurement.	Hidden Power Tools
11: Make final fine-tuning adjustments	Unsharp Masking	Work with both local and fine contrast in the image to improve edge definition and contrast in color and tone.	Filter → Sharpen → Unsharp Mask
12: Save the image	Save As	Save with a new filename.	File → Save As
13: Simplify as appropriate	Merge	Remove extra layers and image content when there are vector layers to preserve.	Layers → Merge Linked, Layers → Merge Visible, Layers → Merge Down
	Flatten	Remove extra layers and image content when there are no vector layers to preserve.	Layers → Flatten Image
	Type To Paths	Globalize type by converting to vector layers.	Hidden Power Tools
14: Optimize the image for final output and use	Mode	Convert to final color space.	Image → Mode submenu
	Levels	Adjust tone.	Enhance → Adjust Brightness/Contrast → Levels
	Blend Mask	Adjust white point.	Hidden Power Tools
	Separations (CMYK and Duotone)	Create separations for print ready files.	Hidden Power Tools
15: Save in output file format	Save As	Save with a new filename.	File → Save As
	Save For Web	Save Web images with limited color and transparency.	File → Save For Web
	DCS Templates	Use custom files to allow unsupported color modes (CMYK and spot color).	Hidden Power Tools

These tools will all be explored in this book as part of the exercises in making image corrections. This listing cuts out many tools, most of which provide redundant (and sometimes inferior) means of completing tasks. If you follow the methods described here you will find that tools other than those on this list are seldom necessary. Several other minor tools (not specifically mentioned) may sneak in at points during the exercises, but are mostly covered in the categories in the list.

One tool that does not fit into any category, but is very useful, is the History palette, shown in Figure 1.1. When doing serious correction and experimentation, it should become a good friend. When you have taken several steps that have not accomplished what you hoped, or you want to compare before and after changes, a single click on the History palette can step you back to an earlier point in the development of the image so you don't have to start all over again. It's a real timesaver and a helpful tool.

Basic Concepts of Tone, Contrast, and Color

Without light, there would be no images. Light is what shapes the subject of images. It strikes an object that you are photographing, reflects back through the camera lens, and creates the exposure for the image. It also helps shape the object, because shadows and highlights reveal object contour. The subtle interplay of tones and contrast gives shape to objects and defines the subject of an image.

Tonal range is the difference between the lightest and darkest image areas. The greater the difference is between the lightest and darkest areas of an image, the greater the tonal range. The way light and dark tones play against one another is *contrast*. The more stark the difference is between light and dark image areas, the greater the contrast. If tonal range and contrast are not balanced correctly, an image will appear too light, too dark, too flat, or too harsh and contrasty, as illustrated in Figure 1.2.

Creating a dynamic image starts with making the most of the tonal range that exists in the image. Contrast (or lack of contrast) between tones within that range helps further define image character. Not every image will have high contrast and a broad tonal range. Some images may be naturally high-key (light, usually with moderate to low contrast), low-key (dark, usually with moderate to low contrast), or simply low contrast. The goal of correction is to maintain the natural character of an image while adjusting tone and contrast to enhance and improve dynamics. If there are 255 possible grays for your image, and you only use 100 of those, the image is really only 40% as dynamic as it might be. If you adjust the tonal range, the image will become more visually dynamic; if you adjust with care, you won't lose the natural quality of the image.

Both tone and contrast work in almost the same way when dealing with color or black-and-white images: You want to make the most of tonal range and dynamics while maintaining image character. The difference is, when you extend the tonal range in a black-and-white image, you get more potential grays; when you make similar adjustments in color images, you get more colors.

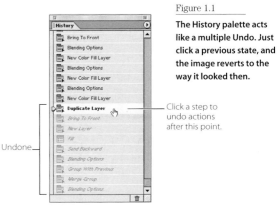

Undone

Figure 1.1

The History palette acts like a multiple Undo. Just click a previous state, and the image reverts to the way it looked then.

Click a step to undo actions after this point.

Figure 1.2

One image can look many different ways, but the best way usually uses full range and flattering contrast.

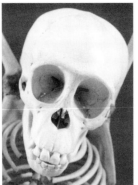

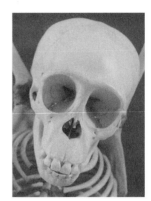

Too light   Too dark   Too flat

Too harsh   Balanced

Color as Tone

Color is a pretty simple thing to manage if you're only picking out clothes, drapes, or upholstery. In those cases it is already mixed and applied for you. If you don't have experience with color mixing, it isn't until the first time you actually try to correct the color of an image that the complexity of color comes alive. If you've never had any training in art and color theory, understanding how color works can be a little confusing. Add to that the fact that there are different color modes (theoretical ways of defining color) and color gets still more complex. However complex, you have to understand color to apply it and achieve the results you want in your images. Because color can be split into simple grayscale components, it is important to understand how grayscale (tone and contrast) can also define color.

For the most part, images that you will work with in color will be in RGB mode. RGB stands for red, green, and blue. It is an additive light-based color theory, where different combinations and intensities of red, green, and blue lights combine to make up the set of available colors. As the red, green, or blue lights are made brighter and applied with more intensity, the resulting color gets brighter, and colors mix in these varying intensities to form other colors. It is a theory that works great with projection, like on your monitor and some projection TVs and the like. Breaking images into their component RGB colors is how your monitor displays color.

Each color you see in an image is made up of these three colors in different combinations. Each of the three colors has just 256 different intensities, which are stored as grayscale information in your image files. Light coming into a camera or sensed by a scanner is actually broken into these three components and stored so the information can be reassembled to reproduce the RGB image on your computer. The theory and practice have been around for quite a while.

One of the earliest photographers to create color images did it in Russia in the early 1900s. Sergei Mikhailovich Prokudin-Gorskii (1863–1944) made glass plates three at a time when he took pictures with a specially designed camera, filtering for the red, green, and blue components of light to record the strength (tone) of each component on what was essentially grayscale film. The plates would record the captured light as grayscale, and then using a special projector, Prokudin-Gorskii would project the images simultaneously with red, green, and blue filters to reproduce the color images on a screen. Figure 1.3 shows one of Prokudin-Gorskii's images; a composited version of this image is also presented in this book's color section. (These plates are from the collection at the U.S. Library of Congress, which can be accessed at `http://lcweb2.loc.gov/pp/prokquery.html`.)

Inside each of your RGB images are the primary source colors: red, green, and blue. These source colors are stored as grayscale representations and mappings of the intensity of red, green, and blue light in every pixel in your image. When you work on color images, the changes that you make affect all three of the source colors at the same time.

Figure 1.3

This image by Prokudin-Gorskii, titled *Man in Uniform, Seated on Chair, Outside*, was taken around 1910 by separating color into grayscale RGB plates. Scans of the glass plates can be composited to achieve a full-color result (as shown in this book's color section).

Red

Green

Blue

Composite

The full version of Photoshop has a palette called Channels, which is another palette like Layers that allows you to get into colors and manipulate them separately (in RGB as well as other color modes). This can be a great tool in making complex color corrections. Although Photoshop Elements doesn't have a Channels palette, this book will show you how to access and alter channel information easily, just as if you had a Channels palette working for you.

Breaking down color information into separations may not always be to your advantage when making corrections. However, the grayscale color components can be separated out of your images, as Prokudin-Gorskii did in creating his plates, by filtering. When they are separate, they can be adjusted one at a time. This can help when correcting color-specific defects, in simplifying an approach to images and corrections, in developing a better understanding of what happens when you apply a tool to color images, and in doing the most complex color alterations and corrections.

Types of Color

Color in your images can be measured in several different ways. In Photoshop Elements, these are *color modes,* which are really just different ways of depicting color and tone. The four modes you can use are Bitmap, Grayscale, Indexed Color, and RGB. Image color mode and file type are two very different things. Knowing which color modes appear in which file types (and which file types to use with a certain color mode) is often essential.

For the most part, people using Photoshop Elements will be working with color images in RGB mode. This mode offers the broadest flexibility for color and tone, and will be the mode most images will originate in (from a camera or by scanning). There are 16 million potential colors in RGB, based on 256 possible tonal variations in each of the three primary colors (256 $\times$ 256 $\times$ 256 = 16,777,216 possible variations). That's one big box of Crayolas! In fact, it is by far the largest color set of any of the color modes you will be working with in Elements. A larger number of colors allows changes that you make to images to blend more evenly.

Generally you will work in RGB for the best access to tools and the most predictable behavior of images. When the image is complete (e.g., all changes you are going to make have been made), then you can consider converting the RGB image to other modes as required for your final purpose. You can save RGB files in many formats, but you will probably most often use TIFF (print), Photoshop (archive), JPEG (Web), and PDF (portability).

Indexed Color is a much more limited color mode than RGB and is almost always associated with GIF Web images. This color set has a maximum of 256 colors. The colors are created as a table using hex values: six-character codes that represent specific colors (see the hex code chart in the Hidden Power tables in the Appendix). The colors cannot be mixed, and must be one or another of the colors in the table. The goal of limiting colors, especially in the case of Web images, is to simplify files and make them smaller. In the case of Web images, this helps transfer them more quickly.

Without any experience in converting to Indexed Color from RGB, it may be obvious that converting all of your 16 million potential colors from RGB into a measly set of 256 colors for Indexed Color may not always produce the best results. In converting to Indexed Color from RGB, almost all of your original color will have to change. Of course, the results can be disastrous to a full-color image. However, there are color tricks (such as dithering) that can make color sets appear larger than they really are. Because color is applied rather than mixed, Indexed Color is a difficult color mode to work in. This color mode will almost always be a last step conversion, and almost always will be done in converting images for display on the Web (when JPEG is not used). They are almost always saved in GIF format.

Grayscale (Figure 1.4) is also limited, but to no color at all. This "color" mode has 256 levels of gray tones that make up all you see in standard black-and-white images, or when working with individual color channels (such as those from RGB images). Generally you should convert images to grayscale when you are printing images without color, so that you can get the best depiction of tone (without depending on the color device to convert color for you). Taking the color out of an image can be simple, but it can also be considered an art, because what looks good in color may not look good at all in a straight conversion to black-and-white. Grayscale images are most often used in black-and-white print jobs.

Bitmap images are like grayscale, but are more strictly formed in black-and-white. There are no grays in a bitmap image: pixels are either white (off) or black (on), as illustrated in Figure 1.5. For the most part, bitmap images are used with line art (pen-and-ink type line drawings). This will probably be the least used color mode of those available. If used, you will probably save in TIFF or BMP formats.

These bitmap images are different from the color bitmaps that used in screen shots and other images on a PC.

a

b

c

Figure 1.4

Grayscale gradients showing white to black gradients in (a) 10 steps (10% darker in each), (b) 25 steps (10 levels darker in each) and (c) 255 steps (every level of gray).

Figure 1.5

The magnification of a portion of the original bitmap image reveals the bitmap patterning.

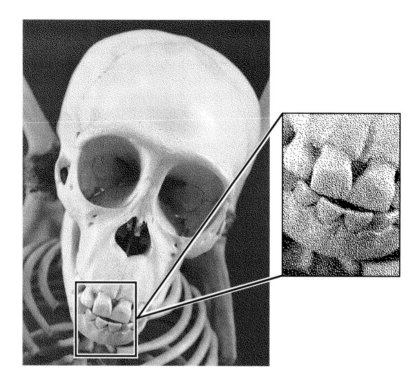

CMYK color mode is not really available to Elements users. It is how color is most often depicted in print. The theory is similar to RGB in that a limited set of colors (cyan, magenta, yellow, and black) are used as inks to create visible color. CMYK at the same time is perceptually the opposite of RGB. While RGB is based on additive color (the more you add, the brighter it gets), CMYK is subtractive (the more ink you add, the darker it gets, because the light striking the color is absorbed). Figure 1.6 shows how two ink halftones combine for a darker result.

Conversion from RGB to CMYK is often a disappointing one, because CMYK can actually portray fewer colors even though there is one more color in the set. The reason for this is probably easiest to understand by simply looking at efficiency. While light is pretty much 100% efficient when projected, the absorption of light by ink pigments is not. Because pigments do not provide perfect light absorption, the color they reflect is not a perfect conversion. Black was added to the CMY color set as an attempt to increase the efficiency of absorption. As an additive, it really produces only redundant color (color that should have been reproducible in a 100% efficient CMY pigment set).

Figure 1.6

Samples of black (45°, left image) and cyan (108°, middle image) halftone dots as grayscale. When the halftone dots are printed over one another (right), colors combine to absorb more light.

There is a supposition that you cannot work with CMYK images in Elements, but this is not entirely true. While the program is not set up to handle CMYK directly, an indirect approach can allow users to make custom CMYK separations and usable CMYK images which may improve printed output. The file format used with CMYK is often TIFF, PDF, or Photoshop EPS. Regretfully none of these will work, directly. However, users can essentially hijack another file format (DCS: Desktop Color Separation) that will allow saving and manipulating files as CMYK.

> Some users wonder—and even worry—about using 16-bit mode for image editing. 16-bit images offer more color detail: where 8-bit can reproduce "only" 16 million colors per pixel, 16-bit can reproduce about 281 trillion. While this difference between 16-bit and 8-bit may be significant for archival purposes, for most cases in the real world, it should not make a noticeable difference in your images. Most output devices can't handle the additional image information, and it is questionable whether technology will meet the 16-bit challenge in the near future, or if human perception can really distinguish between the results. Elements does not support using 16-bit color. The only real gain you would have is in temporarily extending the usable color space for your images while you work on them.

Understanding and Using Color Management

A buzz phrase in image correction is *color management*. If you are not familiar with this term, or if you have heard of it and are embarrassed that you don't know quite what it is, this section will cover all you really need to know. While it is something you should take seriously, it does not have to be as complex or mysterious as it tends to be. This brief discussion will help you get familiar with it, poke it with a stick, and see that it is dangerous if completely ignored. We'll look at your options, get you set up, and get on with the main course of editing images as we pass color management by with a better understanding and a knowing grin.

Color management is supposed to be a means of helping you get better color consistently. By using color management you can have a better chance of your images looking the same from a variety of outputs (print and display). Color management uses a profile that describes how your display handles color to help translate what you see to other devices and how they handle color (via a common color palette and profiles of those other devices). The profile from your monitor can be embedded (saved) with your image file to act as the color interpreter for other devices (monitors and printers).

Every device has its own profile, which acts as the interpreter on its end, essentially so the devices can speak the same color language and adjust for differences. The key to full color management is that every device has to have a profile to be able to interpret other profiles, so the translation will work reliably. The embedded profile will affect images behind the scenes, both to help represent color correctly on screen and to serve as a translator to other devices. In theory, that results in a better image. All this automatic translation sounds very appealing, like I'm serving the chocolate cake first.

This is all nice in theory, but the sad fact is, it doesn't necessarily work in practice. There are a lot of points in image processing where detours or errors can occur. Your profile can get dropped, changed, or ignored, or it can just plain be wrong. Profiling can occur where you don't expect it, and other profiles can be wrong, causing information in your image to be misinterpreted. Any of these can cause unexpected results.

First, you are responsible for building yourself a color profile. You have to set up the profile correctly, and there is no guarantee that you will (even if you follow instructions). Second, every step between saving your image and sending it to the printer has to both respect the color management and process it correctly. This is where the chocolate cake turns to mud pie.

While profiling was planned to function behind the scenes and stay with your image, you can't be sure that the results you get are based on the choices you have made to embed your monitor profile in the image. You also can't be sure that you really want the process to respect your profile (if it is not correct). Embedding a profile doesn't work consistently because it can't be enforced: even if you embed a profile, some device or person along the way can drop your settings. There are devices that don't recognize color management settings; there are services that don't use them in processing. If your results depend on the color management and the wrong color profile is embedded or the profile is missing, you are just as likely—or more likely—to get a bad result than you are without embedding color profiles.

Your only chance for guaranteed success using embedded color profiles is to make a study of how the profiles work, and become intimately knowledgeable about the output types and processes you use. Reading your printer manual is not necessarily intimate knowledge, it goes somewhat deeper than that.

Even with this additional effort, using color management and embedding profiles requires testing. Funny thing is, you have another choice: *not* embedding profiles. Not embedding profiles also requires testing, but it removes the potential complexity of using embedded profiles. In the long run, if you set your system up correctly by calibrating your monitor and creating an ICC profile (which you should do even if you are not embedding profiles in your images), not embedding profiles can actually be more predictable. I find embedding profiles to be an extra half-step that can just as likely trip you up as ease your progress up the stairs—depending on how much you are paying attention. My experience is that you are more likely to trip over that half-step and swear at it than praise it.

None of this is to say that you can't embed profiles with success! You can, and if you do currently, don't change what you do. My perspective on using or not using profiles is a lot like my perspective on images: don't change what works, change what doesn't. If you currently use embedded profiles and everything works fine, stay with it. If you don't, or you have never looked at them, or you don't understand what they are and how to use them, practice color management with the following fast, safe, and effective system:

1. Calibrate your monitor and create a profile (we'll do this in a moment).

2. Don't embed profiles.

To be reasonably successful with color management, all the Photoshop Elements user needs to do is to calibrate, create a monitor profile (which Elements uses for image viewing), and choose how to handle profiles by making a selection in Color Settings. We'll discuss these procedures in the next few sections.

What You See Should Be What You Get

One problem with trusting your visual sense is that it assumes that what you see on screen is the right thing. Regrettably, that is not probable without calibration. All monitors are different, and the settings for display and color will affect what you see. If you haven't calibrated, colors on your screen might look different from colors on someone else's—and worse, they might not match the color that gets printed.

If you are looking at a screen that is shifted green and you depend on the color to be accurate, you will tone down the greens when looking at the screen to make the image look right. This will cause output of any kind to be shifted toward reds. Calibration will help compensate for shifts by flattening the response of your screen.

The goal of calibration is simple: you want to be able to trust what you see on your monitor, within reason. If you can trust what you see, you can mostly use your visual sense to correct your images.

I say "mostly" because even if you've calibrated your monitor, you have merely adjusted it for best performance. You are going to get the most out of your monitor, but the monitor itself may have some limitations. While you probably won't reach perfection, calibrating your monitor gives you a far better chance of at least coming close. With some selective checking, you should be able to feel confident in what you'll get as a result.

Calibrating Your Monitor and Building an ICC Profile

Here I'll show you how to use Adobe Gamma, a utility that comes with Photoshop Elements, to calibrate your monitor. Before you begin, you should know several things about the response and performance of your monitor, including the manufacturer-suggested color temperature, gamma, and phosphor settings. *Color temperature* reflects the monitor display color for the *white point,* which really measures the color of white on your monitor. It is usually 5000, 6500, 7500, or 9300 degrees on the Kelvin scale. It is a characteristic of your display and can subtly affect the appearance of color on screen.

Gamma is a measure of tonal response, often a number with two decimal places between 1 and 3. *Phosphors* are a set of six numbers with x and y coordinates for red, green, and blue; these numbers can be up to three decimal places. These settings vary between monitor brands and models, so don't make assumptions about them or copy someone else's. Find the settings in your manual or contact the manufacturer (via the website or technical support).

> Monitor manufacturers don't always put monitor specs for phosphors, white point, and gamma in the manuals. When you obtain the information, write it down. I usually write the settings right on the cover of the monitor manual for easy reference.

Your monitor should be in an area that will minimize glare, and lighting (except where noted during the calibration) should be as you will have it when you are most frequently using the computer and monitor. Lighting should generally be subdued and indirect if possible. Changes in lighting will require recalibrating the monitor. The monitor can be calibrated to different light conditions, but it is easier to maintain a consistent room lighting than to add it as a variable in color corrections. Extremely bright or overly dark rooms might cause some problems with calibrations and monitor viewing. Optimally, room lighting should be bright enough that you can read and view materials that are not on the screen, yet not so bright that it causes glare or washes out the display. After creating your profile, be sure the lighting where you work remains the same as when you calibrated the monitor.

Before you begin, you should also locate the monitor's brightness, contrast, and color controls. If your monitor has an option to reset to factory settings, do it now.

1. Turn on your monitor and system, and let the monitor warm up for at least 30 minutes.

> Calibration will be slightly different in every operating system and OS version, though the screens will be similar. For example, in Mac OS X, you should use the Display Calibration Assistant. I'll walk you through the Mac OS 9 version, and you can adapt this to your computer.

2. If you haven't done it yet, read the owner's manual for the monitor to see if it provides suggestions for calibration.

3. Open Adobe Gamma by double-clicking the icon in the Control Panel folder. You should see the screen illustrated in Figure 1.7. If Adobe Gamma is not in the Control Panel folder, find it on the Photoshop Elements CD.

4. Click Step By Step. This will lead you through the process of calibrating and creating an ICC profile for your monitor. Click the Next button.

5. In the Description field, type a name for the profile you will be creating (Figure 1.8). You can enter a lot of information here, but it's best to keep it short. I find it handy to name the monitor and add the date, so the profiles are easy to identify. If you use output white point settings (Step 12), you may also want to include this value in the name. Click the Next button.

6. Using the monitor controls, set the contrast all the way up and then adjust brightness until the smaller gray box in the center is dark enough that it is just barely discernable from the larger black box surrounding it (see Figure 1.9). If you notice the white frame beginning to darken at any point, stop darkening the screen. If necessary, adjust the brightness lighter a bit until the frame is bright white again. As you fine-tune this adjustment, it may help to squint or use your peripheral vision to get the center square as dark as possible without losing the brightness of the white frame. When you are satisfied with the adjustments, click the Next button.

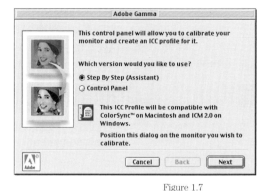

Figure 1.7

The initial Adobe Gamma screen

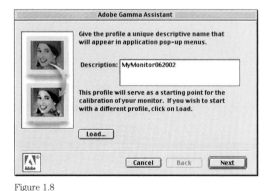

Figure 1.8

Type the profile name in the Description field.

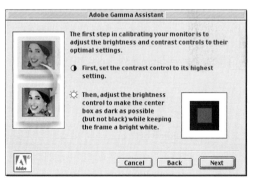

Figure 1.9

Concentric squares help the user adjust the screen contrast by observation while making adjustments to the physical monitor settings.

7. On the screen that appears, select Custom to open the Custom Phosphors screen shown in Figure 1.10.

8. Type the six values obtained from the manufacturer of your monitor in the appropriate fields. You don't really have to know what each number means, but you do have to place each one correctly. Click the OK button to close the Custom Phosphors screen and accept the changes. This returns you to the Adobe Gamma Assistant dialog box.

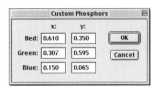

Figure 1.10

Phosphor values describe the monitor's response to color.

9. Click the Next button. The screen that appears (Figure 1.11) allows you to adjust gamma. Check the View Single Gamma Only check box. Using the slider, adjust the appearance of the outer square (the alternating lines of black and white) so that it matches the tone of the 50% black center. Adjust the appearance by squinting at the screen (to blur the box slightly in your vision) while moving the slider. The goal is for the entire square to seem to have a uniform tone.

If you change monitors, you will obviously have to build a new profile. Other less-obvious reasons to build a new profile are: monitor aging and changes in response due to use, replacing your system hard drive, and changing room lighting (or computer placement).

10. In the Gamma field, type the Gamma value you got from the manufacturer. You will be able to enter a two-decimal value, but Adobe Gamma will round the value off when you save the entry.

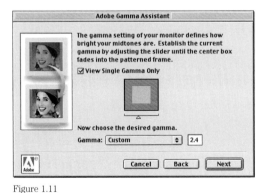

Figure 1.11

Sliders help you visually adjust for the monitor gamma.

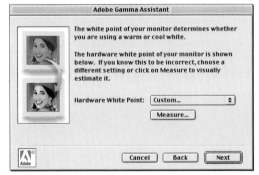

Figure 1.12

White point is a measure of the "color" of the brightest parts of your monitor, measured in degrees Kelvin.

11. Click the Next button. The screen that appears (shown in Figure 1.12) allows adjustment of the monitor's white point. Set the monitor's white point by choosing the value in the drop-down list that corresponds with the number you got from the manufacturer. (If you do not know what value to choose, see the following note.)

A second option on this screen allows you to measure the white point. To do this, dim (or turn off) the lighting in your work area and click the Measure button. A set of three gray squares will appear on a black background. Click the square that seems most flatly gray and repeat until the test closes.

12. Click the Next button. The screen that appears (Figure 1.13) will allow you to select a white point for output. This selection should be based on the color temperature of the intended output media. If you are unsure, or you are creating images for the Web, use the Same As Hardware setting.

13. Click the Next button. The next screen (Figure 1.14) allows you to compare calibration before and after the adjustments you made in the previous steps. Click to toggle the Before and After buttons several times, comparing the appearance of your screen as you toggle back and forth. Specifically, note the grays in the dialog box and see whether the color appears more neutral before or after adjustment. The more neutral (lacking any color, and looking flat gray), the better the calibration.

14. If the before and after results are noticeably different, run through the process again (Steps 3 to 13).

15. Click the Finish button to accept the changes.

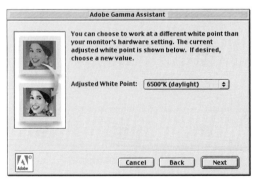

Figure 1.13

Output white point differs from monitor white point. This setting should reflect the color temperature of your output. This may be another monitor, paper, or a projection screen.

Figure 1.14

Compare the Before and After settings by toggling the radio buttons.

> I never calibrate one time and sit back satisfied—even when using a calibration device. I run through the process a few times.

What you have just done is calibrated your monitor and created an ICC profile for it. The calibration helps you to be sure the image information you see on screen is reasonably accurate. The ICC profile is a description of your color space and other data that helps describe how color appears on your system. This information can be used if you embed profiles in your images, to help describe color in your image to other ICC-aware devices.

Although Adobe Gamma is an adequate tool for visual calibration, calibration devices (see the example in Figure 1.15) can measure more accurately than your eye, and will probably measure a greater number of gray levels and create more accurate profiling. The devices take measurements directly from your screen, and create a profile based on those measurements. Using such a device can ensure that your monitor is calibrated properly, and it may actually save some time during calibrations.

Figure 1.15

A calibration device attached to a monitor

Color Preferences

Most Preferences settings in Photoshop Elements are just a matter of personal preference, and they can be changed at any time as you see fit. However, the one you will be required to make a choice about is Color Settings. This is where you can define how Elements handles images with profiles that you open, what color space you want to work in, and whether profiles get embedded in your images by default. The choice you make can be important to your results, and will certainly effect how you work with images.

The Color Settings choices will make themselves known immediately when you first open the program after installing. The dialog box pops up before you do anything. If you have already dismissed this (or want to change preferences after reading this), you can revisit the setting by opening the Color Settings dialog box (Edit → Color Settings), which is shown in Figure 1.16. The three choices seem straightforward enough, but they really don't tell you what they do, and the Help isn't much help.

Figure 1.16

Do most users understand their options here?

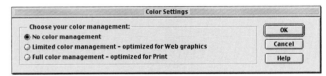

You actually have more than the three options that appear here. If you want to experiment a little, you can open an image using one Color Settings option and close it using another. Changing Color Settings will enforce different rules and create different results. Here are descriptions and some important background information for each choice:

No Color Management This choice ignores any existing profile in an image if one is present when you open it. On saving, Photoshop Elements will not embed a profile with your image. The option to embed a profile is available by choosing Save As from the File menu; to embed a profile, you simply check the Embed Color Profile checkbox. The profile embedded will be based on the ICC profile you created for your monitor. If you change the Color Settings while an image is open, changing to Limited Color Management will offer the option to embed the sRGB profile if using Save As, but will not embed a profile otherwise. Changing to Full Color Management will save a profile fitting to the current color mode (these options are outlined in the following description for Full Color Management).

Limited Color Management Selecting this option will convert to the current profile any profile that exists in an image you are opening. The resulting profile for the image will use the sRGB color space. On Save, no profile will be embedded. The option to embed is available using Save As, and the sRGB profile will be embedded if you choose this option. If you change color management settings while the image is open, changing to No Color Management will allow you the option of saving by manually embedding the profile you created. Changing to Full Color Management will save the image with a profile fitting to the color mode (these options are outlined in the following description for Full Color Management).

Full Color Management Retains a color profile if it is present in an opened image. On Save, the original profile will be retained with the image. The option to disable embedding the profile can be found in the Save As dialog box. Opening a new image (an image with no existing profile) will cause Photoshop Elements to make a decision for the profiling to be retained with the image based on the color mode. These choices are the same when changing Color Settings while an image is open:

- RGB will have the Adobe RGB (1998) profile.

- Indexed Color will have the Adobe RGB (1998) profile.

- Grayscale will have a Dot Gain 20% profile.

- Bitmaps will have no profile.

Notice that if you want to ignore, convert, or retain a profile *and* embed your own (sRGB or Adobe RGB), you can do that by manipulating the Color Settings before and after the image is opened. This may be a pain, and it is something you probably won't do very often, but it can come in handy when you get a bad profile or an opened file does not convert during opening the way you think it should. Attempting to open the image using different settings might improve the initial result.

Color space definitions will be the relative mystery here. A *color space* is really just a defined color set. Some color sets are larger than others, meaning they can encompass more color. You can know the name of the color space, but that may not tell you a lot about what you are working with. sRGB is a limited RGB color space that assumes some limitations of a common RGB monitor to display all RGB colors. Because of inherent limitations in monitor projection, a larger RGB color space may allow you to record color in your files that your monitor can't display. The drawback to that would be that you may be manipulating color that you can't actually see. All this really means is that there are fewer colors in the sRGB color space than in a full-gamut RGB, and that the images you make in sRGB color space are more likely to be compatible with other monitors.

Adobe RGB (1998) is a larger-gamut RGB color space than sRGB. Because it allows a larger number of colors than sRGB, Adobe suggests that it may be a better choice for working with images that are intended for print.

Your ICC profile (you'll see it as the Embed Color Profile choice in the Save As screen when you are using No Color Management) is a custom profile based on the calibration and choices you made while using Adobe Gamma.

You can choose whether to manage color and how to do it. However, the level of complexity and unknowns in working with images seems to rise quite a bit if you choose to embed profiles. Personally, I work with color management off until I get an image that seems to have a profile embedded. In that case, I might try to open the file using different Color Settings to see if I get a better-looking conversion. Otherwise, I stick to the things I normally do because I can depend on them to get consistent results. I never embed a profile (although I might if I were ever to develop a closed workflow where outputs, services, processes, and personnel remained the same).

Resolution

Put as simply as possible, resolution is a measure of potential detail in your images. High resolution suggests that there will be intricate detail; low resolution suggests that detail may be compromised. It would seem, if this description holds, that you would always want high resolution if you consider detail important. But that's not always the case. What you really want is the *correct* resolution, and this depends not only on what size you want the result to be but also on what medium you will be using. Output and display can use image resolution in different ways, so the result doesn't depend only on what the resolution of the image is; it depends on how much there is as well as how it is used.

In print, if you don't have enough resolution to meet the needs of the output, images won't look as sharp as they could; if you have too much, file sizes are unnecessarily large and processing will take longer than it needs to. On the Web, images without enough resolution will be too small; those with too much will be too large. This rule also carries over into other display-based technologies such as film recorders, which makes high-resolution images on film from digital files. You can't really just guess how much image information you need; you have to know the amount you really need and work within those parameters. Understanding what resolution is and how it is used is the only way to use it correctly.

While dpi is really an output term, it's often used casually as a universal term for resolution (spi, ppi, dpi, and even lpi). It can be confusing if you randomly throw out acronyms (abbreviations) when you really mean something specific, but it can also be confusing to use the proper terms consistently. To simplify with better accuracy, use spi when speaking of capture (scan sampling), ppi when discussing digital files, dpi when considering output resolution, and lpi in the context of halftone dot size.

Spi (Samples Per Inch) Capture resolution. The number of scanning and digital capture samples per inch.

Ppi (Pixels Per Inch) Digital file resolution. The assigned number of digital pixel elements to be used in printing or display of an image.

Dpi (Dots Per Inch) Printer resolution. The number of bitmap dot (smallest printing component) an output can create per inch.

Lpi (Lines Per Inch) A measure of halftone dot size. Halftone dots are made of multiple printer dots. The number of rows of halftone dots per inch.

How Image Resolution Is Measured

Image resolution is usually measured in one of several ways: the number of total pixels (image dimension in pixels), the size of the file (number of bytes, kilobytes, or megabytes), or the amount of information per inch (ppi, or pixels per inch). One way of measuring the file size is not necessarily better or worse than another, as long as you can consistently achieve the desired result—without guesswork.

Measuring image resolution in total pixels or file size is not the most intuitive or useful approach for most people working in Elements. Both of these are usually used to measure source image size, such as with scans or images from digital cameras. While the measures tell the quantity of image information in a file, the parameters don't dictate how the information is used. A 2100×1500 image in total pixels could be a 7×5 inch image at 300 ppi, or a 21×15 inch image at 100 ppi—and it can be used that way simultaneously. The number of pixels used in an image measured as total pixels is essentially arbitrary. An image measured with a file size of 12 MB might be about a third larger in RGB than CMYK. In black-and-white (grayscale), a 12 MB image would be much larger still—about four times the size of a 12 MB CMYK image. The lack of a controlling parameter to lock in the size of the image when using total pixels or file size keeps you from knowing exactly what you have and how the image will be applied if you look at file size alone. File size is probably the least-used measure of resolution, and it only really makes sense in a workflow where color mode is static (e.g., images are only either RGB or CMYK).

Most Elements users will use ppi as a measure of image resolution because it is the most compatible in comparing to output resolutions. This type of measure tells how much of the image pixel information should be applied per inch. Because printer resolution is most often a finite measure (based on the printer's dpi: how many printer dots can be made per inch), using ppi measurement makes it easy to determine the optimal match between digital image information and what the printer will need to produce the best results.

What Image Resolution to Use

Some people generalize and suggest using 300 ppi as a standard resolution for images going to print. For Web images is it usually accepted that images should be 72 ppi. While these are pretty good as general-purpose guidelines, they don't tell the entire story. 300 ppi may be more than is necessary for all home printers, and may actually be too little for demanding output (such as film recorder output). Since monitor resolutions can vary, your 72 ppi image on a 96 dpi screen would actually be about 75% of the intended size. Neither choice is very likely to ruin your output, in most cases.

Because output differs, there is no one universal magic formula to figure out what resolution to use. Each output type has a target range (minimum and maximum), based on its capability to process and use image information. If you know that range, you simply use that range as a target when working on an image. Know what your service company or printer manufacturer recommends for output on the devices you use. This may require reading the manuals, or giving a call to the service company to find out.

Table 1.2 shows the approximate resolutions you will want to use for your images depending on how you want to use them. An image sent to a device that uses a specified output resolution should have a specific target ppi. The table shows some real-world examples of output resolution and workable ppi ranges. Calculations for the table were based on the formulas shown in the Calculation Used column; square brackets in the calculations indicate the range of values used to determine the lowest and highest resolution acceptable in that media.

MEDIA	OUTPUT RESOLUTION	APPROXIMATE IMAGE FILE RESOLUTION	CALCULATION USED
Web	72–96 dpi (monitor)	72–96 ppi	ppi = dpi
Inkjet (stochastic)	720 dpi	180–234 ppi	$[1 \text{ to } 1.3] \times (dpi / 4)$
Inkjet (stochastic)	1440 dpi	360–468 ppi	$[1 \text{ to } 1.3] \times (dpi / 4)$
Halftone, low resolution	75–100 lpi	116–200 ppi	$[1.55 \text{ to } 2] \times lpi$
Halftone, normal	133–150 lpi	233–350 ppi	$[1.55 \text{ to } 2] \times lpi$
Halftone, high resolution	175–200 lpi	271–400 ppi	$[1.55 \text{ to } 2] \times lpi$
Lineart	600–3000 dpi	600–1342 ppi	$(dpi/600)^{1/2} \times 600$
Film recorder	4K (35mm)	2731×4096 pixels	Total pixels
Film recorder	8K (6×9)	5461×8192 pixels	Total pixels

Table 1.2

Approximate Resolution for Various Media

Note that these resolutions are suggested and not absolute. Images will still print and display at other resolutions, but the results may not be predictable or efficient. Actual resolution needs may be somewhat flexible based on circumstances, such as paper and equipment used, original image quality, expected results, etc. Be sure to read manufacturer suggestions, and take most of the advice offered by service companies—they should know how to get the best results from their equipment.

Resizing Images

Changing the size of an area that a group of pixels occupies can come in two forms: one causes you to resample an image (using Bicubic, Bilinear, or Nearest Neighbor interpolation), and the other changes the resolution to redistribute pixels over a smaller or larger area. Redistributing pixels does nothing to actually change the content (mathematics) of the image information that is stored; it just suggests that the content will be applied over a different area. Resampling, on the other hand, actually changes the content of your images, and changes it permanently. The larger the amount of resizing (the greater the percentage increase or decrease), the more it affects the image content. One of these two things, redistributing or resampling, has to happen each time you either change the size of the whole image (using Image Size, not Canvas Size) or change the size of a selection by stretching or transforming.

When you upsample or downsample an image or image area and retain the resolution, Photoshop Elements has to interpret and redistribute tonal and color information, either creating (upsample) or removing (downsample) pixels. It does this through interpolation (or decimation), which is really a fancy name for making an educated guess. Resampling an image to make it larger will never fill in information that is not already there, no matter what you do and which plug-in you use. That trick you've seen on TV, where a pixelated image gets clearer and clearer as they zoom in, is reverse engineered. The only thing you can really do to reclaim image detail that you don't already have is reshoot an image or rescan (assuming that the detail is present in what you are scanning). What resampling will do is estimate and average differences between pixels to make a best guess. Details will tend to soften (upsample) or be lost (downsample).

Photoshop Elements has three methods of interpolation—that is, of figuring out how to insert new pixels or remove existing ones as you change an image's size:

Nearest Neighbor Using Nearest Neighbor interpolation, when you resize, Photoshop Elements picks a representative color from the color that is already in the image according to the surrounding color (whether upsample or downsample). There is no averaging to create new colors or tones. It is useful, for example, for controlled upsample of screenshots without blurring.

Bilinear Bilinear interpolation behaves much like Bicubic and is supposed to be faster, but I've never clocked them. During the sampling, new tones and colors can be introduced between existing colors that are not in the original image. This can blur sampling of hard edges, but can provide a smooth transition for tones (Nearest Neighbor might provide a blockier, stepped result). One thing about Bilinear upsampling is that it remains more true to simple averaging between neighboring tones and adds less new qualities to an image than Bicubic (sometimes a good or less good thing). It is useful when you want a straight-forward averaging, which may be useful when downsampling images.

Bicubic The resampling process creates new image information by averaging, like Bilinear, but goes one step further to provide what is perhaps a tiny bit of something like sharpening to the result. This is intended to counteract the blurring result of averaging. It affects change in a greater number of pixels with the same radius setting as Bilinear, but may generally give a better visible result in most cases than Bilinear. It is the real workhorse for sizing images.

While making up information and decimating it sound like bad things, each has their purpose. Usually you should avoid upsampling—especially if the option exists for gaining more detail through a better-targeted source image. However, images can be upsampled with some success, depending on the desired quality—provided the change isn't huge. Upsampling 10% or even 20% may not be noticeable if the source image is sharp. Usually you will only upsample to make up small gaps (if necessary) between the resolution you have in an image and what you really need, or to adjust borrowed image components.

Downsampling, while certainly damaging and compromising to image content, should be less noticeable in your results. Image information indeed gets averaged or eliminated, but if downsizing is being done for the right reason, any details you lose would have been lost on output or display anyway. Detail loss is inherent in the process of downsizing or outputting images at a smaller size: even if the equipment used could reproduce detail at a smaller size, eventually details will pass the limit of the human eye's ability to discern them.

Multipurpose Images

Making images that you'll use with more than one purpose (e.g., print and Web) can cause a little problem. Optimally, you'd like to work with images so that you target the result. Doing so will ensure that you retain all of the actual image detail rather than relying on interpolation or decimation and your choice for sampling type to produce the right results. It is a simple fact that an image going to print on a high-resolution printer should have more information than one at the same size used on the Web, or you will not optimize detail. Your only solutions in working with dual-purpose images are:

- To create two images with specific purpose, or
- To create one image and resize.

Either of these choices poses a trade-off. In creating two images, you sacrifice valuable time by simply trying to achieve similar results in two images using the best process. In creating one image and resizing, you have to allow either interpolation of new image information or decimation, which may not be the optimal process.

You can't work on small images and resize up, because detail will not be present. It is often self-defeating to work on two images to produce the same results (even using a detailed script) because the difference in size and volume of information in the image will produce different results with the same application of tools.

The best way to go about working with multipurpose images is usually to work with them at the highest resolution, and resize them smaller. Working at the higher of two or more resolutions retains the details for the higher-resolution presentations, and decimates detail that will not be reproducible at lower resolutions.

Your Images and Equipment

There are some miscellaneous aspects of working with digital images that may fall into a gray area. Part of working with images on your computer is learning the nuances of systems and software, and having some idea what you expect to do with an image. You are responsible for knowing your equipment and the purpose of your images.

Know Your Equipment

Because all computers and systems are not alike, it is impossible to cover every nuance of every system in every situation in one book. There are innumerable digital cameras on the market, a plethora of ways to get the images off the cameras, and hundreds of home printers to print the result to. Software configurations and utilities can cause problems while solving others, and compatabilities can be an issue with both hardware and software.

If you have trouble getting the images off your camera, or have trouble with your printer or computer, the place to find answers is in the user manual for these devices and through technical support from manufacturers.

The following is a short checklist of maintenance items you should recognize and understand for your computer, peripherals, and software.

Scanners (and analog film)

- Calibrate your scanner per manufacturer suggestions.
- Maintain a regimen for cleaning the scanner and scanned objects.
- Be sure to use proper connections and connection settings.
- Consider having important images scanned by scanning services, which may have better equipment and resolution than you may have at home (e.g., scan negatives and slides to a Kodak PhotoCD rather than on a home flatbed scanner).

Digital cameras

- Choose appropriate settings per manufacturer recommendations, and don't change settings if you don't know what they do.
- Learn about special features and settings by reading the manual.
- Understand image control and exposure.
- Understand how to format camera storage.
- Know how to properly connect a camera to your computer and download images from the camera.

Printers

- Use appropriate paper and inks as suggested by the manufacturer.
- Read maintenance and cleaning suggestions and follow these practices rigorously.
- Don't expect RGB results from a CMYK printer. CMYK is a smaller color space, meaning there are simply fewer colors available.

Computer software and hardware

- Maintain a firewall if using an open Internet connection.

- Use virus protection software to minimize problems with infected digital files, especially if you trade a lot of files. Never open a file from an outside source (even a known source) if it has not been scanned for viruses.

- Maintain a schedule of maintenance for data backup, disk error scanning, and associated digital maintenance (such as defragmenting).

- Check manufacturer websites regularly for software updates, bug fixes, and compatibility notices.

- Keep a log of program installations to help locate software conflicts.

- Don't jump to conclusions. Note multiple problems in the operation of your system. If you have problems with more than one program or device, there may be a common link to the real cause.

- Simplify your system whenever possible by detaching chronically unused peripherals and uninstalling unnecessary software.

Know Your Image

Some matters involved in repairing and compositing images are not really judgment calls, and some are. One thing no book or manual can tell you is exactly what you want to do with an image. While I can suggest proven ways of getting good results, learning to evaluate an image's composition and deciding what to do to improve it will be a judgment call.

Don't ever say it is good enough if it isn't good enough. Give up on an image only when it is not worth the effort to improve it. There is almost nothing you can't do with an image if you have the desire. You can also correct the same image from now until doomsday, improving it in increments all the time. Sometimes putting an image aside for a day or two can give you a new perspective: when you come back to it, you may see solutions you hadn't previously considered. Solutions won't always jump out at you, and sometimes you'll have to manufacture them. In trying to stretch your limitations, no matter what you are attempting to do to an image, chances are you will learn from each solution you attempt.

The more you work with images, the easier and quicker the manipulations will become.

Part II

Wrestling with Image Tone and Contrast

Separating color into tone allows for image repairs beyond the obvious possibility of working with images in black-and-white. It also allows you to ramp up the power of Photoshop Elements by giving you control over what are called Channels in the full version of Photoshop. Understanding the basics of separation in RGB images gives you the power to make other separations, including working with CMYK.

Once you are confident with separation, you can do things to color images that require unique treatment. If your image shows mottling, uneven color, or some other problem that is color- or tone-specific, taking apart the image elements can help you focus on the real problem. It can be the difference between putting a bunch of stitches and some gauze over an image wound and the equivalent of treating it with plastic surgery.

Chapter 2

Separating Color and Tone

Splitting color into tones allows you to change color images to black-and-white, and to work with individual components separately as tone. By doing so, you can simplify image corrections that would be either difficult or impossible. For example, with a little ingenuity you can mask out saturated image areas to adjust areas of purer tone. Or, with pure tones masked, you can limit changes you are making to only a segment of those tones. Before you master complex color separation, you need to learn to handle simple concepts, such as filtering RGB channels and separating luminosity (tone). Once separated, you can work with grayscale components of complex color images. This will allow you to see the importance of tone—not just as black-and-white, but as integral to forming color images.

The Art of Turning Color to Black-and-White

Turning Black-and-White to Color Again

Adding Color to Tone

The Art of Turning Color to Black-and-White

Black-and-white images hold a different kind of interest than color. Sometimes you may want to turn a color image to black-and-white to create black-and-white images or duotones, and other times you may want to remove color from an image so you can colorize it (hand-color, or re-apply existing color to revised image tone).

There is often more to making a good conversion to black-and-white than just choosing Grayscale from the Mode menu. Color images can present about 16 million variations for each pixel, while black-and-white is less robust, in being able to display only 256 levels of tone. Color adds a layer of distinction between objects in an image: things can be a similar tone, or darkness/lightness, but distinct in color. While objects may be easy to distinguish in a color image, they can fail and merge in black-and-white. So when you look at a color image where everything seems nicely defined, and then choose Grayscale, some of the distinct differences wash away with the color. Usually the result—considering how drastic the change is—is surprisingly not catastrophic. Except in extreme cases, you'll still be able to see your subject. Different means of handling the conversion can produce better (and worse) results.

The simplest conversion to tone from color is by either converting the image to Grayscale mode or by desaturating the image (you can use Enhance → Color → Remove Color, or desaturate the image using the Hue/Saturation function). This is a one-step process and each method produces the same results, based on combining tonal values in the red, green, and blue channels of an RGB image in specific percentages.

The result of the straightforward conversion to tone may not result in the black-and-white image you'd expect to see. The converted image can be rather blah, lacking definition and contrast between objects. Looking to other qualities that exist, hidden in the color of the image, can help provide sources for improving the result.

There are various ways to separate out tones based on color, luminosity (brightness or tone), and saturation. Once you learn to make separations, you can use the information to replace, supplement, and combine with other tones to produce improved results. Separating tone can also isolate image components for necessary repairs, and is often a handy technique to use during image restorations.

For our first trick, we'll be doing the impossible by separating a color image into RGB color channels. It is impossible because Photoshop Elements does not have channels, at least not as part of the interface. There is, however, more than one way to coax separate RGB channels out of an image in Elements, and with one of these methods you can reveal the RGB channel information for any image. In this case we'll be separating the channels in the Layers palette. In doing this, you can see how separations work and create at least three sources for working with tone in your image—all at the same time.

Splitting RGB Colors into Tones (or Channels)

Just because a tool is not in the Photoshop Elements program interface does not mean it can't be mimicked or invoked in another way. In the case of channels and separations, the interface for channels may be missing, but the light components of the image are still there. The red, green, and blue color information exists in your color images or else you wouldn't have color. Just like Prokudin-Gorskii, who took an image and separated it into RGB components, you will be able to take any image and split out the components by filtering for red, green, and blue in the layers. This will allow you to mimic channels and take a better look at the tone information as separate color components.

First, we'll look at how to make RGB separations with a long, but rather simple step-by-step process. The process mimics Prokudin-Gorskii's in that you will take an image and separate out the color components by applying filters, in this case using layer modes and a few simple color properties. There is an automated way to do the same thing using the Hidden Power Tools included on the book's companion CD. These tools are provided so that you don't have to do the manual steps for the separation each time you need it. However, don't just skip the steps and go right for the automated tools, because you won't learn anything. What you learn here is imperative in preparing you for more difficult separation and image control challenges to come.

This set of steps was designed to work with a flattened image. Follow along using the sample image `lily.psd` (an orange flower) provided on the CD.

First, create the red channel:

1. Open the image you want to separate.

2. Duplicate the Background layer (Layer → Duplicate Layer). In the dialog box that appears, change the name of the layer to Red. Click OK.

> You'll often need to return to the Background to extract different color information, so duplicating on the first step leaves you the original source to work from.

3. Make a Fill layer by choosing Layer → New Fill Layer → Solid Color. Click OK. When the Color Picker dialog box appears. Set the color to red (255,0,0). Click OK. The image will be red, but we'll fix that in the next few steps.

4. Set the Fill layer mode to Multiply by selecting Multiply from the Blending Mode drop-down list in the upper left of the Layers palette. This will effectively filter the color image for the red light information, isolating it.

5. Merge the layers by choosing Layer → Merge Down (Command/Ctrl+E) to commit the red filtering. We can turn this red light into a channel by adding equal parts of blue and green to the red in the following steps.

6. Duplicate the Red layer (Layer → Duplicate Layer). This will create a layer named Red Copy. You'll need it only temporarily, so there is no need to rename it. Click OK.

7. Make a Hue/Saturation Adjustment layer by choosing Layer → New Adjustment Layer → Hue/Saturation. When the Hue/Saturation dialog box appears, use the sliders or type in the following settings: Hue: 120, Saturation: 0, Lightness: 0. This will change the color of the red component to green without affecting the tone. Click OK.

8. Merge the Hue/ Saturation and Red copy layers by choosing Layer → Merge Down (Command/Ctrl+E). This commits the change of color from red to green without effecting the tone.

9. Set the current layer mode to Screen by selecting Screen from the Blending Mode drop-down list in the upper left of the Layers palette. Screen mode acts by applying layer information as additive light.

10. Duplicate the Red Copy layer (Layer → Duplicate Layer). This will create a layer named Red Copy 2. Again, this is a temporary layer, so there is no need to rename it. Click OK.

11. Make a Hue/Saturation Adjustment layer by choosing Layer → New Adjustment Layer → Hue/Saturation. In the Hue/Saturation dialog box, specify these settings: Hue: 120, Saturation: 0, Lightness: 0. This will change the color of the layer to blue. Click OK.

12. Merge the layers by choosing Layer → Merge Down (Command/Ctrl+E). This commits the change in color from green to blue — still not effecting the tone. The red filtered component is now in the layers palette in equal parts of red green and blue. Combining them correctly (as we'll do in the next steps) will give you the red color channel as black-and-white tone.

13. Activate the Red layer, then link it to Red Copy and Red Copy 2 by clicking the linking box for each copy layer.

14. Merge the linked layers by choosing Layer → Merge Linked. The result will be a single-layer grayscale representation of the red light component in the original image.

Create the green channel

15. Hide the Red layer by clicking its layer visibility toggle (the eyeball icon) .

16. Activate the Background layer, duplicate it (Layer → Duplicate Layer), and rename the duplicate layer to Green. Click OK.

17. Make a Fill layer (Layer → New Fill Layer → Solid Color). The Color Picker dialog box appears. Set the color to green (0,255,0). Click OK. The whole image will be green.

18. Set the layer mode of the Color Fill layer to Multiply to reveal the green light component of your image. Click OK.

19. Merge layers by choosing Layer → Merge Down (Command/Ctrl+E).

20. Duplicate the Green layer (Layer → Duplicate).

21. Make a Hue/Saturation Adjustment layer (Layer → New Adjustment Layer → Hue/Saturation) with these settings: Hue: 120, Saturation: 0, Lightness: 0. This will change the color of the layer to blue.

22. Merge the layers by choosing Layer → Merge Down.

23. Set the layer mode to Screen by selecting Screen from the Blending Mode drop-down list in the upper left of the Layers palette.

24. Duplicate the Green Copy layer.

25. Make a Hue/Saturation adjustment layer with these settings: Hue: 120, Saturation: 0, Lightness: 0. This will change the color of the layer to red.

26. Merge the layers by choosing Layer → Merge Down.

27. Activate the Green layer, and then link it to Green Copy and Green Copy 2 by clicking the linking boxes of the copy layers.

28. Merge the linked layers (Layer → Merge Linked). This will composite the layers into a single layer grayscale representation of the green light component in the original image.

Create the blue channel

29. Hide the Green layer by clicking its visibility toggle.

30. Activate the Background, duplicate it, and name the new layer Blue.

31. Make a Fill layer (Layer → New Fill Layer → Solid Color). The Color Picker dialog box appears. Set the color to blue (0,0,255). Click OK. The whole image will be blue.

32. Set the layer mode to Multiply to reveal the blue light component. Click OK.

33. Merge the layers (Layer → Merge Down).

34. Duplicate the Blue layer (Layer → Duplicate).

35. Make a Hue/Saturation Adjustment layer with these settings: Hue: 120, Saturation 0, Lightness, 0. This will change the color of the layer to red.

36. Merge the layers by choosing Layer → Merge Down (Command/Ctrl+E).

37. Set the current layer mode to Screen.

38. Duplicate the Blue Copy layer.

39. Make a Hue/Saturation Adjustment layer (Layer → New Adjustment Layer → Hue/Saturation) with these settings: Hue: 120, Saturation: 0, Lightness: 0. This will change the color of the layer to green.

40. Merge the layers by choosing Merge Down.

41. Activate the Blue layer, then link the Blue, Blue Copy, and Blue Copy 2 layers.

42. Merge the layers by choosing Layer → Merge Linked.

You have separated the image into three channels, one for each of the primary light components: red, green, and blue. These components can be looked at as a source for making conversion to black-and-white, as well as a source for learning about the nature of light and RGB theory. These are exactly the same components you would get using Channels in Photoshop. Save this image by a different name so you can find it later.

Take a moment to examine the images representing the separate light components, and note the qualitative differences between the red, green, and blue channels. The representations reveal specific qualities about light in each spectrum.

Figure 2.1 shows an image of an orange flower against a green background separated into its components. (See the color representation of this flower in the color section.)

Now that you have seen the separation, you can accomplish the same set of 42 steps in a single click. Just open Hidden Power Tools, open an image, and click Split RGB Channels under the Separations tab of the Hidden Power Tools menu. This will execute the steps for you. Splitting RGB should be done on a flattened, RGB image—other images may be somewhat unpredictable in results and can generate errors.

If you haven't installed the Hidden Power Tools, you can find the tools on the CD and instructions for installing them in the Introduction to this book.

Figure 2.1

These images were created using the separation steps in the previous procedure. Note that the green looks the most like what you might expect as a grayscale conversion.

Red   Green   Blue

Luminosity

Separation for image luminosity is another way to extract valuable tonal information from your images. Luminosity is a component of Lab color, which separates image information into luminosity and balance of two color sets: red and green (the "a" color axis), and blue and yellow (the "b" axis). The idea is to separate the depiction of tone completely from color, and then to measure color as the interplay of opposites. Because this color model considers tone separately from color, the Luminosity component is often a good representation of what we would expect to see in black-and-white.

Photoshop Elements does not have Lab as one of the image color modes. However, like RGB separations, luminosity can be coaxed from an image in more than one way, and can easily be represented using layers. As a purer measure of tone, it is often useful where RGB tone may fail. For example, and as we will see, it is invaluable for color noise reduction in images recorded by digital cameras.

The following steps will allow you to extract luminosity from any RGB image. Use the flower image again (`lily.psd`) with these steps so we can compare the differences in the resulting grayscale.

Extracting Luminosity from Color

1. Open the lily.psd image.

2. Duplicate the Background layer (Layer → Duplicate Layer). This will be a temporary layer so it does not need to be named. Change the layer mode to Luminosity by selecting it from the Blending Mode drop-down list in the upper left of the Layers palette.

3. Activate the Background layer by clicking on it in the layers palette.

4. Create a new layer (Layer → New → Layer). This will create a new layer between the background and the copy. Name the layer Composite, and click OK.

5. Fill the new layer with gray by clicking Edit → Fill and then selecting 50% Gray from the drop-down menu.

6. Duplicate the Composite layer. Name the layer Luminosity, and click OK.

7. Select the Background Copy layer by clicking on it in the layers palette.

8. Merge the Background Copy and the Luminosity layer (Layer → Merge Down).

9. Select Luminosity from the Blending Mode drop-down list in the upper left of the Layers palette.

With the layer mode changed to Luminosity, what will display is the lightness (or L channel from the Lab color model), which is a representation of image tone. Save the resulting file so that you can come back to it later. Comparing this result to the channels of an RGB separation as well as the straight conversion to Grayscale by desaturation (as shown in Figure 2.2) should show some distinct differences in quality. Depending on the source of the image (digital capture or analog), the content of the image, and the quality and quantity of light in the capture, these differences will be more pronounced.

The Luminosity component information can be extracted from an image in a single step by using Hidden Power Tools. Just click Split Luminosity on the Separations tab of the Hidden Power Tools, and the steps for separating luminosity will execute. The tool will create three elements: the Luminosity component, the Color component, and the Composite layer. The Color component is Luminosity's partner: the components work together to create image color and tone in a similar way that RGB channels combine to create an image. The Composite layer is just a canvas for the layer components to present against. To view the image without the color, select the Color layer and click its visibility toggle on the Layers palette to shut the view off. To view the image without the luminosity (essentially this is color saturation), select the Luminosity layer and click its layer visibility toggle 👁 .

The Split Luminosity power tool should be used on flattened, RGB images. We'll look more at the Color component a little later when we look at how saturation information can help in CMYK separation.

Making Black-and-White by Borrowing the Best Tone

Sometimes a simple conversion works just fine for making a color image black-and-white. The most straightforward conversion to black-and-white is accomplished by converting RGB to Grayscale or desaturating. Other opportunities for black-and-white representations of an image may be had from the RGB or luminosity separations. Sometimes a component of one of these conversions will suffice for the conversion, and other times you have to look around and be more creative by borrowing and combining the tones that you can find lurking in various separations. This is where the art of converting to black-and-white comes in.

Figure 2.2

The luminosity or lightness separation (a) for the image shows a somewhat different and often better representation of image tone than simply desaturating the image (b).

a

b

If you look at RGB separations, the most representative component (what you'd expect to see in black-and-white) will most often be the green channel. This is because green is more naturally in the center of the visual spectrum and more closely resembles how humans perceive tone. The red channel is toward the infrared spectra and the blue channel is toward the ultraviolet.

Very often, luminosity will give you an easy source to extract a good representation of tone from any image. It is less prone to color noise, and at times will look surprisingly smooth, even when RGB separations have strong color noise (such as what can happen with images shot with a digital camera in low light).

All of the separation possibilities can show you tonal representations that you may not have considered. Sometimes a subtle adjustment in any of these three representations can yield greatly improved results in what otherwise would have been a straight conversion. These adjustments may be simple changes in tone using correction tools such as Curves (a Hidden Power Tool that we'll look at in chapter 3) or Levels, or the changes may be made by selecting different areas of tonal representation from different separation sources and combining them.

Figure 2.3 shows five possibilities for a simple conversion to black-and-white from a single image, plus one result that combines three of the separations in achieving the result. For simple conversions, the blue and red can usually be discarded right away as sources since they are not always good representations of the way you will perceive image tone. However, red and blue can sometimes be used to make other adjustments (e.g., create selections, create masks, make channel calculations, mix channels, or apply as changes using histories—all of these techniques will be looked at in subsequent chapters). Comparison of the green, luminosity, and grayscale conversion from RGB may reveal different specific advantages. Adjustment of the available tones in more than one of the separated components may affect the best result.

Red · Green · Blue

Luminosity · Desaturate · Composite of three separations

Figure 2.3

Looking at the five simple conversions of image tone can reveal distinct advantages in both representing the images and selecting objects or components.

The composite image takes the background from the luminosity and mixes in the flower, selected from the green channel, with the aid of the red channel as a mask. We will look more at how to specifically make similar adjustments in topics throughout the book.

Turning Black-and-White to Color Again

While separations can be useful for creating black-and-white images, they will be useful for color only if you can recombine the separated components to display color again. Prokudin-Gorskii had a similar problem after making his separations to RGB tones, as discussed in Chapter 1. What he had to do was put his glass plates in a projector and simultaneously project them in near-perfect alignment with appropriate filtering (in the form of color cells) to re-create the color result on a screen.

In Photoshop Elements, you can use layer color and modes to combine the separated RGB elements into a unified color image again. The result can be achieved without actually combining the separated channel tones. This is a great benefit during color correction as it will let you make adjustments to each component and view how those changes effect the color as the changes are made. Layered channels can be combined with layer adjustments targeted at specific channels, and these layers can be effected by other changes simultaneously, including selection and masking.

Compositing Separated Tones into a Color Image

The following procedures should be used on an image that has been separated using the steps for red, green, and blue layer separations in the previous section "Splitting RGB Colors into Tones (or Channels)." These procedures partially reverse the process of creating the original tonal separations. If you are following the step-by-step procedure used at the beginning of this chapter to create the separations, the background layer will be the original full-color image. The background can actually be anything at all as we will be dropping in a Composite layer to block out whatever is there.

This procedure consists of two phases, preparing the RGB layers and then changing tones to projected light.

Prepare the RGB Layers

You should be starting with an image that has Red, Green, Blue, and Background layers, exactly as you will end up with by following the earlier separation procedure, or by opening an image and clicking Split RGB in the Hidden Power Tools.

1. Activate the Background layer of the separated image.

2. Make a new layer (Layer → New → Layer). Name the layer Composite. Click OK. This layer will serve as a canvas for the composite—performing almost the same function as a projection screen.

3. Fill the layer with black by clicking Edit → Fill and then selecting Black from the Contents drop-down list.

4. Reorder the layers if necessary by clicking and dragging them up or down in the list. The layers should be in the following order from top to bottom: Red, Green, Blue, Composite, and Background.

5. Hide the Red and Green layers by turning off their visibility toggles (click the eyeball icons) on the Layers palette.

Changing Tones to Projected Light

Now you need to convert each tonal representation of the image back to a colored light component so they can recombine for a full-color result:

6. Activate the Blue layer and set the color mode to Screen. Applying the layer as a screen will lighten the tone of the black composite layer.

7. Make a Fill layer (Layer → New Fill Layer → Solid Color). Set the mode for the Fill layer to Multiply. Click the Group with Previous checkbox (so it is checked). Click OK.

8. The Color Picker dialog box appears. Set the color to blue (0,0,255). Click OK. Steps 5 through 7 convert the appearance of blue component layer from grayscale tone back to blue. The resulting effect is that the blue tone projects on the Composite layer as the blue light component would.

9. Activate the Green layer and set the layer mode to Screen. This further lightens the tone of the composite.

10. Make a Fill layer (Layer → New Fill Layer → Solid Color). Set the Mode for the fill layer to Multiply. Click the Group With Previous box so that it is checked. Click OK.

11. The Color Picker dialog box appears. Set the color to green (0,255,0). Click OK. Steps 8 through 10 convert the appearance of the green component layer from grayscale tone back to green, and apply the green to the Composite layer as green light.

12. Activate the Red layer and set the layer mode to Screen.

13. Make a Fill layer (Layer → New Fill Layer → Solid Color). Set the Mode for the fill layer to Multiply. Click the Group with Previous checkbox so that the box is checked. Click OK.

14. The Color Picker dialog box appears. Set the color to red (255,0,0). Steps 11 through 13 convert the appearance of the red component layer from grayscale tone back to red, and apply the red tone to the Composite layer as red light.

At this point, the image will appear to be in RGB color in the image window, but the color channels will still be available separately in the Layers palette as tone (see Figure 2.4). To adjust an individual color channel, you can create a new adjustment layer (as many as necessary) between the color layer and the fill layer. You can make any type of adjustment to the tone, as long as it adjusts

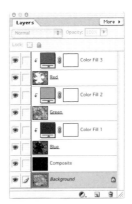

Figure 2.4

The separated colors in the image are successfully combined to recreate the color in layers while being kept separate. This will allow you to work with layers as if they were Photoshop channels.

the individual tone layers directly (Red, Green, and Blue) and not to the fill layers. The result can be converted back to a plain RGB image by flattening.

Steps to change the separated RGB tone to color layers can be accomplished using a single click with Hidden Power Tools. Clicking Preview RGB will complete all of the steps in this procedure. To perform both the separation and the preview of an image in one easy step, click Split RGB w/Preview. The split with preview should be performed on a flattened RGB image. These Hidden Power Tools will be invaluable to you in working through the book and making future image corrections.

Adding Color to Tone

While separations represent the source elements of image color, color can be introduced without using original color components. Colorizing (or hand-coloring) images is usually an artistic approach to adding color to black-and-white images. It differs from recombining RGB tones into color or even adding back the color element of a luminosity separation, in that it is a separate application of color: the color you apply may be a radical change from any color that was originally in the image. The tone of the image becomes a canvas to paint color on.

Color can be applied to tone in a number of different ways, such as using the original color as a source or applying the color with different Photoshop Elements tools. The color application can be done with simple painting tools or with a more complex color application (e.g., Gradient Mapping and/or blending). We'll take a brief look here at applying original color to tone and applying new color, to further an understanding of how color and tone work together.

Applying Original Color

You extracted the tone from an image earlier in the chapter when creating a Luminosity separation (see "Extracting Luminosity from Color" earlier in this chapter). The other byproduct of completing that separation is color. The color component represents the hue and saturation of the image separate from the tone. Hue and saturation might be considered separately as color (perhaps as picked from a color wheel) and the purity or vibrancy of that color.

Isolating and reapplying original color to tone is pretty simple in a Luminosity and color separation—not nearly as complex as re-creating color from RGB separations. Starting with an image that you have extracted luminosity from, your image should have the following layers from the top down: Luminosity, Composite, and Background. Completing the Luminosity separation started earlier is done in a few easy steps to add a new component:

1. Duplicate the Background. Name the layer Color.

2. Move the Color layer to the top of the stack.

3. Change the mode of the Color layer to Color.

In completing these few steps, you have effectively added the color back to the image tone using a separate layer. You can work on the color and lightness (luminosity) components individually. That is, you can take the image tone, and make adjustments to it separate from the color. The color component can be extracted and changed and applied to the original tone, the tone extracted as Luminosity, or the tone created by an RGB preview. Figure 2.5 shows the result of a complete Luminosity and Color separation, with a sample of how adjustment layers could be placed for simple alterations to color and tone.

Figure 2.5

With tonality and color separated, you can effectively control one element without affecting the other.

The Composite layer can be filled with any gray at all (white to black) and result in the same Luminosity effect. That is, if you view Luminosity over white, gray, or black composite backgrounds the result will be the same. If you view the Color layer alone over the composite, however, the tone will affect what you see.

Try this: fill the Composite layer with white, shut off the view for Luminosity and leave Color viewed. The image will turn white, even though the visibility for the color layer is still on. What many would expect is that the color for the image would be applied to the white composite. This is actually what is happening, and the result is very revealing about the Color layer mode—and explains why the results of using Color layers (or tools in Color mode) may not often result in what is expected. The result is very simple and logical.

Color mixes with tone to produce a result. If there is no color, the tone is applied in grayscale. If there is no tone (white), the color is applied, but results in no color value: because there is no tone in pure white, there is no tone in the applied color. The stronger the tone, the darker the applied color, until it turns black. When the image is black, the color layer again shows no effect on the visible result.

If you fill the Composite layer with 50% gray again, you'll see the image color when the Luminosity layer is off. Fill the Composite layer with a gradient from black to white (linear), and the image should show how tonality affects saturation of color. The point is, the display of color is directly dependent on tone: if you want color to display differently (lighter or darker), you'll have to manipulate the tone rather than the color. Making tone darker in an area of color will darken the color; lightening tone will lighten color. If you want another hue (e.g., if you want to turn green to blue), you can adjust that by changing the color layer from the separation without affecting the tone during the process of making the change.

When a color in an image seems wrong, it may be that you need to make a change in the color or tone—or both—to get it right. One or the other won't always work to get you where you want to go. Separating the components gives you more freedom to work with color and tone independently to achieve the desired result. We'll look much more in depth at adjusting color in Chapter 5.

Using Gradient Maps

The most effective ways of handling color additions do not always involve applying flat color. Gradient maps will replace colors and/or tones in an image or image area using a customized color mapping. When the gradient is applied, Elements looks at the tones in the image (Luminosity) and replaces each level of gray with its corresponding gradient color as you've set it up in a one-to-one mapping.

If you have a grayscale image, and you apply a gradient that has 100% red (255,0,0) at half way on the gradient (50%), all of the gray pixels at 50% brightness will display as red. If this gradient blends evenly to black at 0% and white at 100%, the red will fade to pink then white where tones in the image get lighter; the red will darken to brick then black where tones in the image get darker. Gradient application of color and tone can be infinitely more complex than this simple example.

Remapping color and tone often works best in a limited area of an image, such as when using selection or masking. You may want to combine effects by using two or more approaches in conjunction. However, there are instances where entire scenes are influenced almost exclusively by tone/color combinations—such as in sunsets or duotone effects—where the tone in an image can be associated almost exactly one-to-one with color. Although we will look at an example where the gradient affects the whole image, gradient color mapping can also work great for colorizing selected image areas that may have complex color schemes over various tones (such as skin). This can be done with masking (built into the Gradient Map adjustment layers) or with other techniques that we will see later (e.g., History applications).

To work with gradient maps, you need to use the Gradient Editor, which can be opened from the Gradient Map dialog box. Open the Gradient Map dialog box by either directly applying a gradient map (Image → Adjustments → Gradient Map) or applying a gradient map as an Adjustment layer (Layer → New Adjustment Layer → Gradient Map, click OK). When the Gradient Map dialog box is open, click the color bar under Gradient Used For Grayscale Mapping.

Once the Gradient Editor is open, you can edit the current gradient, and create and save custom gradients for reuse. New gradients are created by adding and removing color and transparency stops, choosing a name, and clicking the New button. These new gradients will be stored in the gradient library and will be available whenever you choose gradient functions. Figure 2.6 shows the Gradient Editor dialog box and a breakdown of the major features.

Features in the Gradient Editor are the following:

Buttons Click OK to accept the current values and close the dialog. Click Cancel to revert the gradient to the values that existed in the image prior to opening the Editor. If you have made changes to the gradient and wish to remove them and revert back to the original gradient values, press the Alt key. The Cancel button changes to a Revert button. Click Revert to eliminate all changes and revert to the original values.

Name Enter a name for the current gradient, and then click New to save the gradient (in its current settings) to the Presets list.

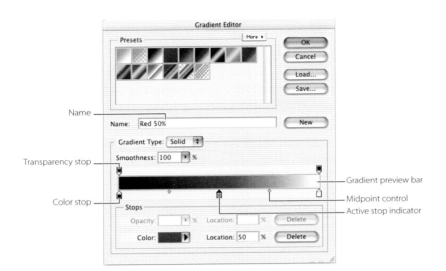

Figure 2.6

The Gradient Editor allows the creation of custom color and tone alterations based on existing image tone.

Opacity and Color Stop icons Opacity Stops are located above the gradient preview bar; Color Stops appear beneath it. The stop with its triangle colored black is the active stop (the stop whose settings appear in the Stops section of the dialog box). You can double-click a color stop to open the Color Picker.

Stops options The Stops options on the top row of the Stops panel on the dialog box show the values for the active Opacity stop. To set its Opacity, enter a number or click the arrow to drop down a slider.

The Stops options on the bottom row apply to the active Color stop. The Color swatch provides a preview of the stop's color; click it to open the Color Picker.

Enter a Location value for either stop type to accurately position the stop (from 0% at the far left to 100% at the far right). Click the Delete button to remove the active stop.

Setting up your gradient requires adding color stops to the bottom of the gradient bar to control the application of color to the tones in the image. To add a color stop, click just below the gradient bar and then drag the stop to the position on the gradient bar where you want to locate it. The color of the stop can be changed in several different ways:

- Sample color directly from the image (moving your cursor over the image changes it to the sample tool).
- Double-click the color stop to open the color picker.
- Make a selection (Foreground, Background, or User Color) from the drop-down menu next to the Color swatch.

The opacity of the color application can be controlled by the opacity stops set on the top of the gradient bar. If you choose color carefully, the colors you apply should affect simply the color you want to see.

The image to which you will be applying the Gradient Map can be converted to grayscale if you like, but this isn't necessary; the map will work on the image tonality independently of current color. In some cases, it may actually be easiest to leave the color in the image so you can use the existing colors as sample color for the enhancement. Different images will require different handling depending on the color that exists and what you want to accomplish. You may want to adjust image tone or separate out image areas before applying gradient maps.

Applying a Gradient Map

The simplest application of a gradient would be using it to make changes in a grayscale image (or part of a separation). In fact, the gradient editor can be used just like a levels or curves adjustment (we'll look at how to make Levels and Curves adjustments in the next chapter). Try this simple Gradient Map application to adjust image tone:

1. Open any flattened black-and-white image (or open a color image, flatten the image, click Split Luminosity in the Hidden Power Tools, shut off the Color layer, and flatten again). If the image is Grayscale, change it to RGB mode.

2. Press D on the keyboard to reset the Foreground and Background colors on the toolbox.

3. Open a Gradient Map by choosing Layer → New Adjustment Layer → Gradient Map. Click OK on the New Layer dialog box. This will open the Gradient Map dialog box with the Foreground-to-Background gradient default.

4. Click the Gradient Used for Grayscale Mapping swatch on the dialog box. This will open the Gradient Editor.

5. Click directly on the white Color Stop at the right of the gradient preview bar. This will reveal a Color Midpoint (small gray diamond) in the center of the bar at the bottom.

When you click a stop to activate it, diamond-shaped markers appear to either side of the stop, between it and the next stop. These midpoints can be adjusted to affect the application of the gradient. Shifting the midpoint to the left increases the influence of the right stop; shifting the midpoint to the right increases the influence of the left stop. Adjust the color markers while viewing the image to get the best results.

6. Position the Gradient Editor so you can see your image, and move the slider right and left of center watching what happens to the image. (You may have to release the slider to see the result). Moving the slider left should lighten the image, and moving it right should darken it.

This simple application remaps the tone of the image based on the position of the slider. You can create more complex tonal adjustments by adding Color and Opacity stops.

Gradient application can readily get far more complex. The best way to see how complex is to look at an example. On the CD, I've provided an image taken at sunrise to complete the following exercise. Open `oceansun.psd` (Figure 2.7), provided on the CD. This example is somewhat of a special case that I picked specifically to show how dramatic a Gradient Map change can be. Because the image is a sunrise, the colors will be limited to mostly reds and yellows. The stops and adjustments will work only on this image. Applying the color with gradients is a little bit of an art and may be steeped in trial and error. I created the result here by placing and adjusting markers, knowing only approximately where they would fall: brighter color in the lighter half of the tone. You will need to experiment a little when placing stops to adjust other images.

First we'll want to darken up the image a little so that the image will accept some more saturated colors because the image seems a little light. Once we've darkened the image, we can apply color to get a dramatic color result. We'll need to make sure existing stops in the gradient are the correct color and add some stops to remap the tone first, and then the color. When we get to the color, we'll make light areas of the image yellow, and deepen that color toward red to imitate the effect sunrise lighting produces.

Figure 2.7

The colors in the original sunrise are dulled yellows, oranges, and grays, but the results can be made more dramatic using a Gradient Map.

Adjust the contrast and darken the image

1. Create a Gradient Map Adjustment layer by choosing Layer → New Adjustment Layer → Gradient Map. Click OK on the New Layer dialog box. This will open the Gradient Map dialog box.

2. Open the Gradient Editor by clicking the gradient bar in the Gradient Used For Grayscale Mapping preview section.

3. Double-click the 0% color stop (at the bottom left) to open the Color Picker dialog box, and change the color to black (RGB 0,0,0). (In this example image, it will already be set to black.) Click OK to close the Color Picker.

4. Add a color stop to the gradient by clicking below the gradient preview bar. Set the position of the stop to 40% by typing 40 in the Location field.

5. Double-click on the new color stop to open the Color Picker dialog box. Change the color of the stop to HSB 0,0,33 (33% bright). (HSB is an alternative color scheme representing hue, saturation, and brightness.) Making this change will darken the tones at the 40% position from 40% to 33% bright. Click OK to accept the changes and close the Color Picker.

6. Add another color stop to the gradient by clicking below the gradient preview bar. Set the position of the stop to 60% by typing 60 in the Location field.

7. Double-click on the new color stop to open the Color Picker. Change the color of the stop to HSB 0,0,55 to change the tone 5% darker at this point, from 60% to 55%. Click OK to accept the changes and close the Color Picker.

8. Double-click on the 100% color stop (at the bottom right) to activate it and open the Color Picker.

9. Change the color of the stop if necessary to white RGB 255,255,255 or HSB 0,0,100 (your stop may already be set to these settings). Click OK to close the Color Picker. At this point the Gradient Editor should look something like Figure 2.8.

10. Click OK on the Gradient Editor to close it and accept the changes to the gradient.

11. Click OK on the Gradient Map dialog box to close it and accept the changes for the new layer. At this point, the image should be notably darker; it should resemble Figure 2.9.

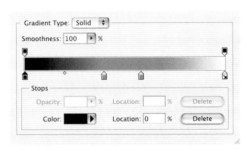

Figure 2.8

The change in the gradient increases the influence of the darker tones.

Figure 2.9

**The gradient mapping
has adjusted the tones
according to the stops
placed in the gradient.**

Recolor the altered tone

12. Create another Gradient Map Adjustment layer (Layer → New Adjustment Layer →
    Gradient Map).

13. Click OK in the New Layer dialog box to open the Gradient Map dialog box.

14. Click OK in the Gradient Map dialog box to close it and create the new layer.

15. Change the layer opacity to 50% using the Opacity slider on the layers palette. This will
    allow you to intentionally apply strong colors rather than muted ones to achieve your
    result. You can adjust the opacity again later to make the color stronger or weaker, as
    desired.

16. Change the layer mode to Color using the Mode drop-down list. This will apply the color
    in the gradient rather than forcing adjustment of tone and color—which may be much
    harder to control.

17. Double-click the layer thumbnail for the active layer on the Layers palette. This will
    open the Gradient Map dialog box.

18. Open the Gradient Editor by clicking the gradient bar in the Gradient Used For
    Grayscale Mapping preview.

19. Double-click the 0% color stop (at bottom left) and change the color to dark gray (RGB 40,40,40). This will lighten the darkest areas of the image so they won't be absolute black. Click OK to close the Color Picker. The color can be changed in the Color Picker by typing the values into the RGB boxes after opening the picker using any of the methods described earlier.

20. Add a color stop to the gradient by clicking below the gradient preview bar. Set the position of the stop to 25% by typing 25 in the Location field.

21. Double-click on the stop and change its color to RGB 25,30,90. This is a deep blue that will be used to keep a bluish tone in the water and in the darkest parts of the clouds. Click OK to close the Color Picker.

22. Add a color stop to the gradient by clicking below the gradient preview bar. Set the position of the stop to 40% by typing 40 in the Location field.

23. Double-click on the stop and change its color to RGB 145,115,120. This is a muted red that helps serve as a transition between blue and orange. Click OK to close the Color Picker.

24. Add a color stop to the gradient by clicking below the gradient preview bar. Set the position of the stop to 60% by typing 60 in the Location field.

25. Double-click on the stop and change its color to RGB 255,90,0. This color begins the more dramatic color highlighting by saturating the brighter portions of the image in orange. Click OK to close the Color Picker.

26. Add a color stop to the gradient by clicking below the gradient preview bar. Set the position of the stop to 85% by typing 85 in the Location field.

27. Double-click on the stop and change its color to RGB 250,250,20. Yellow will be used to add some spark to the somewhat drab highlights in the original. Click OK to close the Color Picker.

28. Double-click on the 100% (white) stop and change its color to RGB 245,245,200. This is not quite white, and can stop the sun from looking too burned in and bright in the image. Click OK to close the Color Picker to activate it. At this point the Gradient Editor should look something like Figure 2.10.

29. Click OK on the Gradient Editor to accept the changes to the gradient.

30. Click OK on the Gradient Map dialog box to close it and accept the changes for the new layer.

The result of the changes made in Steps 12 through 30 can be seen in the color section. You should have a result that shows a golden-orange sunrise. The result in the color section shows an opacity of 40% for the color gradient layer, which was adjusted after the color mapping was accepted—one of the great advantages of using layered corrections is the ability to adjust after the fact. Setting color markers is obviously the most involved step in the process. It will be useful to go back and experiment by adjusting the color and position of the gradient stops to see the effect each adjustment has on the image. You may want to use additional stops to effect changes you may prefer and experiment with Gradient Map opacity. Leave this image open for now; you'll need it for the next procedure.

Figure 2.10

Positioning of the stops should look like this after you have completed Step 28.

To add more control, you might want to experiment with separating control of the sky and sea. In the example, you can control the effects in the sky separately from the effects in the sea. A simple masking of image areas can allow you to adjust the colors in each with different gradients to improve the realism of the result. Because the horizon is flat, selecting one image area can be done quickly using the Polygonal Lasso.

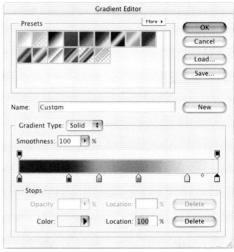

Creating a Mask for Gradients

The selections outlined in this procedure are very much specific to this image. Your selections should be made on an image-to-image basis, according to the content you want to apply effects to. Begin this procedure using the image from the previous procedure, with the contrast adjusted and tones altered.

1. Commit the grayscale changes to the background by merging Gradient Map 1 with the background.

2. Duplicate Gradient Map 2 and change the name of the duplicate layer to Sky Gradient.

3. Click and drag the lower-right corner of the image window to reveal the image matte, as shown in Figure 2.11. You may have to zoom out from the image if you are in close (200%+) to make the image smaller before attempting to view the matte.

4. Choose the Polygonal Lasso tool, then select the Anti-Aliased option and change the Feathering to 2 pixels on the Options bar.

Figure 2.11

Clicking and dragging the corner of the image window reveals the image matte.

5. Click the Lasso tool to the left of the image just outside the image, right at the horizon line on the image matte.

6. Move the cursor to the right of the image and click just outside the image on the image matte, right at the horizon line.

7. Complete the selection by clicking outside the image at the bottom-right corner, the bottom-left corner, and then back at the point of origin, as shown in Figure 2.12.

8. Change the foreground color to black.

9. Choose the Paint Bucket tool and click it in the selected area. This will mask out the sea for this gradient. The effect of the mask will be to hide (mask) the gradient effect for this layer over the sea.

10. Select the inverse of the area that is currently selected (Select → Inverse).

11. Activate the Gradient Map 1 layer by clicking it. Change the name of the layer to Sea Gradient.

12. Fill the sky area of the mask using the Paint Bucket tool. The effect of the fill will hide the gradient effect of this layer over the sky.

This will effectively mask the sky separately from the sea using the same gradient map with two complementary masks, allowing a 2-pixel blend where the edges of the mask meet. After the masking has been completed, making adjustments to either of the gradient maps will affect the sky and sea separately. In the image used for this example, as the separate gradient maps provide an opportunity to remove any residual blue from the clouds in the sky without affecting the color of the sea. As the clouds would tend to be either a warmer color (red to yellow) or simply flat gray, rather than a sea blue, this extra control can help shift the color to make it more realistic.

By applying gradients using masking and multiple gradient layers, and by working with layer modes and opacity, you can achieve some very complex results. Of course, this example is only the tip of the iceberg when it comes to applying color to tone. Combined with a variety of other tools you will use for enhancing and replacing color (which we will explore in later chapters) your ability to control the result is limitless. One thing should be clear: The foundation for color application is tone. Perhaps that fact makes it much more apparent why the tone components of an image are so important to achieving results. You must be able to control tone as a basis for image color.

Figure 2.12

Click points A, B, C, and D to complete the selection.

Chapter 3

Manipulating Image Tones

Manipulating tone with confidence makes all the difference in getting the results you want in black-and-white and color. Adjusting tone starts with evaluating the image to define your purpose, and moves through steps to make changes based on that evaluation. Two things to keep in mind:

- For every action, there is a reaction.

- You might have to break it to fix it.

The first point is an adaptation of one of Newton's laws of physics. Every general adjustment you make will affect what you are adjusting as well as other tones. The second is based on my experience with "fixing" appliances by disabling broken functions. In images, a fix doesn't always make everything in an image better, but it should improve the appearance of the image. Sometimes you must do something destructive to an image to enable a repair.

Do Minor Cleanup First

Evaluating Image Tones

Redistributing Tone with Levels

Snapping and Fading Contrast with Curves

(Un)Sharpening and Boosting Contrast

Reduce Image Noise for Smoother Tone

Adding Image Noise for Realism

Masking with Image Tone

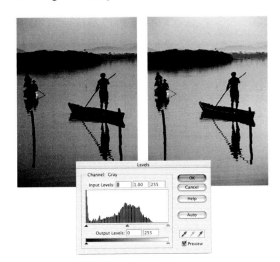

Do Minor Cleanup First

Before adjusting an image, it is often good to do a quick once-over to remove things that just shouldn't be there, such as extra image area, damage, and dust. This quick evaluation can also involve first cropping the image and then removing, or touching up, other damage. Care in touch-up at this point permanently removes unwanted elements so they will not be present in any later purpose you have for the image.

A simple, direct method of taking care of minor damage is to clone or duplicate image areas. With *cloning*, you sample information from one part of an image and then apply that information to another part of the image that might be damaged or missing. Cloning covers up the problem with other, problem-free image information. It can solve any type of minor damage, including dings, dirt, digital noise, and tears, as long as you have something to clone from that is a close match to the spot you are fixing. You can also use simple duplication to select an area of an image and copy it to another area to correct damage. Careful cloning or duplication can allow you to patch an image seamlessly without creating noticeable patterns.

Image areas with tone and color complexities (such as skin tones) require careful selection of replacement areas in order to make unnoticeable repairs. Substitutions can come from within the same image or from another image with similar qualities. All cloning and duplication corrections follow the same basic steps:

1. Define the damaged area.
2. Locate a suitable replacement.
3. Obtain a sample of the replacement.
4. Apply the replacement to the damaged area.

DO SOME DAMAGE CONTROL BY PLANNING AHEAD

You can avoid a lot of trouble with your digital images before you create them. Don't get into the habit of just thinking, "I'll clean it up later digitally!" A quick wipe with a clean cloth can clear troublesome debris from an image you are scanning, or from the scanner glass, just as you might wipe crumbs from a chair before you sit down. The same idea applies to taking images with a digital camera; be sure your lens is clean before you point it at anything, wipe off dusty or dirty objects that will be in your images, and be sure you take the time to focus so your subject is as crisp and clear as possible. Taking these steps can save a lot of detail work later. Obviously you can't expect anything to be pristine. Dust and finger smudges can appear at any point where the image makes a physical rather than electronic transfer (on the subject, on your lens, on the scanner glass, on the surface of a print or negative, etc.). But once you've taken the image or scanned it, any minor nagging defects that worked their way into your image will always remain until you remove them. The moments you spend preparing to create an image, the cleaner the image will be and the fewer problems you will have to correct, which saves lots of time at the computer.

Images can be cropped to remove damage, but also to improve composition. The idea of composition is discussed later along with the tools in Chapter 7.

Correcting By Using the Clone Stamp Tool

The Clone Stamp tool samples from a spot that you define in the image and copies image information in the shape of the brush you've chosen for the tool. This will help you take care of dust, flecked dirt, scratches, and many other minor image problems.

To select the area you will be cloning from, hold down the Option/Alt key with the cursor directly over what you will be cloning, then click the mouse to set the coordinates for the sample. The sample can be taken in the same image or another image, or from a different layer in the same image. Release the Option/Alt key and place the cursor over the target (the damaged area to be repaired). When you click the mouse again, the sample area will be applied to the target area. The distance and angle between the sample and brush will lock in with that relationship until you change the sample. To change the sample angle and distance, hold down the Option/Alt key and create a new sample. Both the clone-from and clone-to areas show on the image while you hold down the mouse button to apply the tool. This way, you can monitor accurately what area will be copied as well as the result. See Figure 3.1.

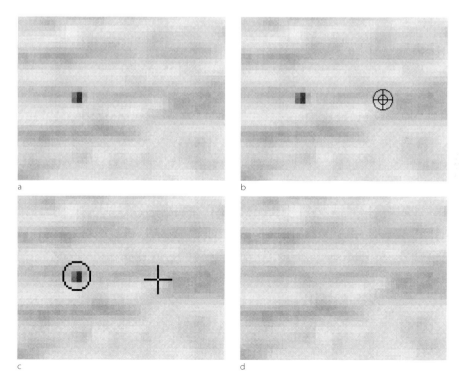

a

b

c

d

Figure 3.1

Identify a damaged area (a), sample the replacement (b), and apply (c) to achieve a repaired image (d).

A practice image called `wavedirt.psd` is supplied on the CD. It is a scan of just the corner of an image that was apparently taken with a dirty lens. It may look simple, but the patterning and shading can prove to be tricky. The entire process of correction is as follows:

1. Choose the Clone Stamp tool.

2. Change the image view to 200%–300%. This size ensures that you are viewing all of the pixel information on screen to make accurate applications.

3. Choose a brush. Brush size for dust correction should be somewhat larger than the width of the damage. In most cases, use a slightly soft brush (85%–95% hardness) so that corrections feather slightly into the surroundings as they are applied.

4. Choose a clone-from area. The area you clone from should be clear of damage and dust, or you will just copy that damage to the spot you are cloning to.

5. Apply the Clone Stamp tool to the spot you would like to repair by positioning the cursor over the damage and clicking the mouse. This sets the cloning angle and distance and applies the correction. Holding the mouse button down and dragging will apply the cloning over the area you drag across, maintaining the angle and distance between the sample and application points.

Your setting for Painting Cursors on the Display & Cursors preferences (Edit → Preferences → Display & Cursors) will effect the way the Clone Stamp Tool appears on your screen. Standard shows the tool icon ⬆ during application, Precise shows a cross-hair -¦- and Brush Size shows the shape of the brush being applied ◯. All three tools display the sample icon ⊕ when holding down the Option/Alt key to sample the image.

The Clone Stamp tool duplicates the sample point when you apply the tool. It is as though the image freezes in the computer memory as a source for the application. When you release the mouse and apply the tool again, the image freezes as a new source maintaining the distance and angle used for the previous sample. The freeze lasts for as long as you hold down the mouse button.

For the best results, hold down the mouse button only as long as you have to; click over the damage and release. Click new sample points as often as necessary, but try to do so frequently. Changing the angle between the sample and application point can help reduce the possibility of creating undesirable patterns.

For most corrections, choose the following options for the Clone Stamp tool:

- Aligned cloning (clones from sample point to application point using a set distance and angle)

- Use All Layers

- A soft brush (85%–95% hard)

- Brush spacing set to 1%
- Normal mode
- 100% opacity

> Brush options can only be set when using the Brush tool. To get the brush you want, choose the Brush tool, set up the options (by clicking More Options on the Options bar) and then save the brush by clicking the brush preview and choosing New Brush from the pop-up menu. Once the brush is saved, you can use it with other tools.

You will most often use the Clone Stamp tool in Normal mode, but there are instances where other modes can serve a purpose. For example, using Lighten mode when stamping from slightly darker portions of an image can lessen the impact of black spots without darkening lighter areas.

It may make corrections easier if you use another layer to hold the corrections. To do this, create a new layer above the one where you want to apply the correction, then apply the tool. Any changes will be applied to the new layer. You can view before and after by toggling on and off the view for the layer. Making corrections on a separate layer will also allow you to make other adjustments (such as applying filters or layer modes) while preserving your original image.

> If your brush has a soft edge, the actual effects of the brush application extend outside the brush size shown onscreen.

If you are stamping with Lighten to lighten dark spots in a light image area, try to clone from an area a little darker than the area you are cloning to. If you are stamping with Darken to darken light specks in a dark image area, try to clone from an area a little lighter than the area you are cloning to. The corrections will affect only the specks while keeping the general tone of the area unchanged.

Correcting By Duplication

It is sometimes advantageous to make corrections by copying and pasting larger areas of an image rather than painstakingly removing each speck of dust one at a time with the Clone Stamp tool.

Preselecting a large area of damage that you want to correct will allow you to find the best available replacement area and make quick work of repairs. The order of your approach and some basic techniques will remain the same:

1. Identify the problem area in the image and the intended replacement.

2. Click on a selection tool. The lasso tool is often a good choice, because irregular selections tend to blend more easily when pasted. Set the tool to feather the selection, this will soften the edge of the sample. Usually you have to feather only a few pixels (3–5), depending on the resolution of the image.

3. Make a selection with the selection tool around the general area of the image you want to replace. Making this selection will ensure that you get a "patch" that is sized to cover the damage, almost like a template. Make it a bit larger than the damage so you can have some leeway in blending pasted areas.

4. Move the selection tool over the selection, and the icon will change to the selection move icon ▶▫▫. Click and drag the selection over to the area of the image to be used as a replacement. Choosing exactly where to place the selection can involve rotating, flipping or carefully sizing the selection. You may want to note the changes you make if you transform the selection so you can reverse them when you paste the replacement. The options bar will show changes that you make.

5. Copy the selected area.

6. Paste. This will create a new layer containing the image area you will use as a patch. Because the patch is on its own layer, you can size and position it (by reversing the changes made in Step 4), or use the Eraser tool and a slightly soft brush to remove and blend the patch with the area being covered. Layer modes can also be employed (e.g., lighten and darken).

7. Repeat Steps 1 through 6 as needed to repair the image.

You may want to try several different solutions to the same problem areas if time permits and the area that you are patching is large or if you have more than one option for making the correction. Make the first patch, then turn off the visibility for its layer. After making the next patch, you can compare the two by turning the layer views on or off. Don't be afraid to mix patches using more than one, if it works.

> It is often best to work on an image area in stages, first removing smaller problems and then working up to larger ones. This approach allows you to remove minor problems and then use those corrected image areas to repair larger areas of the image, without duplicating old damage and problems to other areas of the image.

Evaluating Image Tones

Evaluating the tone, color (as part of tone), or other qualities of an image can help you make better corrections. At times you'll need to make precise measurements of image information, and at others you'll have to evaluate the general appearance of the image. The Eyedropper tool (used in conjunction with the Info palette) and the Histogram feature can provide just about all the image information you'll need to make adjustments.

Using the Eyedropper for Evaluation

The Eyedropper, located in the Toolbox, makes it easy to gather information about individual pixels or small pixel groupings. Simply click the Eyedropper tool and put the cursor over the image area you want to measure, and the Eyedropper will sample the composite of the visible layers and display the information in the Info palette (Figure 3.2). It can be helpful in evaluating an image periodically throughout the correction process. For example, comparing grayscale values for sample and target areas before cloning or duplicating can give you a good idea whether those areas are a good match before you make the clone or patch.

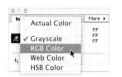

Figure 3.2

The Palette Options pop-up menu on the Info palette allows you to choose or change color references between Grayscale (luminosity), RGB, Web Color, and HSB.

From the drop-down list on the options bar, you can select a sample size: Point Sample (samples the pixel at the tip of the tool icon), 3 By 3 Average, and 5 By 5 Average. These options are also available by pointing the Eyedropper at an image and clicking the right mouse button (PC), or holding down the Control key and left clicking (Mac). The Average options look at a square of pixels (with the tip of the tool icon as the center pixel) and then average those to determine the result. In certain cases where tone is noisy, such as skin tones, it is better to sample with a broader sample size to get a better average reading of the tones you want to measure. Using a sample size that is too small might make confusing samples: values between one pixel and the next might change too rapidly to make sense.

1. Select the Eyedropper tool (I).

2. Choose the sample size from the drop-down list on the options bar.

3. Bring the Info palette to the front by selecting it from the Window menu or by clicking the tab in the palette well.

4. Spot-check with the Eyedropper by passing the cursor over various areas of the image while noting the values in the Info palette.

Evaluating Images with Histograms

The Histogram feature (Image → Histogram) graphs the number of pixels for each level throughout the entire range of the image as a mapping of the 256 available levels of gray. A histogram is also available in the Levels dialog box (Enhance → Brightness/Contrast → Levels). The height of each line in the graph represents the number of pixels with particular luminescence. A histogram can help describe the tonality and integrity of an image, pointing out both image qualities and abnormalities that may need to be corrected.

For example, a graph can tell whether an image is naturally bright (high-key) or dark (low-key), whether the contrast is neutral or high. If the qualities are desirable, histograms can help you maintain those qualities by reevaluating the image later in the correction process. While image qualities may be relatively apparent to the naked eye, histograms also help you determine whether an image has been damaged in processing or if it shows some other limitation, such as not taking full advantage of tonal range.

Aberrations can present themselves as uncharacteristic shifts, lack of balance, or gaps in the information. A histogram that contains many peaks and valleys, gaps in information, and /or clipping (spikes in information that run off the chart) may represent some form of image damage, limitation, or loss of image information. If the damage appears extreme, the image might need correction, or could have insufficient tonal range for manipulation, correction, and use.

Evaluating a histogram is as easy as looking at it. Characteristics become obvious in a quick visual evaluation of the graph. The following examples show a basic blueprint for specific image types, such as high-key, low-key, high-contrast, low-contrast, and images with damaged information.

> It is possible to evaluate a section of an image by selecting it with the selection tools. The histogram charts results only for the active or selected portion of an image.

A histogram that is weighted toward the black or dark end of the graph—and that does not show gaps in tonality at the light end of the graph—represents a low-key (dark) image. These are often images taken in low light, such as around a campfire or birthday cake. Figure 3.3 shows an example of a low-key image and the histogram that represents it.

Figure 3.3

A low-key image

A histogram that is skewed to the light (right) end of the graph represents a high-key (light) image, such as the one in Figure 3.4. Beach shots with lots of light sand or snowy winter scenes are good examples of high-key images.

A histogram that peaks in the dark and light areas while having lower pixel density in the middle of the graph (like the one in Figure 3.5) is representative of a high-contrast image. Harsh lighting in direct sunlight can create a chasm between lights and darks, which is a typical example of high contrast—although not necessarily a desirable one. A silhouette, where a figure is shown lit from behind, is another example.

A histogram that shows a peak in the center (Figure 3.6) is low-contrast and medium-key. These images are dominated by mid-tones. Images shot on an overcast day can often have a low-contrast appearance.

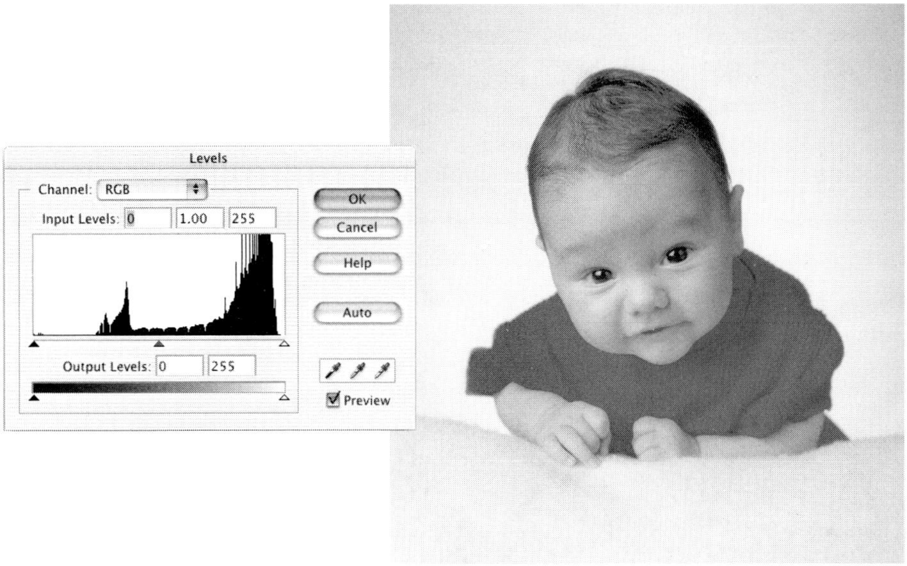

Figure 3.4

A high-key image

Figure 3.5

A high-contrast image

Figure 3.6

A low-contrast, medium-key image

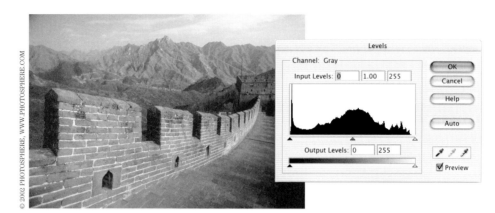

Figure 3.7

A full toned image

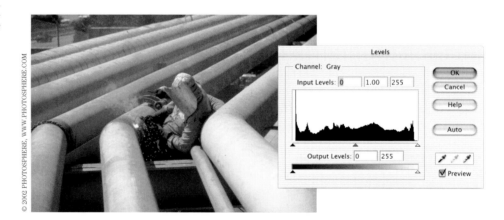

An image with a mix of global and local contrast displays as a flattened graph in a histogram with few peaks and valleys; see Figure 3.7 for an example. Images with full tonal range can have quite a bit of local contrast as opposed to high total contrast.

The histograms in Figure 3.8 show image information from an image that has been altered by limiting the number of tones it contains (such as using the Indexed Color mode). Gaps between tones on the histogram suggest that the image has limitations. These types of gaps can be symptomatic of other damage, such as poor scanning.

Histogram graphs should have some information for every level from the right to the left of the graphing, or else the tonality is not covering the potential dynamic range. Abnormalities might not always represent problems, but they are certainly good indications of unusual conditions. If the histogram shows a gap, it suggests that image information is missing or damaged. Intermittent gaps (like those in the histogram created by reducing colors in Figure 3.8) can suggest a cause or origin of the image damage. While it is possible for gaps in tone to be a natural state for the image, it is unlikely. Anomalies can result from capture problems, such as bad scanning (faulty techniques or equipment), incorrect image exposure, filter use, or unusual lighting conditions. Anomalies can also be the result of image processing: mode conversions, corrections, poorly applied filters, etc.

The most common tendencies in image histograms that you can use to effect image improvements are shortened tonal ranges and clipping.

Shortened tonal range is represented by a histogram that does not have information across the entire 256 levels of gray, with a gap at either the light or dark end of the graph or both. A shortened tonal range is an indication that the image is not taking full advantage of the shades of gray available (0% to 100% black). The image in Figure 3.9 shows some potential for stronger contrast. The histogram has a shortened tonal range, confirming the visual inspection. The tonality of the image can probably be adjusted successfully to make the image more dynamic.

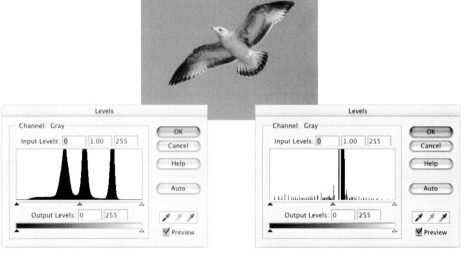

The histogram for the image in RGB

The histogram for the image in 64 colors

Figure 3.8

These histograms represent the original tone and a conversion to 64 grays.

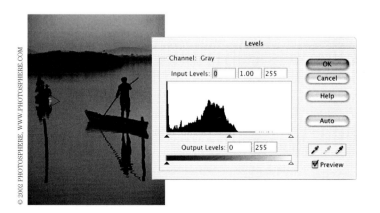

Figure 3.9

Potential problems with this image are revealed through its histogram.

Clipping is similar to, but perhaps the opposite of, a shortened tonal range. When levels of image detail get combined as pure white or black, the result is usually that some of the extreme highlights or shadow details may be lost. This may be caused by any number of processes that occur in obtaining, opening, or resaving an image, such as over- or under-exposing an already high-contrast scene (wedding images, for instance, where the groom is in black and the bride in white). However, clipping may not always determine that an image is damaged; it may just show a concentration of information in a specific level. The key to keep in mind is that when the histogram confirms possible image damage, it is something you can explore, and it may lead the way toward a course of correction.

> Do not be overzealous in accepting the appearance of the histogram as an absolute judge of the image; be sure to make a visual assessment as well and use the two assessments in tandem. The visual assessment should override the digital one, especially if you get good results in tests and can trust the view of your monitor.

Even if you evaluate an image and feel you need to make corrections, that doesn't tell you where to begin or what to do to make the corrections. The next task is to define what you want to do and how to accomplish your ends.

Although sometimes it is a mistake to drastically alter tonal range, shifting the range—even radically—can work to the benefit of the image by improving contrast and dynamic range. While correction may temporarily skew an image's key and/or contrast, several corrections can be made in succession to achieve the desired result. First we'll look at using Levels and then the more sophisticated Curves, and we'll evaluate how each of these tools affects tonal correction.

Redistributing Tone with Levels

Tonal correction will often give black-and-white images broader tonal range and stronger overall contrast. After you correct minor flaws and evaluate the image both visually and with histograms, the next step in correction should be to open the Levels dialog box to make a general tonal correction. Proper use of levels can quickly fix tonal range and the general brightness and contrast of an image.

1. Open a black-and-white image for corrections.

2. Complete dust corrections, cropping, and minor alterations.

3. Create an adjustment layer for adjusting levels (Layer → New Adjustment Layer → Levels).

4. Make an inspection of the image visually (on the monitor) and using the histogram, noting the image qualities (the image key, contrast, and potential damage). If there are no concerns about the histogram and image damage, skip to Step 6.

5. If the histogram seems out of character with the image or shows hints of damage, consider rescanning, replacing the image, or weeding out the source of the trouble.

6. Correct shortened tonal range by adjusting the Levels sliders.

7. Adjust the mid-tone slider on the Levels graph to manipulate the overall brightness of the image.

Of the steps here, all but Steps 6 and 7 have been covered previously. To understand the effects such changes have on an image, it will be best to look at an example. Look back at the image and histogram in Figure 3.9. The image was originally in color, and the warm tones in the color made the low-key appearance interesting. However, once converted to black-and-white, the image became dark and murky. This is confirmed by the histogram, which shows a decided skew toward the dark end of the graph and a gap between midtones and highlights.

Moving the Levels sliders to the left will lighten the image; moving them to the right will darken the image. Where exactly to place the slider is a matter of what you want to accomplish. Changes can be conservative or quite radical. To correct a shortened tonal range, simply move the end slider on the side of the gap in toward the graph to where the graph information becomes solid (see Figure 3.10).

When you commit your changes by clicking OK, Photoshop Elements redistributes the tones over the total available range (0 to 255 levels of gray). Redistribution of the tonal information in an image from a thinner to a broader range will necessarily create some gaps in the presentation of the image information as the information is redistributed (see Figure 3.11).

This Levels change is one you can make strictly by looking at the appearance of the histogram and adjusting accordingly. The purpose is to take full advantage of the tonal range. The change will intensify overall contrast and broaden the dynamic range of the image. It may, however, affect the apparent key or contrast of the image.

> One possible means of smoothing inconsistent tonality caused by redistribution is to apply a slight (less than 1-pixel radius) Blur or Sharpen filter to the image. This will, however, change fine detail and distort edges depending on the severity of the application of either filter.

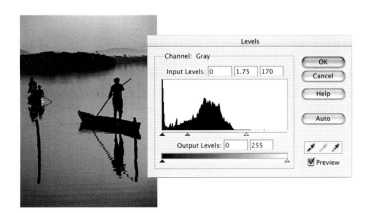

Figure 3.10

The levels sliders let you quickly redefine the white and black points in an image and redistribute tone.

Figure 3.11

Gaps can suggest that image information is adjusted, but can also signify damage (or just that you've got the Use Cache For Histograms preference checked in the Image Cache preferences).

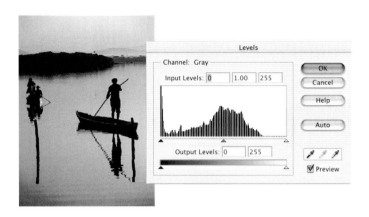

It may be possible and desirable to go even further with this levels correction. When a histogram presents a "tail" toward the shadows or highlights, it can often be clipped in part or whole. Tails on the histogram often represent scattered highlight or shadow information—generally attributable to image noise rather than actual image detail. Snipping the information turns it to absolute white for a highlight, or absolute black for a shadow. Generally, you will want to cut an entire tail when the graph represents scattered pixels; however, it is sometimes desirable to eliminate none, some, or all of a solid tail, depending on the image and the length of the tail.

As a general rule, the longer the tail, the less (proportionally) you should cut off. For example, whereas you may completely remove a tail that covers 15 levels, you might trim half or less of a tail that covers 50 pixels, or 33% of one that covers 100 levels. Cutting proportionally in this way will help retain image integrity and character.

Don't feel that you have to crop a tail in an image just because it exists. If the results seem too drastic after cutting a tail, then they are. Put simply: Do crop a tail that improves the image; don't crop a tail that compromises the image.

After adjusting tonal range, images can be adjusted for overall brightness as well. A black-and-white image that appears too dark or light can be corrected by using the middle slider in the Levels tool. Moving the slider to the left lightens midtones, whereas moving it to the right darkens them. This may seem slightly counterintuitive; however, it makes a lot of sense. The idea is that you are moving the median so that more levels of tone fall within the lighter or darker half of the tonal range.

Be careful not to abuse this tool—there are other, and perhaps better, ways of controlling the midtones (such as using Curves, as described in the next section). As a guide, try not to move the midtone slider more than 25 levels in any direction when making corrections. This keeps the redistribution small and more forgiving. You can always come back and lighten or darken an image later.

While Levels adjustments can be made automatically, it is suggested that you do not use automation. Automated tools may get it right sometimes, but there will be many images where personal judgment should prevail. Auto-corrections have no means to determine what "looks good."

Snapping and Fading Contrast with Curves

Curves is the ideal tool to help fine-tune and reshape the tonal distribution of an image. Whereas levels have only three slider points to change, curves can have many and can allow you to control different tonal levels separately. Curves is both a more versatile correction tool and a more dangerous one than Levels because of its power. However, using Curves can help remove steps in corrections because you can make numerous corrections to various parts of image tone in one application.

Because the Curves tool is powerful, applying it requires a little more savvy. It also requires installing Hidden Power Tools, because normally you can't get to Curves using the Photoshop Elements interface. Apply Curves with the following steps:

1. Open an image and determine through inspection and measurement what needs to be altered.

2. Click the uppermost layer on the image to highlight it. It is fine if this image is the background.

3. Open the Hidden Power Tools and click the Tools tab.

4. Click Curves. This opens the New Layer dialog box.

5. Click OK. This opens the Curves dialog box and creates a new Curves Adjustment layer in the Layers palette. See Figure 3.12.

6. Set points on the curve to redistribute image information. (See the following sections, "Using the Curves Interface" and "Manipulating Curves," for more information.)

7. Click OK to accept changes and close the dialog box.

Steps 1 through 6 create a Curves layer for the image. You will be able to manipulate the curve until you accept the changes in step 7, at which point the curve will become uneditable. To make further changes, you can either add another Curves layer or delete the layer and replace it. Shutting off the View for the layer temporarily shuts off the curve.

Before looking at how to apply Curves, we need to look briefly at the interface and how to manipulate the curve.

Figure 3.12

The Curves dialog box

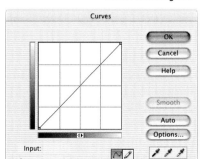

Using the Curves Interface

The line that runs from the lower left to the upper right corner of the Curves dialog box represents tonal response. On the initial screen there will be two points, one at black and one at white. When you alter the line (which we'll do in a moment), you alter the tonal response of the image.

If you move your cursor over the graph, you'll note that the Input and Output numbers below the graph change according to the position of the cursor. These numbers represent the vertical (Output) and horizontal (Input) positions on the graph. Look at the gradient below the Curves dialog box and click the arrows in the center if it does not look like Figure 3.12. Once that is set, if you roll the cursor above the line, the Input number will be lower than the Output; if you roll the cursor below the line, the Input number will be higher than the Output. As you roll the cursor on the line, Input will equal Output.

The Curve graph can be in two modes, percentage and levels of gray. Percentage measures the percentage of black (0-100%) and levels of gray measures the number of levels of brightness (0-255). The percentage graph runs light to dark: higher percentage means more black. The levels graph runs dark to light: more levels means brighter tone. You can switch between grayscale in levels and grayscale in percentages by clicking the arrow button in the center of the gradient bar below the graph. Photoshop Elements will remember this setting for the next time you use the Curves dialog.

Change to levels display and move the cursor around the graph until you are at an Input/Output reading of 128,128. This will be the center of the graph. Clicking the mouse at that point will place a new point on the line, and will change the Input/Output readings to fields that represent the position of the current point. If you click on the same point and drag (holding the mouse button down), you can move the point and the curve. As you move the curve, the tonality of the image shifts according to the change in position. When viewing levels, the image will get lighter as you shift the arc of the curve upward and darker as you shift the arc of the curve down (see Figure 3.13). When viewing percentages, the relationship is reversed.

Figure 3.13

When the curve is displayed in levels of gray (rather than percentages), reducing the volume under the curve darkens the image (left). This relationship reverses when the curve displays percentages (right).

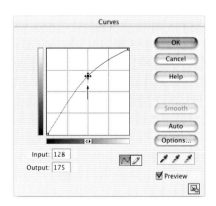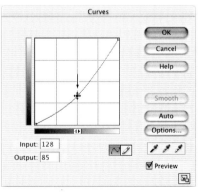

You can manipulate the position of points by typing numbers into the Input and Output fields. If you highlight the Input and type 63, then press Tab and type 63, the response of the curve will flatten, and the point will move to the 75% black hash.

Without closing the dialog box, move your cursor over the image. Your cursor will become the Eyedropper tool. Look for a place in the image that is close to 50% gray. When you have located the spot, hold down the Command/Ctrl key and click the mouse. A new point will be created on the curve representing the tone sampled in the image.

To add a point:

- Hold Command/Ctrl and click to sample the image.

- Move the cursor over the curve and click.

To move a point:

- Click on the point and drag.

- Highlight the point (by clicking it) and change the Input/Output numbers.

- Highlight the point (by clicking it) and press the keyboard arrows in the direction you want to move the point. Hold the Shift key to move 10 levels in the arrow direction.

To remove a point:

- Position the cursor over the point, hold Command/Ctrl, and click.

- Highlight the point (by clicking it) and press Delete.

- Click and drag the point off the dialog box.

Although there are a few other features in the Curves dialog box, these will be all you'll need to understand to make specific adjustments.

Manipulating Curves

Specific tonal distribution changes that you make with Curves can be far more flexible than changes you can effect with Levels. If Levels is considered as a tool to affect the tonal range of the image, Curves can be considered the tool for effecting change in contrast.

A simple way to look at curves is that contrast increases in the tonal range between points where the curve is steeper and contrast decreases in the tonal range where the curve flattens out. The curve in Figure 3.14 will increase contrast in the image midtones (between 25% and 75% black).

Figure 3.15 shows a curve that will decrease contrast in the midtones over the same range. Note that the increase in contrast over the midtones in Figure 3.14 decreases the contrast in the highlights (191 to 255 levels) and shadows (0 to 63 levels); in Figure 3.15, decreasing the contrast increases the contrast in the highlights and shadows.

Midtones   Shadows   Highlights

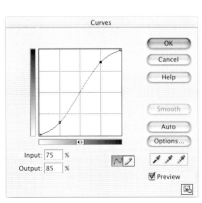

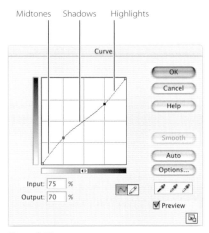

Figure 3.14

A steeper rise in the curve between Input values of 25% and 75% makes contrast sharper through the midtones.

Figure 3.15

Decreasing midtone contrast increases contrast in shadows and highlights.

Figure 3.16

Anchoring the curve with extra points that just hold the curve in place can reduce the effect of an equal and opposite reaction to your changes.

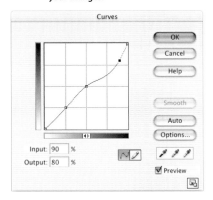

All points that you put on a curve will not necessarily be for moving the curve. At times it will be useful to place anchors on the curve to keep the tone in that area of the image from changing, or to act as a pivot for adjustments. For example, anchors set in the highlight and midtone can keep the tone in the highlight from changing while you adjust shadows (See Figure 3.16).

Corrections in contrast over shorter ranges should be evaluated with the Eyedropper to help limit the correction to that range. For example, if shadows seem somewhat flat or highlights lack detail, there might be a reason to strengthen the contrast just in those ranges. To measure the range, measure the brightest and darkest areas of the tonal range you want to include by dragging the Eyedropper. Test samples in areas near the light and dark side of the range, and note what the values are. When you determine the range, set anchor points either by using samples or by clicking the curve and entering sample values (as Input). Sample values will be shown in grayscale percentages on the Info palette, so they will have to be converted to levels. To make the conversion from percentages to levels, you can multiply a percentage by 2.55.

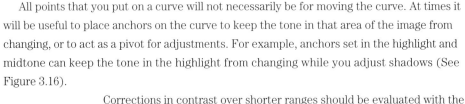

The Sample Size setting for the Eyedropper tool affects the result of samples used with curves. In most cases, you should use a sample of 3 or 5 pixels rather than a point sample. Control-click/right-click to bring up the Sample Size menu.

The image used in the following procedure (see `contrastfix.psd` on the CD) was taken in direct sunlight, making for a high-contrast exposure. Your goal is to slow the transition from highlight to shadow, as well as lighten the image.

1. Open the image you want to correct (see Figure 3.17).

2. Set the options for the Eyedropper and Info palette. For this example I chose a sample of 3 by 3 for the Eyedropper and changed one of the Info palette colors to K (Grayscale).

3. Open the Hidden Power Tools and click Curves.

4. Click OK when the New Layer dialog box appears.

5. Sample the bright end of the range you want to correct (see Figure 3.18) and create a curve point.

6. Sample the dark end of the range you want to correct (see Figure 3.19) and create a curve point.

7. Adjust the position of the curve points to effect the desired change. In Figure 3.20, the 51% (134 levels) point was changed to an output of 33% (171 levels).

8. Repeat steps 5 through 7 to continue adding points and adjusting other tonal relationships.

9. Click OK to accept the changes in the curve.

10. Add additional curves using steps 3 through 9 to make further modifications to the tone as necessary. See Figure 3.21.

Keeping a curve as a smooth cascade is more likely to create good results. Jagged curves tend to be unpredictable and will more likely produce special effects than corrections. If changes seem extreme or become difficult, make them over the course of several applications of Curves rather than just in one shot. This will allow you to compare adjustments by toggling layer views, as well as allowing you to fine tune.

Figure 3.17

This image was taken in direct sunlight and shows harsh shadows.

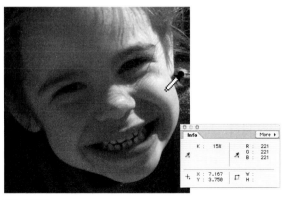

Figure 3.18

The highlighted area of the cheek is the lightest portion of the area that will be changed.

Figure 3.19

Decreasing contrast over the transition between highlight and shadow increases detail.

Figure 3.20

The changes in the curve lighten the image and reduce contrast in the midtones while improving contrast in the highlight and shadow detail.

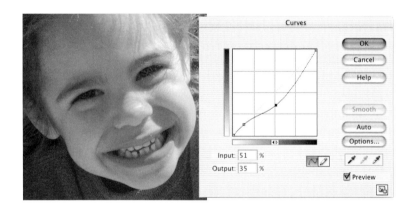

Figure 3.21

The result of several curve applications has improved the tonality of the image by lessening the harsh contrast between light and dark while enhancing contrast in selected areas.

(Un)Sharpening and Boosting Contrast

The sharpening filters in Photoshop Elements are not magic. They will not take a wildly out-of-focus image and snap it back into focus. This is not to say that it is impossible to use filters to improve the appearance of an image; however, you should not expect a miraculous recovery. Although they can help the appearance of sharpness in the image, there are actually several uses for sharpening tools.

Sharpening—specifically the Unsharp Mask filter—enhances contrast. The filters strengthen local contrast in an image based on the difference between adjacent tones and the radius and percentage you select in the dialog box. This enhancement is useful not only for improving the appearance of slightly blurry images, but also for adjusting images after resizing and for increasing contrast between image elements in low-contrast images. In other words, while the filter can help with sharpening, it can also be used as an intelligent tool for enhancing image contrast.

> Although there are other sharpening tools (the freehand Sharpen tool, and the Sharpen, Sharpen Edges, and Sharpen More filters), I find them somewhat less valuable because they lack controls. They do nothing that you can't do using the Unsharp Mask filter.

The Unsharp Mask Dialog Box

The Unsharp Mask dialog box (Filter → Sharpen → Unsharp Mask) has three sliders: Amount, Radius, and Threshold (see Figure 3.22). The Amount can be between 1% and 500% and determines how much effect neighboring pixels will have on one another. The setting is affected by choices for radius and threshold: the higher the percentage, the greater the effect. The Radius can be from 0.1 to 250 pixels and works similarly to a feather radius: the farther out from the center of the radius, the weaker the effect. The Threshold option affects the way pixels work against each other based on their relative difference. The threshold notes the number of levels by which neighboring pixels must differ to have an effect on the pixel being looked at. For example, a low threshold (0) would allow neighboring pixels to freely affect one another if there is a difference; a high threshold (255) keeps pixels from affecting one another. The dialog box offers preview and zoom buttons in addition to the sliders.

The goal of sharpening is to improve, not reclaim, an image. The effect will work more or less effectively depending on the content of the image.

Generally, you will want to choose a setting with a low threshold, which is measured in levels. This means Photoshop Elements will look at the number of levels of difference in the surrounding pixels, and if the number of levels is greater than the threshold, it will apply sharpening based on the settings for Radius and Amount.

Figure 3.22

The Unsharp Mask dialog box (Filter → Sharpen → Unsharp Mask)

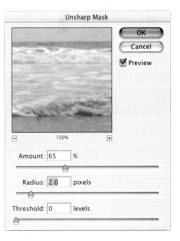

The name Unsharp Mask comes from the traditional darkroom process where an inverted, blurred (unsharp) duplicate of the original image was sandwiched to mask the exposure during printing. This helped target and adjust (sharpen) contrast differences.

You should usually keep the Threshold setting between 0 and 5—toward the lower end of this range. Often you will want to use zero tolerance, but some tolerance (1 or 2) will keep Photoshop from sharpening what is otherwise image noise. Sharpening noise will only make the image noisier. With that in mind, the noisier the image, generally the greater the threshold you should use. The only time you will set the threshold higher than 5 is when you want to limit the effect of the filter to high-contrast areas of the image to play up existing contrast and separation of image elements.

Radius and Amount might be set quite differently depending on what you are trying to achieve and the ppi and content of the image. In many cases, you might actually apply the filter twice: once with a low radius for general sharpening, and once with a higher radius for broader enhancement of image contrast.

Affecting Sharpness with the Unsharp Mask Filter

Sharpening an image with the Unsharp Mask filter depends on Elements recognizing and enhancing existing edges in an image. In other words, if the image is too blurry to recognize, the filter can't tell where the edge is, so it can't tell what to enhance. This is why the filter works best on images that are already characteristically sharp.

Although settings can vary depending on the type of image and desired effect, you will probably normally maintain the following settings in images that have average busyness and contrast:

Radius	0.5% to 1.5% of the ppi
Amount	50% to 100%

For example, a 300ppi image would have a target range for the Radius of about 1.5 to 4.5 pixels; a 72ppi image of the same size and similar content would have a Radius of about 0.35 pixel to 1 pixel. Note that these are rough guidelines, but they work for a variety of situations. If the content of the image is not busy, lacks focus, and/or is lower-contrast, you can tend toward the high end of the ranges; if the image is busier, is relatively sharp, and has high contrast, you would probably tend toward the low end.

Figure 3.23 shows an image before and after sharpening. Before sharpening, the image appears slightly soft, and perhaps a bit lacking in contrast. A single application of the Unsharp Mask filter in the midpoint for the suggested range increases the contrast and seems to boost the sharpness (see Figure 3.23).

A *halo* effect occurs when the Unsharp Mask is applied too strongly over image areas where flatly dark portions of an image meet flatly light portions of an image (see Figure 3.24). Often it is more apparent when the applied Radius is short—or not long enough to dissipate without being obvious. Not only will the halo tend to blow out (or clip) areas of images, but the image will also distort and the effect will become unpleasant.

Staying within the guidelines helps you avoid the potential problems with over-sharpening and creating halos in high-contrast areas of your images. Better to sharpen a little several times or try other measures to accomplish your effects than to sharpen hastily and heavily and damage the image.

Raising Local Contrast with Sharpening

Sharpening with the Unsharp Mask filter has a much different effect on an image than applying Curves or Levels, as the effect actually compares adjacent pixels. It does less to sharpen the details than it does to enhance differences that already exist in the image. This effect works well with low-contrast images, or images that seem to somehow lack dynamics.

Figure 3.23

Sharpness and contrast in this image appear to improve with an application of Unsharp Mask.

Figure 3.24

The original image and an over-sharpened counterpart: While some sharpening effects may be desirable, a halo effect probably will not be.

When you are adjusting local contrast with the Unsharp Mask, the Radius might be much higher than suggested for normal sharpening (15% to 40% of the ppi), and the amount between 10% and 35%. Again, these are just suggested ranges. The goal of the settings is to increase the radius beyond the distance where a halo is noticeable, and to keep the effect from causing damage (hence the low intensity, or Amount).

Figure 3.25 shows a somewhat low-contrast image of a ship and corrections using the Unsharp Mask filter. While it looks okay in color, the image lacks a little pop in black-and-white. By raising the local contrast using the Unsharp Mask, the image elements will have more separation from one another. Two applications of Unsharp Mask—one to build local contrast, and one to sharpen—make quick work of what would otherwise be an arduous task in masking to separate this boat from its surroundings.

The third image adds slight Levels and Curves adjustments to finish up the adjustment. Curves were used to make a simple enhancement to the contrast that Unsharp Mask brought out, and Levels were used to adjust final brightness. Some tone was replaced quickly by duplicating the original, moving it to the top of the stack, setting it to darken, and lowering the Opacity to 10%; this effectively filled in areas that sharpening had forced to clip (go to 0% gray).

Figure 3.25

The original boat is a little dull (a). After raising the local contrast with the **Unsharp Mask** (using a broad radius and low percentage), the boat stands out better from the surroundings (b). The filter is then applied again (c), but this time to sharpen the image (using a short radius and higher percentage).

Managing Image Noise

Having noise in an image can mean a number of things, from having many objects in an image to something more akin to random digitized information—like you might get when turning your TV on without a signal or antenna. Unlike editing clutter from an image, the concepts here will help you to reduce and eliminate undesirable patterning and texture in an image.

At times you may want to edit out, reduce, or even add image noise to achieve particular effects in your images. To do this, you will use Blur and Add Noise filters, often in conjunction with other image editing functions, like layer blending, selection, masking, and perhaps a few Hidden Power Tools.

The Gaussian Blur filter (Filter → Blur → Gaussian Blur) can effectively blur images or image areas. It does this by averaging the effects of pixels over a Radius, which you define using a slider on the dialog box: the greater the radius, the more intense the effect of the blur. As a result of averaging pixels, blurring removes or lessens the effect of image noise by lowering the contrast of adjacent pixels. This averaging softens image edges or smoothes hard lines between areas of contrast, and can obliterate image details. Essentially, this is the opposite of Sharpening, which builds existing contrast.

The Add Noise filter (Filter → Noise → Add Noise) generates image noise by randomizing color assignments for pixels. There are several choices in the Add Noise dialog box for controlling the effect. The Amount is related to Percentage, and defines the range of variation possible in creating the noise distribution. As the Amount goes up, the application of the noise is potentially more radical. Very strong applications of noise, like blur, can obliterate detail—in this case by wiping it out with random behavior rather than averaging. Noise applications can swiftly become something of a special effect, depending on the ppi of the image. An image with a higher ppi will be able to withstand stronger applications of the filter.

Generation of noise will be affected by the Distribution Type. A *Uniform* distribution changes the values of individual pixels by selecting a random number within the range defined by the amount. This number can be the original value plus or minus the amount for each channel of color. For example, applying an Amount of 25 to a 50% gray image (128 levels) in Grayscale will result in values between 103 and 153 levels of gray for any pixel, each value generated at random.

A *Gaussian* distribution changes the values of individual pixels by selecting a random number based on a Gaussian function. The function creates a tendency to select from the center of the range, but can also deviate more strongly from that norm. While the quantitative effects to each pixel can actually extend beyond what is dictated by Amount, the total effect is the same—just with greater peaks and valleys in the deviation. Because deviations can potentially be broader, Gaussian noise can appear to be a stronger effect than the Uniform distribution with the same Amount setting as shown in Figure 3.26.

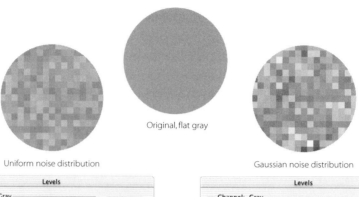

Original, flat gray

Uniform noise distribution

Gaussian noise distribution

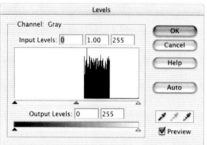

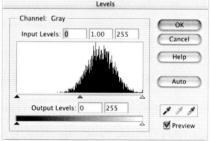

Figure 3.26

A magnification of a 25% gray area shown with Uniform and Gaussian noise distributions of 10%. The histograms show the flat application of noise in the Uniform distribution and the bell-shaped application in Gaussian distribution.

The *Monochromatic* option applies the filter to only the tonal elements in the image without changing the color. For example, this would keep an RGB image that has been desaturated from generating color noise when the filter is run.

So far, neither adding noise nor blurring may sound like a desirable thing, because either would seem to be damaging to an image. However, used in a controlled fashion, both can enhance an image and make results more realistic.

An image or image area that is affected by JPEG compression can be restored, somewhat, by blurring. In this case, blurring could potentially dissipate artifacts generated by compression. In a similar way, some types of digital noise can be lessened or removed, as might be effects of film grain, halftone printing, and paper texture. Blurring can also help in isolating image subjects by imitating effects of focus, like depth of field.

On the other side of the coin, most image tones that look natural in an image are not completely flat when you look at them close up. When you attempt to add new elements to an image, such as by painting them in with flat tones or creating an area with blends (for example, to replace a sky), the elements can tend to look *too* perfect. The result is that the repair will look like a repair. Applying noise can mimic a more natural look by randomizing and effectively dithering image information. Additionally, you can use Add Noise to create texture or graininess (e.g., mimic film grain).

As strange as it may seem, sometimes when blurring won't solve a problem that you may have thought required noise reduction, applying noise can. Even more often, applying both blur and noise can do the job.

Blur and Add Noise filters can be used effectively along with other functions to produce the best results. For example, you might make a selection of a particularly noisy area of an image to isolate it before applying a blur. After using Blur, you may need to use the Add Noise filter to fix the blurred areas so that they don't seem flat. You also might make use of a layer mode, mask, or other feature.

Both Add Noise and Blur are best if applied lightly, and in combination. Figure 3.27 shows a repair in which noise was used to make an image correction blend better, after a blur was applied. The skin on the subject is not bad, but it could appear much more youthful with gentler pores.

A selection was made of the subject's face (mostly using the red channel as a mask). With the selection loaded, the area of the subject's skin was copied and pasted to its own layer to isolate it. Once isolated, the copied skin was blurred. The results smoothed the skin, but left it too flat. Noise was added, using Uniform distribution with the Monochromatic box checked. This returns some of the texture to the skin without leaving it looking too flat and fake.

Figure 3.27

Original image and (a) the image blurred, (b) then noise added and Opacity adjusted (c).

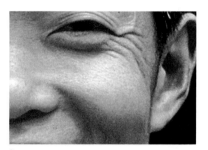

a

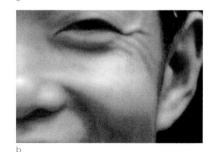

b

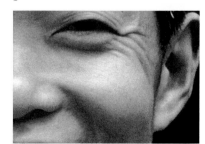

c

The appearance of the pores is softened first, using the Blur filter to remove noise. Next, the Add Noise filter is used to gently replace some of what was lost in the texture. The result is much smoother skin, and a somewhat more youthful smile.

Several effects, including erasing information on the new layer or masking, could have been used to bring back the details that were getting covered. However, Blend Masking, a Hidden Power Tool was applied to the layer to allow the character of wrinkles to blend through based on tone. Again, combinations of tool applications and functions generally work best in achieving goals in an image because no one tool can do it all. We'll see more of Blend Masking in the following section.

Masking with Image Tone

Masks are very much like selections, in that they can help you isolate image areas and work on them without affecting other parts of the image. You saw an example of how this can help you target image changes by isolating the sky from the water in the Gradient Map example in Chapter 2, "Separating Color Into Tone." One frustration with using Photoshop Elements is that it allows you to use masks only in conjunction with adjustment layers, and does not freely allow the user to mask any layer in an image. It also doesn't allow you to work fluidly with alpha channels, which are places the full-version of Photoshop can store masks and selections. While you can save a selection in Elements 2, you still can't attach a mask to any old layer.

Hidden Power Tools to the rescue!

The Hidden Power Blend Mask is a unique solution to this problem based on layer clipping and layer transparency. It allows you to make white areas of a layer transparent with a single click. It leaves black solid and turns levels of gray to semi-transparent pixels—the darker the pixel, the less transparent it is. These semi-transparent layers can then be grouped with other image content to be used as high-tech cookie cutters to reveal only what you want to see from the original image in a separate layer.

Because it is based on tone, the Blend Mask tool gives you the power to mask exact areas of an image based on any image quality that you can isolate as tone. Clever manipulation of tone using curves can allow you to target specific image areas based on particular qualities. These qualities can influence an image whether the image is color or black-and-white.

So what does this do for you? Well, say you have a color image that looks a little flat in the shadows. You know there is image detail there, but you can't seem to coax it out no matter what you try: every time you make a change that helps the area you are trying to affect, the other image areas go sour. Creating a mask for the shadows (75%–100% black) would allow you to isolate the dark portion of the image so you can make changes there without affecting anything else.

Figure 3.28 shows an image that could benefit from correction in just the shadow area. To mask just the shadow, you can create a Blend Mask using Hidden Power Tools. Several power tools converge here to create your image-editing advantage.

1. Open the sample image (`horsehead.psd`) from the CD.

2. Create a Luminosity layer by clicking Add Luminosity in Hidden Power Tools. Change the name of the Luminosity layer to Masking Tone.

3. Create a new layer above the background and name it Mask.

4. Turn off the visibility for the Background layer.

5. Activate the Masking Tone layer and click Curves on the Tools tab of the Hidden Power Tools to create a curve adjustment layer. Be sure to click the Group With Previous checkbox when the New Layer dialogue opens.

6. Click on the center of the curve graph to create a new point on the curve. If the curve is displaying as levels, click the arrow to change to percentage display.

7. Change the position of the current point to 75,100 (Input/Output), by typing these values in the appropriate fields as shown in Figure 3.29.

8. Create another point on the curve by clicking near the center of the graph.

9. Change the position of the point to 73,0 by typing the values into the Input and Output fields as shown in Figure 3.30.

Figure 3.28

This image of a giant bronze horse was taken with the sun as a backlight, leaving the detail of the shadow a little flat.

Figure 3.29

Darkening the image is just the beginning of creating your mask.

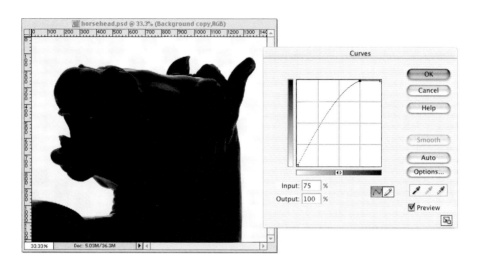

Figure 3.30

Shifting the position of this point will create stark contrast between the shadow (75%–100% black) and the rest of the image (0%–74% black).

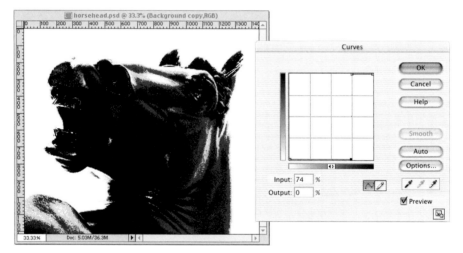

10. Accept the changes to the curve by clicking OK.

11. Merge the Curve with the Masking Tone layer (Layer → Merge Down) to commit the curve changes.

12. Click Clear Grayscale on the Hidden Power Tools. This will remove the white and grays from the Masking Tone layer to reveal the transparency grid. Only portions of the image that are 75%–100% black based on luminosity will be opaque.

13. Merge the Masking Tone layer with the Mask layer. This will commit the transparency of the adjustment to the tone as a mask.

14. Turn on the visibility for the Background layer.

15. Duplicate the Background layer and name it Isolated Shadows.

16. Move the Isolated Shadows layer to the top of the layer stack.

17. Group the Isolated Shadows layer with the Mask layer. This completes the masking, and the layers should look as they do in Figure 3.31.

Figure 3.31

When Steps 1 to 17 are complete, your masking should show the Isolated Shadows layer grouped with the Mask layer.

If you turn off the visibility for the Background layer at this point, the shadows will show without the non-shadow portions of the image. You can make adjustments to the color or tone in the shadow area by applying changes to the Isolated Shadows layer, but be sure to group adjustment layers. Commit the changes by flattening the image. The Blend Mask Hidden Power Tool will perform steps 2-17 for you, but you won't always want to just run full speed through this masking process. If you want to convert a black-and-white layer to a masking layer, the Transparent Grayscale Hidden Power Tool will do that.

Masks and black-and-white representations can be created to target and exclude all sorts of image information. The key to targeting your masked information is the Blend Mask tool, which affects the layer transparency, and the application of the curve. Curves can help you create complex masks based entirely on tonal components. For example, if you wanted to mask only the middle tones in an image, the curve would look like Figure 3.32.

Not only can you work with components separated from your original image, but you can also combine the results to target even more specific image areas. For example, say you want to adjust color in the midtones for a particular color component. You could target the midtones and make a color shift, but that would affect all other color in the image; You could use Hue/Saturation set to a component color, but that would limit you to using only Hue/Saturation for the correction.

Figure 3.32

This curve applied to luminosity will allow you to isolate midtones.

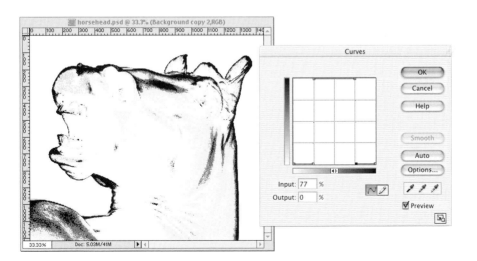

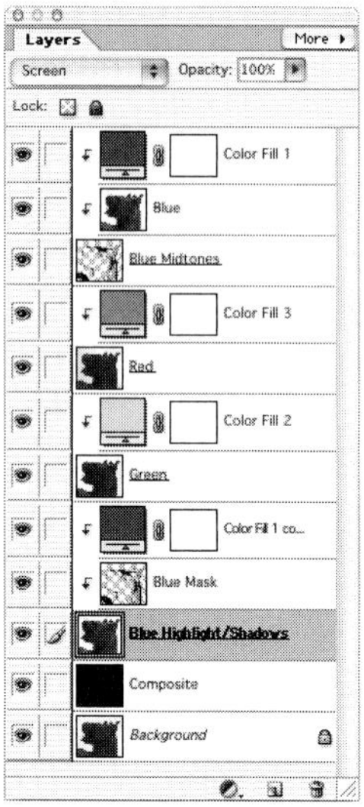

Figure 3.33

Multiple mask applications allow you to accurately target changes in your images.

Using the midtone mask could help you isolate the midtones in a color or luminosity component so you have more freedom to make corrections in a specific area of the image. All you have to do is make the masking component, and apply. You could isolate the midtones on the blue component of the RGB separation as follows:

1. Open the image you want to correct as a flattened RGB image.

2. Click Blend Mask on the Hidden Power Tools and set the Curve to look like Figure 3.32 when it appears. Allow the masking to complete. This will create the midtone mask.

3. Duplicate the background to a new image (using Duplicate Layer in the layers pop-up menu), and separate the image by clicking Split RGB w/Preview.

4. Activate the original document and duplicate the Mask to the separated image two times. Name the duplicates Layer 1, and Blue Midtones.

5. Activate the new document and create a new layer below Layer 1. Fill it with white and name it Blue Mask.

6. Merge Layer 1 and the Blue Mask, then drag it between the Blue layer and its Color Fill layer. Change the mode to Multiply. This will blot out the influence of the Blue layer midtones.

7. Duplicate the Blue layer, change the Blue copy layer name to Blue Highlight/Shadow. The Highlight/Shadow layer will remain grouped with the Blue Mask and Fill layers.

8. Change the mode of the Blue layer to Normal and drag it above Blue Midtones, then group Blue and Blue Midtones. Change the mode of Blue Midtones to Screen.

9. Duplicate the Blue Highlight/Shadow layer's Color Fill layer and drag the duplicate above the Blue layer, then group the Blue and Color Fill copy layers.

Once you have completed these steps, the masking will have been used to effectively isolate the blue midtones. The layer stack will look like Figure 3.33 and the image will look exactly the same as the original. However, if you add a Levels adjustment layer above the Blue layer, and you'll be able to adjust the blue midtones in isolation from the rest of the image color—without effecting the highlight and shadow. In other words, you are free, at this point to replace just that portion of the image with any tone or color that you want. In a similar way, you could create masking for highlights, shadows, and any combination of color and tone to accurately target an image area for change.

These changes and more are possible, and they become important when attempting more complicated color separations and application. We'll implement some interesting uses of this type of masking in the next few chapters.

Part III

Serious Color Correction

The term "color correction" suggests that there is a correct color in the first place. You may consider "correct" to be what you saw with your eyes when taking an image. But your eyes can adjust to color and lighting conditions so they are not good at judging the quality of color in a scene.

It would be nice if there were a quantitative measure of "correctness" that would guarantee the best color, because that would make correction easier. However, in actuality, what looks best won't necessarily match the original color, and in some cases matching color will not be what you'll want to do at all. You can match the color of prints, slides, and transparencies by measuring with sophisticated devices, but correcting to specific color doesn't guarantee that the color will look its best. In this section we'll look at ways that you might apply color correction for both technical and artistic success using techniques that expand on those you learned in Chapter 3.

Chapter 4 **Applying Tonal Manipulations to Color**

Chapter 5 **Color-Specific Correction Tools**

Chapter 4

Applying Tonal Manipulations to Color

If you look at separations into RGB as a basis for forming color, color is just a slightly more complex version of black and white. The difference ends up being that there are three grayscale images sandwiched together to make a color representation. If you consider the three black-and-white parts of your color image separately, and make basic correction to the tones, it is interesting to note that correction for color follows. The Levels and Curves manipulations and techniques from Chapter 3 can be implemented in almost exactly the same way in adjusting color. Correcting color in an RGB image involves adjusting the tone in each of the RGB channels, just like you adjust the dynamic range for tone in grayscale. This type of correction will adjust many color saturation and brightness problems and can often balance color to compensate for color shifts caused by lighting. In the next sections, we'll look at the techniques for performing this type of correction as well as the reasons why it works.

Minor Cleanup for Color Images

Levels Correction for Color

Curves Correction for Color

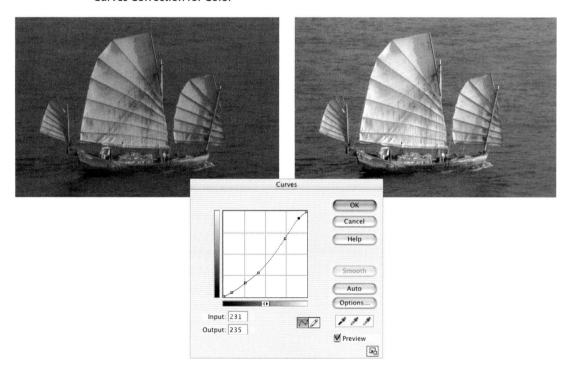

Minor Cleanup for Color Images

The place to start in doing minor cleanup is to get rid of what absolutely should not be in the image. Cleanup for color images is very similar to the techniques already describe for cleaning tone. Basically, you use the Rubber Stamp tool to clear out spots and minor debris by stamping over them with good replacements. Because you are trying to match red, green, and blue tones all at the same time, you have to be careful in selecting the source for replacement color. Making the corrections in a new layer can help by allowing you to fine-tune any changes. The Use All Layers option for the Clone Stamp tool should remain turned on.

Other options for cleanup can present themselves in separated channels more readily than on a color composite. Looking at RGB tones or Luminosity and Color separations may reveal color-specific noise or other damage (such as stains on scanned prints). All you have to do is split the channels using Hidden Power Tools, then examine the separations individually to see if there is any damage.

To view the grayscale for a specific channel, turn off the visibility for the two other color channels and the color fill associated with the channel (see Figure 4.1).

The Prokudin-Gorskii images from Chapter 1 (`Gorskii.psd`) are a great example of how correcting in separated tones may be useful. The glass plates in Gorskii's images have unique information because they were taken separately. Therefore, each color plate has unique damage from dust and scratches, as the red plate shows in Figure 4.2. In that case (certainly a rare one) it is actually better and easier to correct much of the damage in the separated tones as RGB because the damage will stand out more clearly than it will in color.

> Splitting out the channels is often good for removing color-related problems, such as stains on scanned prints or colored blemishes. We'll see more of the advantages when looking at more intensive color correction later in this chapter.

Once you have stamped out damage in the channels—and as long as you have made each correction carefully, so it is undetectable in each of the individual tones—the result should appear undetectable in the composite image as well. When the changes are complete, merge the separation back to a single layer by flattening the image before moving on to other corrections. Although you can switch back and forth between working with the separations and the composite without harming the image, you should avoid making a lot of separation changes at this point because it wastes time. This should usually be a simple, quick cleanup before getting on to the main course of correcting color.

Figure 4.1

To view the Blue channel, turn off the visibility for the Red and Green channels as well as the blue color fill.

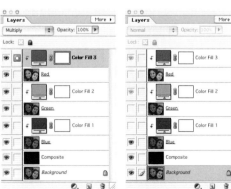

Figure 4.2

A defect in the red plate shows up prominently in the original scan of the Gorskii image.

Digital noise is sometimes a problem in images, and this may be something else that you will want to clean up at this point. Figure 4.3 shows a close-up of an image that was not taken in the best conditions. JPEG compression settings were not high, but they were high enough to accentuate the noise. Although the image isn't bad, it can be much better. The separation into RGB for this image can make it very clear that you have mostly color noise on your hands (You can see the original image as `vince.psd` on the CD, as well as before and after corrections in the color section.)

Cleaning up or improving such obvious problems may be something to consider at this point, or you might wait to do it after levels correction. It depends on how much help the image needs—the more help it needs, the less you should consider doing anything drastic before basic color correction. Doing too much before basic corrections can potentially cause even greater problems later on.

There are many more things that you can do in addition to the few steps we will go through here for correcting the color noise. For example, you might mask skin tone areas to apply smoothing to some of the tone or sharpen the image. But that type of correction, being more complex, is a good example of what it might be better for you to do later on, after initial color correction with levels. You will be able to better judge when to flip-flop your basic correction steps as you gain additional experience with correction.

1. Open `vince.psd` from the CD.
2. Split luminosity and color by clicking Split Luminosity in the Hidden Power Tools.

3. Activate the Color layer by clicking on it in the Layers palette.

4. Apply a Gaussian Blur (Filter → Blur → Gaussian Blur). This will blur the color information in the image while keeping the tone intact. The results of these steps appear in Figure 4.4.

As the tone holds the detail in place, the color can be smoothed out without dropping the appearance of the image. When you are done, flatten the image and save it with a different name before continuing any other corrections. This will keep you from saving over the original if it turns out that you want to go back and see what happens if you don't correct the noise first.

Figure 4.3

This image shows digital noise even in black and white. Separating the channels of the image into RGB (using the Split RGB Channels Hidden Power Tool) makes it apparent where the damage is. The worst of the channels is the discouraging blue channel (e).

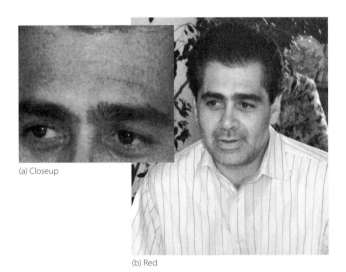

(a) Closeup

(b) Red

(c) Green

(d) Blue

(e) Blue Close-up

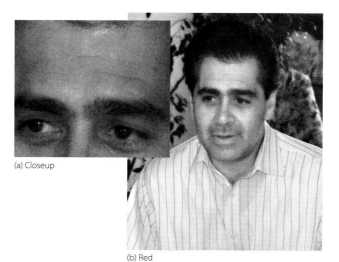

(a) Closeup

(b) Red

Figure 4.4

A great improvement can be seen in the color channels if you flatten the image again and separate the RGB. Note the dramatic change in the blue channel (e), and, surprisingly, you do not lose detail.

(c) Green

(e) Blue Close-up

(d) Blue

There is a noise reduction tool in the Hidden Power Tools that will perform the noise reduction steps for you while allowing you to choose how much blur to apply. When you need it, just click Reduce Color Noise in the Hidden Power Tools. The image will automatically flatten and commit the changes so that you will be ready for additional corrections.

Levels Correction for Color

Object color is a result of light. Brightness of 100% indicates a 100% intensity of red, green, and blue light components. Brightness of 0% indicates a 0% intensity of red, green, and blue. If the color in a scene runs from white to black (a full dynamic range), all of the tones must have

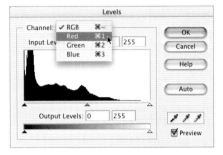

Figure 4.5

Selecting a channel color from the drop-down list in the Levels dialog box reveals the histogram specific to that channel and confines the effects of your adjustments to what you have selected without making separations.

a full range as well. Levels corrections for each channel optimize dynamic range, and correcting with Curves can fine-tune the quality of color.

If you followed the discussion of correcting tonality with levels in Chapter 3, making the leap to correcting color with Levels is a small step. It brings together the concept of separations from Chapter 2 with the corrective steps for Levels in Chapter 3. You want to apply Levels to the image tone as separate red, green, and blue components, and treat them as you would a black-and-white image.

The Levels dialog box makes it easy to apply corrections to the separate channels, and saves you the step of separating the colors into tone. All you have to do is open the Levels dialog box and correct the red, green, and blue channels for your image individually. You can do this by selecting the channels one at a time from the Channels drop-down list (see Figure 4.5). Make adjustments to each channel just as you would for a grayscale correction. Don't bother correcting the RGB composite; this will be taken care of if you do the Levels properly.

To apply corrections to separate channels:

1. Open the image you want to correct.

2. Complete minor cleanup.

3. Choose Enhance → Brightness/Contrast → Levels. This will open the Levels dialog box.

4. Select Red from the Channels drop list. This will reveal the histogram for the red channel.

5. Make a Levels correction for the channel using the guidelines provided in Chapter 3 for making grayscale corrections with Levels. The correction should be done by evaluating the Histogram.

6. Repeat Steps 4 and 5 for the Green and Blue channels.

7. Accept the changes by clicking OK. This will close the dialog box.

When the correction is complete, the image should show increased dynamic range, stronger saturation, and a better likeness to realistic color (color balance)—as long as there was something to correct. Again, this correction may not get you entirely where you want to be. You'll probably have additional corrections to make.

When making a Levels correction for color you must remember that:

- Making a correction might easily remove a desired color shift.

- You will want to make similar adjustments to histogram tails in the red, green, and blue channels to retain desired color shifts.

There are certain times when this type of Levels correction doesn't improve the image. Examples include extreme lighting conditions or adjustments that were made intentionally—such as in a sunset, or when an effect was achieved by color filtering (to purposely shift color in the image at the time it was taken).

Using a color version of the same image we worked with in the example for level correction of tone in Chapter 3, the Levels adjustment would probably look something like the sets of screens shown in Figure 4.6. (The result for the color image can be seen in the color section of this book.) The Levels correction in RGB will also improve the black-and-white result. Make the corrections yourself using the `boat.psd` image included on the CD.

If you make a Levels correction using the guidelines we looked at for correcting tone in Chapter 3, the color in this image will spring back to life on your screen. In effect, all you are doing is redistributing the black-and-white tones in the red, green, and blue components to achieve a better dynamic range. Because light in the most dynamic image will run from white to black, your correction in Levels is just enabling the image to look its best.

Figure 4.6

The corrections on the top row remove half the tail from each channel; the corrections below remove the entire tail. Color balance results from using a consistent approach to correcting image channels.

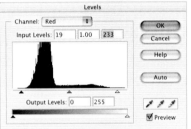 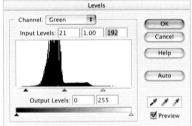 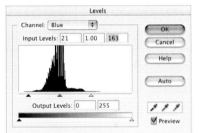

Half clipping

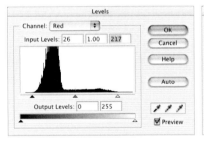 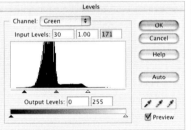 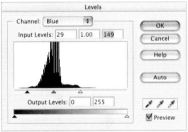

Full clipping

Original image   After full clipping

In the corrections for Figure 4.6 the rules are pretty clear-cut. Because the image doesn't have a decided skew, and there is a reasonable similarity in the quality of the histograms for red, green, and blue, the common rules hold. In Figure 4.7, however, the histograms are very different for the RGB channels and require some unusual treatment. The image is a close-up of a rose, and it is decidedly skewed toward reds. The first application of Levels is just a straight cut of the histogram tails, treating each Channel as if it were a black-and-white image. However, a better result is achieved by doing an additional adjustment to the RGB. Because the first adjustment makes the shadows seem pale, the image requires a shift in the midtones to

Figure 4.7

Visual evaluation of the results suggests an additional change in the composite level.

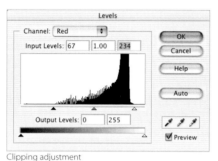

Clipping adjustment

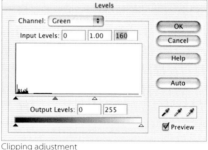

Clipping adjustment

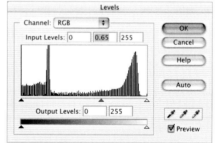

Clipping adjustment

Midtone adjustment

Original image

After adjustment

compensate—thereby pushing more image information toward the shadows. Once that's accomplished, the tone of the image seems more natural and balanced. See the result of these Levels applications in the color section. Use the image `rose.psd` on the CD to work the results for yourself.

Curves Correction for Color

Color casts in an image can result in flatness or unnatural color. A cast might be the result of poor image processing, varied lighting conditions (photos taken under fluorescent bulbs, for example), aging of the original medium (such as paper yellowing), or any number of other things. Basic color correction with Levels often takes care of a lot of these problems. But color casts and shifts between the lightest and darkest parts of an image are often a little more complex than looking at a Histogram or doing a linear color correction in Levels. Curves have an added level of complexity that makes them perfect tools for fine-tuning color.

The problem lies in knowing exactly what to do with your curve. It is very difficult to just look at an image and envision how a correction curve should look to fix problems in the image. While it may even be easy to determine what looks wrong, correcting it can easily remain a puzzle.

For example, say you are looking at an image and the color of the subject's skin just looks wrong. If the skin tone looks wrong, the image will look wrong. If there were a reference that you could use to correct skin tone perfectly, everything else in the image would also fall in line.

However, there is no absolute reference for skin tone. There are ways to estimate and approximate, but if approximations were good, you could just put your trust in the image you have on screen and correct completely by eye. The difference in skin tones is vast. Not only does skin tone have many colors and shades in general, the same person can have different skin tones at different times (such as having a tan, or looking pale or flushed). This being the case, there is no value that can be used as an accurate reference.

The best references to use in your image when you are considering making changes in image color are grays. Grays can act as references because they are easy to measure: they will have even amounts of red, green, and blue. When you measure with the Eyedropper, the R, G, and B values displayed in the Info palette should all be the same—or very nearly so.

In a perfect world, you could find areas of your image that would be grays of exactly 25% (64,64,64), 50% (128,128,128), and 75% (192,192,192) black when corrected. You could then take measurements from these areas of your digital image to use as references for correction. All you'd have to do is set accurate white and black points and then correct the sampled gray areas to a flat tone. As a result, your images would color balance nicely. However, it usually isn't too easy to find gray references unless you place them right in your image. While you can do this using a reference card (a gray card, usually 18% gray, but anything of a standard flat tone will work), it is not something that everyone will take the time to do.

Grays that already exist in the image can be used as reasonable substitutes for a reference card. If you look closely, you may find something that should be a flat shade of gray, such as a steel flag pole, chrome on a car, asphalt …anything that should be flat gray can be useful for color evaluation. White and black objects (such as paper or car tires) can work, too, as long as they are not over- or underexposed, respectively. While objects can also vary in color to some degree and sometimes drastically (such as the mossy side of a tree), they will often be easier to judge and correct for than skin tones.

Once you determine a target gray in your image, Curves can help you easily adjust image color. All you have to do is measure the tone and color of the gray object, and then adjust the curves to flatten the color response. Flattening the color response can be done by shifting the curves to correct the gray while ignoring everything else in the image.

To determine the values for a gray object to use in correcting an image, do the following:

1. Examine the image to locate an object that should be closest to gray.

2. Be sure the Info palette is visible and that one of the sample types is set to RGB Color (RGB).

3. Select the Eyedropper from the toolbox. Select a sample option depending on the size and resolution of the image. Larger images with more resolution can usually stand broader sample areas.

4. Point the tip of the Eyedropper at the gray reference area in the image.

5. Note the grayscale and RGB values shown on the Info palette.

6. Make an RGB separation (using Split RGB in Hidden Power Tools).

7. Adjust the Red, Green, and Blue layers with Curves so that the color tones reflect an average of the RGB values sampled at the reference area.

For example, say there is a flagpole in your image and you will be using it to make your color correction with Curves. You sample the tone and find that the area is 41% gray (looking at the Grayscale) and that RGB values in that area are 170,150,160. If the image is a good exposure, you'll probably want to stay close to the 41% gray when you are done with the correction. To get the gray to be flat (no color) in that zone, you'll want to make the RGB values equal.

Because you want the gray to be flat, you can average the RGB values to get a target (170 + 160 + 150 = 480; 480 / 3 = 160). Add curves one at a time, grouped to the layered channels to change the value of the tones according to the numbers. Here are the values for the curves and a sample of what the curves would look like in Figure 4.8:

COLOR	INPUT	OUTPUT
Red	170	160
Green	150	160
Blue	160	160

Because of this level of control, your choice in the selection of a gray reference is very important to the outcome of your color correction. For example, if you choose a gray that in reality is supposed to be slightly green and you don't allow for that in the correction, your final corrections will end up somewhat warm. Again, visual inspection must work hand in hand with the numbers to achieve the best result.

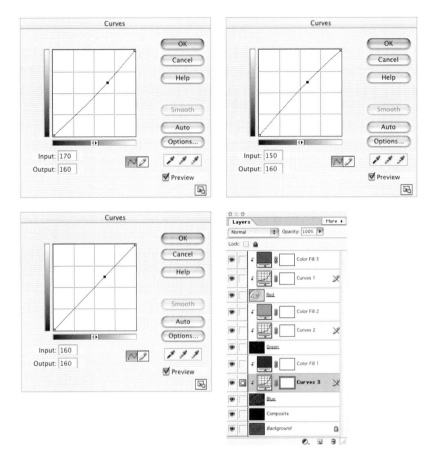

Figure 4.8

Adjustments would be made by changing the numbers in three Curves dialog boxes, one for each channel of your separation.

You'll note in this discussion that gray measures are given in percentages and RGB measures are given in levels. The levels graph can work in either levels of gray or percentages. You can toggle between the two, and even use the curve to make the calculation for you (by placing a point on the curve and then clicking the percentage/level toggle on the bar below the curve graph). If you want to convert gray percentages (P) to levels (L) manually for your calculations, subtract the percent from 100 and multiply by 2.55: $(100 - P) \times 2.55 = L$. To convert levels to percentages, use $100 - (L / 2.55) = P$.

You also may want to allow for accuracy in the image. Because you are making an assumption about the gray (that it is indeed a flat gray rather than one with a slight tone), you may want to make an adjustment only by using a percentage. Doing so may keep you from over-adjusting. This concept is similar to not cropping off all of a large tail in Levels. If the difference in the colors is broad, or skewed to one of the channels, it may be preferable to average 50 or 75% of the difference. The more positive you are that the value you are measuring should be

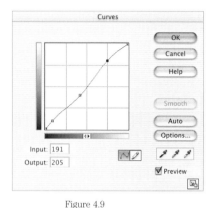

Figure 4.9

If using several sample grays, place them on the curve for each channel in one step. This shows a Red correction for three measured values at 25, 101, and 205 levels.

gray, the stronger the percentage of change you should apply. If you are positive the object is gray, make the change 100% of the difference. Scaling back to 50 or 75% respects some of the measurement of the gray color in the image.

Using the previous example, take the difference between the measured and average value, multiply that figure by the percentage, and add it to the measured value:

target value = measured value + ([average value – measured value] × percentage)

In the case of the Red channel, which measures 170, your equation would look like the following if using 75% of the difference (the average value is still 160). Your solution would look like this:

target value = 170 + ([160 – 170] × 0.75), or 170 – 7.5 = 163

Using an Output value of 163 makes the red change only 75% of the way, leaving some respect for the value you measured in the image. The following list shows the target values for making the change with 75% strength (respecting 25% of the original measurement):

COLOR	INPUT	OUTPUT
Red	170	163
Green	150	158
Blue	160	160

The more gray points you measure, the more accurate your balance in the resulting color corrections will be. If you measure several key gray spots, you should make the corrections all at once by placing as many points on each curve as you have key spots. Do this instead of returning to the process several times, as shown on the curve in Figure 4.9. This will make sure that you are changing the measured spots relative to one another; if you change the values sequentially on separate curves, the changes will occur independently and simply won't work right. When measuring one level of gray, try to make it a midtone; if you are measuring two, use a lighter and darker gray; if you are measuring three, use quartertones (25%, 50%, and 75%, or 63, 128, and 191 levels). The more evenly you divide the gray levels used for the correction, the better. The more levels of gray you correct for, the more accurate your correction will appear.

The following example uses the image from Figure 4.10 that was photographed by including a homemade 25%, 50%, 75% gray card in the image. The image was then opened as a digital image, corrected for Levels, and then the gray card was measured and those measured results were applied as curves to make a correction. Use the `bleedingheart.psd` file on the CD to follow along.

> You can make your own gray card by making an image with scaled tones (e.g., 25, 50, and 75% gray) and then printing that image with black ink only on your printer. This won't be entirely accurate, as black ink can have color and color can be influenced by the whiteness of the paper, but it can certainly work well in many situations.

Figure 4.10

The gray card (shown to the right) can help balance color at three levels of gray.

Use the following steps to adjust the curves according to your gray selection.

1. Measure the gray. Because there is a gray card in the example, there is an absolute reference. These are the original measurements:

Color	25%	50%	75%
Red	228	129	43
Green	210	151	91
Blue	209	143	78

2. Average the gray value for each tone (add the RGB values at each percentage and divide by 3). The results are 216 levels at 25%, 141 levels at 50%, and 71 levels at 75%.

3. Determine the target values for a flat gray (convert the measured tones at the average sample). Each curve will have three points, with the input reflecting the measured tone and the output reflecting the desired (averaged) result. Table 4.1 plots the points.

4. Separate the image into its RGB components by using Split RGB Channels in Hidden Power Tools.

5. Activate and view only the Red component in the layers.

Table 4.1

Example Curves Settings for the Sample

COLOR	INPUT	OUTPUT
Red	228	216
Red	129	141
Red	43	71
Green	210	216
Green	151	141
Green	91	71
Blue	209	216
Blue	143	141
Blue	78	71

6. Click Curves on the Tools tab of the Hidden Power Tools. Click the Group With Previous Layer checkbox and click OK.

7. In the Curves dialog box that appears, add three points to the curve. You can do this by holding Command/Ctrl and clicking once on each of the card swatches in the sample image, or add them by clicking right on the curve itself.

8. Ensure that the Input and Output fields are set to level values, not percentages (you can change between levels and percentages by clicking the toggle switch on the bar below the curve graph). Click each of the points one at a time and change the Input and Output values to match those in the chart. Do this by entering the values from the chart in the Input and Output fields.

9. Repeat steps 6 through 8 for the Green and Blue layer components, viewing each layer individually by turning off the visibility for the other layers.

After all the corrections performed using the card, you will have corrected for white and black, as well as 25%, 50%, and 75% gray. This gives you five reference points that should result in some pretty accurate color. This technique should be more accurate than using just one reference point, and can account for complex lighting. For example, if you take a picture in a royal blue room where there is incandescent lighting, ambient light (reflected) might tend to be blue, while direct light would be warm (or a little red). Highlights would tend toward red, while shadows would tend toward blue. Making multipoint corrections will allow you to compensate for color difference and shifts at more points, leading to color that is more correct overall.

At this point, click Preview RGB in the Hidden Power Tools to add color back to the image without flattening the layer channels. The preview should show improved color. Check it by toggling the visibility for the correction layers on and off.

When you are done correcting the color, the image can be corrected for luminosity as well. You can make corrections for tonal shift based on new black (K) measurements, or by using the RGB averages. If using measured percentages, you will take new samples of the gray card using the K measurement in the Info palette; if you are using the averages (as I'll do here) you just use the RGB averages you already determined. Use the following steps:

1. Activate the Background layer for the RGB separated image by clicking on it.

2. Click Add Luminosity on the Separations tab of the Hidden Power Tools. This will create a Luminosity layer at the top of the stack.

3. With the Luminosity layer active, click Curves on the Tools tab of the Hidden Power Tools. Click the Group With Previous Layer checkbox and click OK.

4. Determine the values you will be using. You are adjusting to 25%, 50%, and 75% (191,128,63) for the card swatches based on the average RGB values (216, 141, and 71). So your value chart would look like this:

Color	Input	Output
Luminosity	216	191
Luminosity	141	128
Luminosity	71	63

5. Adjust the tone. Add three points to the curve by holding down Command/Ctrl and clicking on the three card swatches or by clicking on the curve. Then change the Input and Output values to the numbers determined in Step 4.

The result of this correction will darken the image. Although it is based on measurement from the original, you may or may not want to keep that change. Click the view toggle for the Luminosity layer to compare before and after. To go somewhere in between, change the Opacity of the Luminosity layer using the Opacity slider on the Layers palette.

You can split the RGB and Luminosity to make your corrections all in one separation by clicking Split RGBL in Hidden Power Tools before making any adjustments. (RGBL stands for Red, Green, Blue, and Luminosity.) Making this separation will allow you to make correction to the Luminosity separately from color while controlling both color and tone.

While Levels and Curves corrections are excellent tools, one problem you will note with making corrections absolutely by the numbers is that although it may seem pretty accurate, it may not produce the most pleasing color. If you have no idea where to start your correction, the techniques we've looked at here are definitely a fine start, as they will get you moving in the right direction. Because of other considerations (such as the limitations of the CMYK color space), you may actually get better color by replacing colors and tones, or by making corrections not so strictly tied to measurements, or in some cases by altering color completely. Making targeted and selective tone and color corrections can help with these additional changes, and we'll look at those approaches in the next chapter.

Chapter 5
Color-Specific Correction Tools

After making general corrections with Levels and/or Curves, it is time to get specific about color. You can make changes with Levels and Curves as part of later steps in corrections, but chances are that any additional changes you make will need to be targeted to a specific image area. Splitting channels is helpful for general color correction and grayscale conversion, but there are other ways that separations can help you work with color and tone in images to get the best result. In a similar way that separation may help affect changes in grayscale images, you can use portions of a separation to target specific areas of an image, and thereby affect the color results.

Using Hue/Saturation for Color Adjustments

Adjusting Color Balance

Painting in Color Changes: History Brush Application

Making Duotones

RGB Channel Calculations and Mixing

Separating CMYK Color

Using CMYK Color

Using Hue/Saturation for Color Adjustments

Hue/Saturation is a powerful but easy to use color-correction method. It allows the user to adjust color based on hue, saturation, and brightness (HSB measurements are used on the Color Picker along with RGB, and are used to mix color—often in painting. Hue changes between colors as if you are selecting color from a 360° color wheel. Saturation controls the density of the color; greater saturation means that the color in an image has the potential to be richer; however, the actual appearance of color is influenced by tone. Brightness (which is actually lightness) affects the tone in the image. Hue/Saturation can be confined to affecting only a specific range of color, using the Edit drop-down list in the Hue/Saturation dialog box (see Figure 5.1).

The Hue/Saturation feature can help with color corrections by providing visual feedback and a relatively easy interface. When using the Hue/Saturation dialog box, all you have to do is adjust the sliders and use the image on screen as a preview to watch what happens as a result of your adjustments. The hitch is that for the most part, as long as you have made proper Levels corrections, you won't have much to bother with. Levels adjustments will have corrected for saturation, hue, and lightness (brightness). Although it may not be the best use of the feature, you can open the Hue/Saturation dialog box and play with the sliders to see if you happen to stumble on an adjustment that improves the image. Testing adjustments using Hue/Saturation can yield pleasant surprises.

Unless you are targeting a color change using selection or masking, global adjustments to hue, saturation, and brightness will tend to involve only a slight movement of any of the sliders—unless you are looking to achieve a special effect. You might be a little wilder with your experimentation if the subject in the image is something like a flower or a seashell—that may not have a specific color reference (unlike, for example, skin tone—which can't be a specific color like green or purple unless painted). In making straightforward changes, adjusting Hue will often throw the color out of balance swiftly, and adjusting Lightness may provide too drastic and primitive a change in tone. Lightness is actually the least attractive adjustment for most images when used by itself. However, you may get some pleasant effects from increasing Saturation in some images.

Figure 5.1

The Hue/Saturation dialog box

1. Select the appropriate portion of the image to target your corrections. You can either:

   - Flatten your image (choose Layer→ Flatten Image) or select the top layer in the stack if adjusting the whole image (press Option+Shift+]/Alt+Shift+] to activate the top layer, or just click on it).

   - Activate the layer you want to correct by clicking it in the Layers palette, if making a selective change based on layer content.

2. Open the Hue/Saturation dialog box by creating a Hue/Saturation adjustment layer. Select Layer → New Adjustment Layer → Hue/Saturation. If targeting a specific layer for change, check Group With Previous on the New Layer dialog box.

3. When the Hue/Saturation dialog box is open, attempt to adjust the Saturation by moving the slider a few points to the right of the center position to see if greater saturation improves the color dynamic.

Admittedly, this procedure isn't terribly exciting. The result is that you will get more saturated color, and either prefer it, or not. One other option on Hue/Saturation is the Colorize option. The Colorize option is like applying a layer filled with a single color set to Overlay mode (at 50% Opacity). The difference is that you can adjust the Color, Saturation and Lightness sliders on the Hue/Saturation dialog box to achieve the color effect you want rather than selecting a color from the Color Picker.

The Hue/Saturation function also offers some unique opportunities for selective correction when used in combination with other features and tools. Snapshots in the Hidden Power Tools (as we'll see later in the chapter) and Luminosity/Color separations help make selective corrections, and this is where the real power of Hue/Saturation is. That's what we'll look at in the next section.

Saturation Masking

If you want to make a selective color change (if you have a specific color or color range that you want to change or freeze in a shot), you may target those colors using Hue/Saturation to help in creating a mask. You can make more drastic changes than you normally would in targeted colors because the rest of the image won't change. Clever use of the Saturation slider on the Hue/Saturation dialog box can help you quickly create masks based on hue. These masks can help you target image areas based on color so you can make corrections and changes using other features and tools.

The image in Figure 5.2 has several distinct colors that might be adjusted independently. (You'll have to take a look in the color section to see the color detail.) The image (`bottle.psd`) is provided on the CD for your experimentation and so you can follow along with the masking procedure. In the example, the color of the bottles is already a rich blue. If you want to keep it that way while making other changes, you can target other areas by freezing (masking out) the color of the bottles. This will allow you to alter color in the other parts of the image without affecting the bottles. Just a warning, as we go along this image will look quite awful before it gets better.

The steps involved in creating a mask based on color and saturation are basically the same for any image:

1. Preparation: Prepare the image for making a color range choice by adding some key layers.

2. Choose a color range. Select the color range you want to either keep from change or affect changes to using Hue/Saturation functions.

3. Use the color range selection and preparations to create a useful color mask.

Figure 5.2

This image offers
several opportunities
for hue-based
color isolation.

Preparation

To prepare this image you'll set up a few layers that may seem extraneous. The sole purpose of these layers will be to commit changes you make using layer blending options. Until you commit the changes by merging layers, the changes are only an appearance. You need to commit the changes to use them.

1. Open a flattened image, or flatten an open one. For this example, I used `bottle.psd`, found on the CD.

2. Duplicate the background. You'll use this layer to select the target colors for masking and to create the mask. Name the layer Saturated Colors.

3. Activate the background (press Option+Shift+[/Alt+Shift+[).

4. Create a new layer. Name it Mask. This layer should remain transparent until the final steps of the exercise, and then it will become the mask.

5. Create another new Fill Layer and fill it with gray (put 50% H in the HSB fields in the color picker; S and B should be 0%). Name this Commit Mode 2.

6. Duplicate the Commit Mode 2 layer created in Step 5. Name this Commit Mode 1. There are two changes to commit using layer modes, and this upper layer will be the first in line.

Choosing a Color Range

Now that you have prepared the image, you can choose the colors to be excluded or masked out and made safe from change. You will temporarily desaturate the areas of the image you want to keep as they are, leaving only the color that should be changed visible. The remaining saturated colors will be used to create your mask.

7. Activate the Saturated Colors layer by clicking on it and select Layer→ New Adjustment Layer→ Hue/Saturation. This will initiate the creation of a Hue/Saturation adjustment layer at the top of the layer stack.

8. Check the Group With Previous box in the New Layer dialog box when it appears, and click OK to continue. The Hue/Saturation dialog box will open.

Figure 5.3

For the example, Blues was selected as the closest range for the current target for masking the blue bottles; the sliders automatically set to that range.

9. Select the Blues option from the Edit drop-down menu. The object of this step is to enable the color sliders at the bottom of the Hue Saturation screen. You can do this by selecting any color other than Master from the drop-down list. I suggest Blues for this example, because it is closest to our target range for masking the bottles. We'll make adjustments to the range in a moment. When making changes in other images, try to choose the color that best matches the color you want to freeze. When you make the selection from the drop-down list, note that the eyedroppers become available in the dialog box and that the color bar at the bottom reveals sliders as in Figure 5.3. The sliders on the color bar represent the color range that will be affected by changes made to the Hue, Saturation, and Lightness.

10. Drag the Saturation slider in the Hue/Saturation dialog box all the way to the left. If you have selected a good representation of the color you want to work with, the color will desaturate. Don't let that worry you; it is actually starting to build your mask, which will be based on desaturated areas of the image.

11. Adjust the range of color that you want to keep from change—in other words, the color(s) that you want to add to the mask. In this image, use the Add To Sample eyedropper to click on anything left in the image that is blue. Most blue things should have been included already, but there may be areas such as in the vase that you would like to include (see Figure 5.4). If you make a mistake, clean it up by changing to the Subtract From Sample eyedropper, adjust the sliders manually to contract the range by clicking and dragging them, or just start over by holding down the Option/Alt key and clicking the Reset button. All color that you add to the color range will appear to desaturate in the image; any colors removed from the range will turn back to the original color. Color range adjustment can be accomplished in any of the following ways:

    *   Use the Add To Sample eyedropper. To do this, click the plus eyedropper icon ✎ and use that to sample colors from the image to add to the range, as shown in Figure 5.4.

    *   Use the Subtract From Sample eyedropper ✎. To do this, click the minus eyedropper icon and use that to sample colors from the image to remove from the range.

Figure 5.4

There are blues in the pitcher/vase that you may want to include as well. Dragging the Add To Sample eyedropper over the vase will include these blues (actually cyan) as well.

- Adjust the sliders manually. To do this, click on the slider and drag it to move. The close-up of the color range slider in Figure 5.5 shows some details of the slider. The color bar above the slider shows the range of color being affected, and the color bar below the slider shows the results of how that affects the color spectrum. The dark gray area between the absolute markers (the rectangular markers on the inside) shows the range that will be affected 100% by changes on the dialog. The gray area between the absolute markers and the fade point markers (the triangular markers on the outside) shows where the color range will be affected in decreasing intensity (100%–0%). Everything outside the range of the markers will not be affected.

Figure 5.5

Close-up of the color range sliders

12. Once the range is set (see Figure 5.6) and the colors you want to freeze are desaturated, accept the changes for the dialog box by clicking OK.

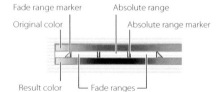

Fade range marker   Absolute range

Original color   Absolute range marker

Result color   └ Fade ranges ┘

You can imitate my result by changing the color range to match the settings shown in Figure 5.6. However, the point is to create the mask—not necessarily to match my results exactly. Depending on how you made the color selections, your range may be slightly different, and that's okay.

Creating the Mask

With the color range you want to freeze desaturated, you can use the image color saturation that is left to create a mask.

Figure 5.6

After adjusting the range using the eye-droppers, the sliders will have shifted posi-tion to represent the range you have selected. The name of the color choice has automatically changed here to **Cyan 2**, to reflect a custom color range.

13. Merge the Hue/Saturation change with the Saturated Colors layer below by pressing Command+E/Ctrl+E. This will lock in the changes and show the original image with the selected color range as black.

14. Change the Mode of the Saturated Colors layer to Color (select Color from the drop-down mode list at the top of the Layers palette). This will show image color saturation against a 50% gray background. The gray represents unsaturated image areas and image areas you want to freeze.

15. Merge the Saturated Colors and Commit Mode 1 layers by pressing Command+E/Ctrl+E. This will lock in the changes. The name of the layer should be Commit Mode 1.

16. Change the Mode of the Commit Mode 1 layer to Difference. Difference will compare the pixels in the layer with the pixels below. If there is no difference, the result will be black. The greater the difference, the lighter the result will be. The unsaturated areas of the image and blue bottles will appear as black.

17. Merge the Commit Mode 1 and Commit Mode 2 layers to commit the changes. The resulting layer should be named Commit Mode 2.

18. Open the Levels dialog box (Enhance → Adjust Brightness/Contrast → Levels or Command+L/Ctrl+L) and make a Levels adjustment by pushing the white (right) RGB slider to 128. This will intensify the saturation of the color areas (everything that isn't gray).

19. Click the Drop Black tool on the Hidden Power Tools. This will remove black from appearing in the current layer, revealing the blue from the bottles and other unsaturated areas of the image below.

> The Drop Black function makes pixels up to 2 levels completely transparent, and then fades the opacity of dark pixels between 3 and 31 levels. This is done to help blend the saturation masking between saturated and unsaturated areas.

20. Merge the Mask layer and the Commit Mode 2 layer. This will commit the Drop Black changes and leave part of the mask layer transparent. The resulting layer should be named Mask.

21. Duplicate the Background. Change the name to Unmasked Color.

22. Move Unmasked Color to the top of the layer stack.

23. Group the duplicate with previous by pressing Command/Ctrl+G.

Figure 5.7

Many changes result in just these few layers, but the mask result is very powerful and useful.

Figure 5.8

This layer palette shows how to set up Hue/Saturation adjustments made to the masked color range and Color Balance for the Unmasked Color.

Steps 21 to 23 recolor the masked image area. In the end, the Layers palette should look like Figure 5.7.

If you turn off the visibility for the background at this point, you will see the area that you have isolated in original color. Chances are that the complexity of the area is nothing you would have wanted to select manually. You can make changes to the area freely by grouping the layers that appear above the Unmasked Color layer in the Layers palette. You can actually make changes to the bottles by grouping changes with the Background layer.

For example, if you want to make a Hue/Saturation adjustment layer change to the blue bottles and a Color Balance change to the rest of the image (Unmasked Color), the placement for these adjustment layers is shown in Figure 5.8.

Saturation masking allows you to mask any color in any image so you can work on distinct colors separately within the image. This is different from working with separated color as you do when separating RGB tones, because you are isolating colors that may have information in red, green, and blue components all at the same time. Not only can this method be used to isolate specific colors, but it can also be used to make selections of objects based on color. Masks you create can be loaded as selections by pressing the Command/Ctrl key and clicking on the Mask layer.

A function is provided in the Hidden Power Tools to quickly work through the previous procedures and create the saturation mask. Just click Saturation Masking on the Hidden Power Tools and you will be walked through all the steps. Although this tool allows you to make saturation masks with the click of a button, it is recommended that you practice this manual technique first, and preferably more than once. For example, try isolating the red or yellow flowers in the image (the red is a challenge). Understanding how this works is invaluable when working on other images that need isolated corrections, or when working on complex separations such as creating the K (black) component in CMYK (which we'll be doing later in this chapter).

Adjusting Color Balance

Adjusting image color balance allows the user to compensate for color shifts that may have occurred in a given image, or to add shifts that create a pleasing look. It is a far more useful tool for direct color correction and changes than the Hue/Saturation tool (used without masking). The one problem with Color Balance is that, like Curves, it is missing from the Photoshop Elements interface. But Hidden Power Tools allows the user to access Color Balance by simply clicking Color Balance in the Hidden Power Tools menu. This will open the Color Balance dialog box (see Figure 5.9) and will create an adjustment layer. When the changes are accepted and the dialog box is closed, the adjustment layer cannot be edited.

The Color Balance is easier and friendlier to work with when making color adjustments than Hue/Saturation. It is also often more effective at bringing out pleasing color by removing counter color — or colors that effectively work against one another in your images. It is great for finessing, rather than manhandling, color elements. Color Balance allows the user to balance highlights, shadows, and midtones for cyan/red, magenta/green and yellow/blue. If yellowish highlights have been tainted by blue, they flatten and muddy toward green. Shifting the color back can make the color seem more vibrant. All the user really has to do is open the dialog box and experiment with application to pick the most pleasing result.

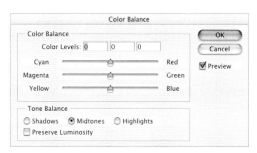

Figure 5.9

The Color Balance dialog box looks much like the Hue/Saturation dialog box, but the controls produce very different results.

To make adjustments, open your image, open the Color Balance dialog box (by clicking Color Balance on the Hidden Power Tools menu), and try the following:

1. Starting with the Midtones checked, make a radical shift in the top slider (Cyan/Red). Slide from approximately –50 to +50 and watch the effect on the image. This gives you an idea as to whether a move with the slider makes a change that seems visually pleasing in the color of the image overall.

2. Pick either –50 or +50 as the more pleasing. Compare as many times as you need to make the decision.

3. When you have selected the more pleasing slider position, compare it to the mid-point between the two original selections. In this case, that would be a comparison between the center (0) and the point you found more pleasing (–50 to 0, or 0 to +50).

Figure 5.10

If the better choice was +50, your next comparison would be between +25 and +50. The winner of that decision goes against +38.

4. Make a few such comparisons, picking the best of your two choices and each time dividing the field in half until you arrive at a final result. See Figure 5.10.

5. Repeat Steps 2 through 4 for the Magenta/Green and Yellow/Blue sliders.

6. Repeat Steps 1 through 5 for Highlights and then for the Shadows.

7. To be reasonably sure you've made the best choices (you won't be able to open the dialog box again once you have closed it), run through steps 1 through 6 a second time. This will help you to adjust for balance changes you made.

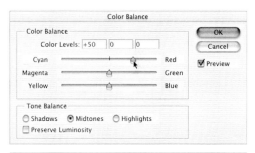

8. Click OK to accept the changes.

9. Compare the image before and after the correction by toggling the view for the Color Balance layer.

While the application here may seem conceptually simplistic, as long as your monitor can be reasonably trusted, you will find that this trial and error method can greatly improve your images—in tone, contrast and color. You'll also get good rather quickly in determining the best slider positions, and will spend very little time doing comparisons. This adjustment can be used in conjunction

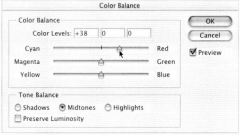

with other tools to achieve targeted results as well. For example, you might use it in combination with a hue-based color mask created with Hue/Saturation. These types of combinations give you infinite control over image color results.

Painting in Color Changes: History Brush Application

Sometimes it is easiest to get the color you want in different portions of an image with different corrections. You may find that making one part of an image look good comes at the expense of absolutely ruining the color in the rest of your image. This little dilemma might make it seem that there is no way to make a compromise between the two without it ending up compromising the image color or making complicated selections. As it turns out, there isn't a reason you have to settle for a compromise.

There is a way to make a change to your image and freeze those changes so you can use them later. Using some Hidden Power Tools you can then paint only a portion of the color back in. The full version of Photoshop allows you to do this with something called the History Brush. The History Brush lets you select a *snapshot* (a frozen History state) of your image as the source for painting and then apply that version of the image back into your present image. It allows you to do all sorts of things like color changes or spot application of filters (apply the filter, take a snapshot to use as a source, then jump back to the original image and paint changes in as desired).

Photoshop Elements doesn't have a History Brush tool and has no way to take snapshots. But why should that stop you? Using Hidden Power Tools, you can freeze your image in a way similar to taking snapshots by clicking the Snapshot tool. The tool allows you to freeze an image as it looks on screen so the image information doesn't disappear as you progress through changes in the image. The shots are saved in layers, and the visibility is turned off so that you can return to them as needed. Using layer masking allows you to easily imitate the History Brush: you can group the snapshot to an empty layer and use brushes to fill in the mask. As the mask layer becomes solid, it will look like you are painting back changes stored in the snapshots of your images.

To take a snapshot of your image, be sure it looks like you want it to, and then click Snapshot on the Hidden Power Tools. When you take a snapshot, several things will happen in the image. Whatever you see on screen will be merged (retaining transparency, if any) and a copy of that will be stored in a new layer. The snapshot layer will be stored at the top of the layer stack, above and grouped with a Snapshot Mask layer. The image information will be hidden because the mask is empty and the view will be off. Leave the snapshots in storage until you want to apply them. The rest of the image will be exactly as it was when you clicked to make the snapshot. See Figure 5.11.

Between snapshots, you have several options for continuing to work and make changes and corrections:

- Leave everything as it is and just keep making changes.

- Throw out the changes you made to achieve the snapshot by deleting those layers (leaving the snapshot, of course) and then make new changes.

Figure 5.11

After taking a snapshot of the background, the layers look like this. You can have multiple snapshots.

- Retain the changes and start with the original background.

- Retain the changes and start from the snapshot.

Your choice depends on how much information you really want to keep, and how you like to work. If you just keep going from where you are, there is a possibility that you will remove information you might want to use later. On the other hand, if you are sure there is nothing you want to retain, tossing out the changes will keep the important information in the snapshot and make your image a little more lean.

You may want to retain some or all of the layers used in making the changes so that you can make adjustments (for instance, if you want to reshoot Snapshot 1 with additional changes or in a different style). You might also want to retain them if you just aren't done with the image yet (such as if you have to go to work and can't complete what you are working on right then). To retain the layers used in making the changes, just leave them there. Use a duplicate of the background or a snapshot to keep working. Duplicate the background so you will be able to return to the original image, or duplicate the snapshot to continue working from where you were. After duplicating the source (snapshot or background), drag it just below the snapshots in the layer stack. The layers will look like Figure 5.12.

Technically, you can save the image with all the layers and changes—which is something histories don't allow in Photoshop or Elements. You may want to thin these out as you go along to keep the file size small. Although retaining histories and layers can be an important time saver, it can also fatten your image heartily. Be sure you need what you save.

The purpose and application of this type of change may be best looked at in an example. We can run through an application of the tools in context, and you can see how they work.

Figure 5.13 shows a butterfly. In the color section you can see that by coincidence this butterfly landed on an object that was nearly the same color as itself. While the color is interesting, you may prefer a little more variety to make the butterfly stand out more. Because the color of the background is similar to the butterfly, Hue/Saturation masking wouldn't get your change done, because it would select both the color in the butterfly and the background. And while you could make some sort of complicated selection, there are much easier ways.

Start by making a general correction to the image to be sure you are starting with the best representation of tone and color. With that complete, it is time to start exploring opportunities to change the image.

Preparation First off, do some exploring and experimenting. Instead of working with complicated selections, you can simply adjust different versions of your image to create sources for the color you'd rather see in specific areas of the image. Taking snapshots will store the changes, which you can later use to recall and apply to your image.

Application Once the source color is all set up in the original image, you can paint the color back into the original image using brushes.

Figure 5.12

With Background copy 2 blotting out the changes made earlier, you can step back to the original image without losing previous corrections.

Figure 5.13

A blue butterfly rests on a blue background, but you might want some more interesting color distinction.

Preparation

To prepare for changes to the butterfly, you will make some corrections to separate areas of color and freeze those changes by taking snapshots. Each snapshot can focus on a different color or element that you will want to work back in later.

1. Open the butterfly image (find it on the accompanying CD: `butterfly.psd`) and duplicate the background. You should work on this duplicate. Leaving the background alone will allow you to return to the original later to adjust for different colors.

2. Adjust the color of the image so that the dark portion of the butterfly looks how you want it to look. Don't worry at all about what you do to the blue—or any other color, for that matter. Don't bother to use selection or other masking. You can use any tools or filters that you want, but in this case, use the Color Balance Hidden Power Tool to achieve the change. I added yellows and reds to the shadow to warm up the black.

3. Once the dark portion of the butterfly looks how you want it to look, take another snapshot by clicking Snapshot from Hidden Power Tools. This will be your source for the dark portion of the butterfly. Name the snapshot Dark Portion. It will appear at the top of the layer stack.

4. Make changes to adjust the wing color for the butterfly to however you would like to see it. This may require deleting and enhancing other changes that you made to create the Dark Portion. You may want to duplicate the background and drag it below the Snapshot

Mask layer to give you a fresh starting point. This is a good time to use Hue/Saturation to make the change. Again, adjust the color on the wings and ignore everything else.

5. Make a snapshot of the image when you have completed the change for the wing color. Name it Wings.

6. Make changes to the image to target just the color for the spots on the bottom of the wings. Again you may need to duplicate the background or remove other color changes. I used Hue/Saturation, selected Red from the Edit menu, and fiddled with the sliders to get a brighter, more saturated red.

7. Make a snapshot of the image when you have completed the change for the wing color. Name it Spots.

You can continue to make changes for other elements in the image, but these will do for the example.

Application

With the snapshots created, you are ready to apply them to make your changes.

8. View the original image background. This may require turning off visibility for the other layers, or you can duplicate the background layer and bring it up below the snapshots.

9. Click the Snapshot Mask layer for the snapshot source you want to apply. This will activate the visibility for the Snapshot Mask. Start with the Wings snapshot, because the resulting change will be the most dramatic.

10. Choose a painting tool (the Airbrush is a personal favorite) and a brush for the application. I chose a brush size of 200 that is fairly soft (30% hardness).

> Brush selection and dynamics in Step 10 matter, and should make sense for your application. If you are going to be painting back image areas that are large and mostly open, select a large brush; if you are painting back smaller areas, choose a smaller brush. Solidity also matters: an opaque brush will create an opaque mask, and a brush that is soft and/or applied with less than 100% opacity will only partially mask an area.

11. Although it doesn't really matter, choose white for the foreground color. Any color will work, but the idea of masking is usually based on black-and-white, where white represents unmasked areas.

12. Paint over the wing area in the image by clicking and dragging the paintbrush. The color from your snapshot source will fill in as you go. To compare the change before and after, toggle the visibility of the Snapshot Mask layer for the snapshot you are working with.

13. Choose the next source by clicking the Snapshot Mask for that snapshot. Repeat Steps 10 through 12.

After you have painted in information from the Dark Portion, Wings, and Spots snapshots, your butterfly should look significantly different. By the time you are done you should have painted back all the interesting color that you have from the different sources. This is eons easier than making complex color selections, and often a lot more fun.

You can adjust your results by touching up the mask using the Eraser tool, and changing layer modes and opacity. When you do, make the changes on the *Snapshot Mask* layer, not the snapshot. If you change the snapshot, all it will do is reveal the content of the mask (which would be white, if you took the suggestions I made previously).

Snapshots can be very simple in concept but can allow you to paint in corrections, filter applications, and make other color corrections and changes. A snapshot can be used to spot-apply any change, and is a versatile tool for spot corrections.

Making Duotones

A duotone is an image where two colors are applied as tone to create a colored effect in an image. The idea behind duotones is to create a richer feel for black-and-white images, perhaps to add a little color and maybe even increase the dynamic range of a printed image. Duotone effects in non-digital image processing are achieved by toning prints in photography (sepia toning as well as other special processes) or applying two or more inks in print based on image tone. We'll look at how to control duotone results digitally and in print. Although there is some information on printing and halftones here, you may want to take a look at chapter 9 for more.

Creating a duotone digitally in Photoshop Elements can be done a number of different ways. For example, you can rather quickly emulate a sepia tone by opening Hue/Saturation, clicking the Colorize option, and shifting the slider to achieve a duotone effect (see the Hue/Saturation palette in Figure 5.14). When you print to an inkjet printer, the result will often be satisfactory.

You could apply a color in a Fill layer set to Color mode, or you could also do some experimenting with colorizing using Gradient Maps. Although these methods may achieve the effect of duotone color, and the image might print out just fine on your home inkjet, the method does not produce a true duotone and it may not be the best solution for other purposes.

Certainly duotones can simply be pleasing to the eye, but they also pose specific advantages in halftone printing. Making images duotone can actually help make images print better on presses. Using more than one ink to print your halftone images takes advantage of multiple screening angles, which can do a better job of presenting ink and color. Other advantages to using duotone over black ink alone include lessening the appearance of halftone dots and increasing ink coverage. Duotone effects can also help with correcting and emphasizing subtle tonal detail.

Figure 5.14

Clicking Colorize and setting the Hue to about 10 will give a decent sepia tone with any black-and-white image.

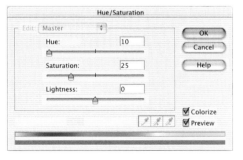

When printing on printing presses using halftones, using two black inks can improve a printed image because the two sets of dots will be screened differently, for better application of inks. (You'll learn more about halftone dots in Chapter 9, "Options for Printing.")

When duotone images are used in spot color print jobs the purpose is probably to limit color due to budget constraints. To create effective duotones for this purpose, you have to be able to control the color separation for two inks (such as black and a spot color). If not, you will have to pay a technician to do the separation for you, or worse, pay for four-color work (CMYK printing) on a two-color job. But, because there is no built-in duotone handling in Photoshop Elements, there is really no direct way to save the separate plates for duotone colors. Add to the difficulty the fact that there really isn't a means to handle spot color in Elements in the first place, and you've got a problem. Luckily it is another one that you can solve with Hidden Power Tools.

Solving the problem and understanding the application requires a little knowledge of duotoning as well as working with separations and spot color. We'll take a look at the whole process, from how to break down and apply spot color inks in preview to how to get actual duotone print effects on your inkjet printer and on a press using Photoshop Elements alone.

Background on Duotones

When you create a duotone, you replace the single tone of an image with two tones. A key to the difference between duotone color and four-color printing (CMYK) is that CMYK color printing attempts to imitate color that already exists in the image or a scene. Duotoning is different because it is a means of adding color to image tone: inks are applied using variations on existing image tonality. The mix of the inks is controlled using curves to dictate how the individual inks are emphasized in specific image tones. The effect of duotoning will be more like colorization in that the tone of the image is influenced by color rather than representing realistic color.

The effect and success of duotones is controlled by selecting and mixing color and successfully influencing how the colors interplay. Interplay is created by manipulating application curves that define how intensely the selected ink is to be applied over specific image tones. Setting curves without some sort of technique or method might prove quite fruitless and frustrating. Likewise, problems can result if you pick color you like rather than color that will be effective. Your plan should be:

1. Select inks that are compatible and that can accomplish your goal in duotoning.

2. Set up the image and apply curves to make the most of the inks you have chosen in the image you have.

Although there is a little art to experimenting with color selection and application, there is some pretty straightforward science as well. A 25% gray ink at 100% strength still shows at 25% gray when printed, it just covers 100% of the paper (see Figure 5.15). It can never get darker than 25% gray unless mixed with another color. With this in mind, any color affects an image mostly in tonal areas that are lighter than the 100% strength of the color. That is, a 25% gray ink will be able to more effectively influence tonality in 1%–25% grays—although it will affect darker colors that it mixes with, it will be less effective in manipulating the image over that tonal range. A dark color can represent lighter tones, but the opposite can never happen. A rule of thumb should be to use at least one color that is dark or black for your duotone so you can maintain the dynamic range in the image.

When choosing color, work with color that is harmonious and sensible. Select color that can blend effectively to produce a smooth white-to-black gradient (see Figure 5.16). For example, you might choose black, and light yellowish-orange; or black and sky blue. The emphasis of the colors in the duotone should be in their effective tonal range. Harmony between colors will make it easier to set up effective blends and it will allow you to work effectively with various levels of image tone. If you chose difficult color combinations or have unrealistic expectations, you can make twice as much work in getting the blends to be effective—or you may simply make it impossible.

You will most often want to use colors with varied tone rather than all dark or all medium-toned inks. In a simplistic view, the lighter colors you use will emphasize the contrast and tone in the brighter or highlight/midtone range of the image, and the darker colors will emphasize the shadow details. Splitting the effective range of the colors you pick can improve your image by providing colors with varying specialties. If you select a light color and a dark color for a duotone, the light color can be run with a greater density in the lighter image areas and the dark in the shadows. This will help you to most effectively work with (rather than against) image tone. The mixture of inks can give the image more of the feel of a continuous tone image and create more of a photographic appearance.

The colors used in duotones are often called "spot colors," although actual commercial color book names are also often used (such as PANTONE, TRUMATCH, Focoltone, and so on). These colors are standards and can be matched by your printing service. To use specific colors, you'll have to get an RGB equivalent from a color book or a printing service.

Figure 5.15

Magnification shows black ink—100% black—printed at 25% gray (left) and gray ink—25% black—printed at 25% gray in halftone printing (right).

Figure 5.16

Unrealistic expectations can yield bad results in your duotones. You want blended tones to be able to flow evenly from dark to light (a). Bad choices can limit tonal range (b) or lead to color being applied inappropriately (c).

Curves serve as translators for how ink density is to be applied. The curves are applied to the original tone of an image to target application strength. Throughout the tonal range, the inks blend to form shades and tones, which can be finessed to the advantage of the image. A rule of thumb is: if you want to apply a 25% gray ink, curves should show high intensity at 25% on the curve graphing for that ink (as shown in Figure 5.17).

Deciding how to set the curves is part art and part science. Darker inks are often steeply graded in the shadow tones, whereas lighter inks are more steeply graded in lighter tones. This will use the ink in its most effective area and help it to render the tone dynamically (the steepness of the ink application curve affects contrast). If you use two shades of black ink, for example, you probably want to de-emphasize the total density of the inks or you will darken the image; however, when using two dark inks, setting both curves the same way may not take advantage of potential dynamics in the image. Figure 5.18 shows a sample of curve settings used in a scenario with two dark inks.

Experimenting with curves for application of color can yield some pleasant and subtle toning effects.

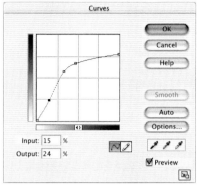

Figure 5.17

Depending on the color, desired effect, and image, the curve can be even steeper than shown here.

Applying Duotone Effects

To build a separation-ready duotone in Photoshop Elements, you have to use the image tonality along with some tricks that we've seen hints of both in using curves and in making RGB separations. Curves are used to create the tone for the separate inks, and RGB preview techniques are used to look at the results of how inks will combine. When the preview looks the way you want it to look, separations can be provided to your printing service as grayscale image plates.

1. Open an image that is black-and-white, or convert a color image to black-and-white by the methods described in Chapter 2, "Separating Color Into Tone." Be sure the image tone is corrected—you won't want to do this afterward as it will change the look of the color application. See the sample image shown in Figure 5.19. This image is available on the CD (`duotoning.psd`).

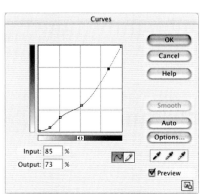
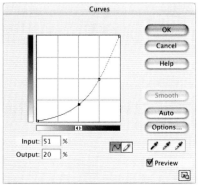

Figure 5.18

The curve with the hump (left) is used to emphasize contrast in a small portion of the highlight area so those tones don't flatten out.

Figure 5.19

**People are often good
subjects for duotones.**

2. Copy the flattened background two times. If you were creating a Tritone (three inks) or Quadtone (four inks), you would duplicate as many times as there are inks you want to apply.

3. Rename the layers to identify the colors/tones you expect to apply. I simply called them Black and Spot 1.

4. Change the Mode of the layer at the top of the layer stack (Spot 1) to Multiply. This will assure that the application of the upper color makes the result darker, as it would when printing.

5. Create a new layer, and fill it with the color you want to apply. Name the layer according to the color you are applying. This way if you come back to it several years later, you'll know what you did without a lot of analysis. In the example, to create something of a sepia tone I used an RGB close to Pantone 472 (255, 155, 125 as RGB). This layer will be used to apply a color or tone to the upper layer.

6. Change the mode of the color layer to Screen and group it with the Spot 1 layer. Using the Screen mode will lighten the layer. You need to do this because you have started with a grayscale image, and the layer color of Spot 1 will technically be black. Because any color you pick will be lighter than black, using Screen mode will replace the black ink with the color ink you are applying.

When stacking colors, arrange them from darkest at the bottom to lightest at the top. This will help your organization and application.

7. Activate the Black layer by clicking on it.

8. Click Curves on the Tool tab of Hidden Power Tools to open a curve and check Group With Previous.

9. Apply a curve to adjust the results. See Figure 5.20 for the curve used in the example. The idea here would be to lower the influence of the black overall, while using it to emphasize contrast in the darker half of the image.

10. Activate the Spot 1 layer.

11. Click Curves on the Tool tab of Hidden Power Tools to open a curve. Group With Previous should be already checked.

12. Apply a curve to adjust the results. The lighter ink should have stronger influence and contrast in the lighter tones, and this is reflected in the use of the curves pictured in Figure 5.21.

The final result of this procedure can be seen in the color section. Your Layers palette should look like Figure 5.22 when you are done. As far as layer order, the curves should be above the tone they are adjusting and between the tone and color. Should you need more

Figure 5.20

The curve for the dark ink lightens the influence so that later ink adjustments will interplay.

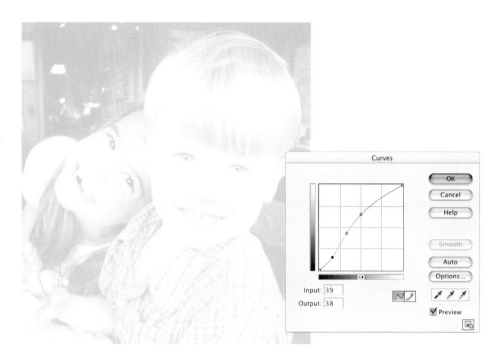

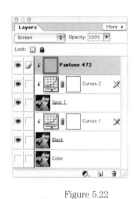

Figure 5.22

The result of the example should look like this in layers.

adjustments, add another curve to the ink layer that needs adjustment. You can add as many adjustments as you want and test different combinations by toggling the visibility for any of the layers. If you want more spot colors (to create a Tritone or Quadtone), duplicate the setup for Spot 1. If you want the black to be a spot color, add a color layer above the curve for the Black adjustment. The adjustments may require some fiddling before they look just right.

Again, this type of work on individual color separations can serve many different purposes: achieving the effect of adding color to a black-and-white image, working within the limitations of a two-color print job, enhancing printed results by using two inks and screens rather than one, and gaining the opportunity to enhance image tone by influencing ink coverage and ink contrasts. If you are just colorizing an image to get a duotone effect, you probably won't have to go through the trouble; if you want a true duotone that can be separated into specific inks, this is the way to go.

Hidden Power Tools provide functions for creating duotone images. Just start with a flattened RGB image that has been converted to black and white, and click on the Duotone Setup (on the separations tab). The power tool will lead you through the process of setting up the layer stack.

Be sure to try to blend inks so that the influence of one ink can pick up where the next leaves off. As part of the process, you may want to use a gradient bar to judge the quality of the gradient you are creating when combining the colors. I have provided a sample gradient bar (`Duotone_Preview_Bar.psd`) on the CD. You can use this to check how smooth your mixing is or to actually develop curves for application in duotones. To test your duotone curves, just open the preview image and drag the curves and colors to it from the duotone you are working on. You will have to arrange and group the layers to match what you created. To use it to develop curves, create the curves right in the preview file and then drag them to the duotone you are creating. The gradient should appear relatively smooth and even—unless you are using the duotone for some type of image correction or special effect. The bar is more useful for seeing where the curves may be failing (and need adjustment) than in generating effective duotones. To test the duotone right in the image, click Duotone Bar on the Hidden Power Tools.

Even when applying the same color to different images, you can't always apply it with the same curves. The result really depends on the image. What works fine for normal and low-key images may not work as well for high-key images, which would probably suffer from the attention to shadow detail. Curves need to be created dependent on the overall tonality of the image on an individual basis—otherwise I'd just create a push-button effect. Generally high-key images should be set to emphasize detail in the highlight areas and low-key images should be set to emphasize detail in the shadows. Experimentation and experience with setting the curves will make it easier and more intuitive.

Printing Duotones

To print your duotones, you could just flatten them and send to the printer, but you'd have done all that extra work for nothing. What you have in the layers by the time you are done with the previous procedure is a *bona fide* separation. You should treat it that way. This means using it as separate plates.

A great home experiment is to print the separated colors one at a time to see the results. To do this, leave one color on (see Figure 5.23), flatten the image, and save as an RGB (you can use Grayscale mode for black ink) with the name of the color. Do this for each color. When you are done, print these to your printer one at a time: *on the same sheet!* Print light colors first, and follow with darker. You will want to use photo-quality paper and allow sufficient drying time in between. If you use lower-quality paper, it is likely that the paper will not handle the ink well and the result might be murky and over-saturated. In putting down the colors one at a time, you will build your print similar to the way it will be created on a printing press. As long as your printer has reasonably accurate paper gripping, you'll get a pretty refined result.

Blacks will probably be richer and darker in print because the inks will go on heavier than they would be if printed in one pass. The printed effect is that there actually is a greater tonal range,

Figure 5.23

View only one color result at a time before flattening and saving.

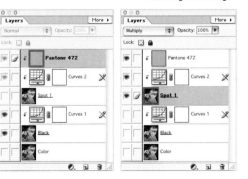

because the blacks will be darker—even though you are dealing with the same number of different levels of grays in the image. This works somewhat like putting on multiple coats of paint.

For use with an image setter and for making film or creating printing plates, you'll want to make grayscale images from your result. Do it like this: Leave one color on, shut off any coloring for it, flatten the image, and save it as a grayscale with the name of the color. Do this for each color. You'll note that the 'light' layers get dark when you do this (see Figure 5.24), and that's what is supposed to happen. What you are seeing is how the application of the color ink will look in grayscale—as real separation plates. This shows the tonal representation as a percentage of ink (0-100 percent) rather than the color as you would normally expect to see it.

Figure 5.24

Shutting off the color (a) and other layers (c), then flattening gives you grayscale depictions of the Spot 1 color plate. (b) is the Spot 1 plate and (c) is the black.

a

b

c

Figure 5.25

This image had flat medium tones (left), but applying a duotone helped make an adjustment that better defined the differences and lightened the result (right).

As long as you tell your printing service which file is which, they can actually create film for printing or impose the image without a lot of trouble. There is one other way to put these files together to avoid problems when submitting the them by turning them into EPS files. We'll take a closer look at that technique in the section on CMYK later in this chapter.

Using Duotone for Tonal Corrections

Duotone curves can be used to make subtle changes and corrections in difficult black-and-white images. Although the images will not retain the richness of duotoning or the effect of multiple inks, creating duotone effects to correct grayscale images can help strengthen subtle detail, and some of this may be retained in the grayscale result. Consider the duotone curves to be an important part of your grayscale correction arsenal.

For example, if you have an image with subtle highlight detail (such as a wedding picture where dress detail can become somewhat washed out or faded due to harsh flash lighting), you can create a duotone to change the image emphasis in different tones. Just open the image in black-and-white, and then create a duotone. For the wedding picture example, you'd pick a black and light-gray ink for your colors. Use the light gray to emphasize the highlight area of the image. This can work in images where tones seem to flatten too much, as in Figure 5.25.

RGB Channel Calculations and Mixing

Channel calculations and mixing in the full version of Photoshop are ways to adjust color or tone based on channel representations. What the two features have in common is that they pose one channel against another to establish a result.

Calculations in Photoshop will create a result channel by performing an operation that involves up to three channels (two primary channels and a mask). The simplest calculations can be a way of combining masks or selections. For example, say you see a situation where

you can easily make two selections separately, but you want to use the selections both together and separately. Calculations would let you make the separate selections and then duplicate and combine them by using layer functions. See Figure 5.26.

Mixing is an adjustment where you change one color channel based on combining it in percentages with other channels. For example, say you have an image where a bright red flower appears over a lush green background. The problem with the image is that in real life, the flower is actually purple. Assuming this is a problem with the image, if you separate and look at the RGB channels, you'll find that the red channel is white (saturated) where the flowers are and the blue channel is dark or black (unsaturated). You could mix some of the red channel into the blue to lighten the blue channel, increasing the blue saturation in the flowers. The result will, of course, shade the color of the flower toward purple—although you may have to exercise other control (such as masking) to get the result you want.

Calculations are usually a means of producing masks based on image color or content. Therefore, you'll handle them a little differently than you would normally handle channel mixing. Channel mixing is often more suited to color correction. The functions allow you to render simple changes, complex image results, and fine adjustments. The real advantage is that you use tone that already exists in the image; the tone can act as a complex, natural selection to enhance your image in ways that would be much more difficult otherwise.

One of the most frightening things about calculations and mixing are the names and the descriptions. If you have followed the concepts behind separations to this point, you have actually applied what are very simple calculations. However, how to use calculations and mixing in layers may not be entirely obvious. Once you've taken a look at how to do calculations and mixing, they are really easier to control and they offer more options the Hidden Power way than if you were working with the full version of Photoshop. Because you work in layers, the results are more visual, and they simply make more sense to use because you can see exactly what is happening as you make the changes. You are also not limited to using just a few components and you can mix and match any way you find convenient. The key is the setup in layers.

We'll look at Calculations first, and mixing will fall right in line. When we're all done, we'll look at an example of how calculations work by building an unsharp mask using traditional darkroom techniques that you can use on any image—in combination with or as a substitute for the Unsharp mask filter.

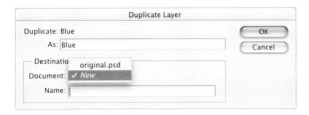

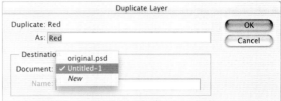

Figure 5.27

The target for the first channel is a new image (left). The target for the second channel can be the image created in the first duplication (right).

Calculations Setup and Application

Practically the whole problem in Calculations is the setup and deciding what to do, and what you'll want to do at any time depends on your image and purpose. Setting up calculations requires that you have channels (or grayscale representations) that you want to use in creating a result. Your source can be selections, masks, and/or separations. All you do is duplicating the parts you want to use for the calculations and use layer modes to combine them. You'll want the gray tone for each color you involve in the calculation rather than the color version.

1. Decide what you want to do to the image and which separation pieces it will involve. These can be separated color components (red, green, blue, luminosity, etc.), layer masks you have saved, etc. The source should be converted to grayscale.

2. Duplicate the channels you will be using to a new image. Duplicating the first channel to a new image (see Figure 5.27), and then duplicate the second channel by targeting the new image created by the first duplication.

3. Arrange the channel layers in order of effect. For example, if you want to darken one layer based on the other, put the layer that will be doing the darkening on top. In this case you would change the mode to Darken. If you are looking to create other effects, you would choose the appropriate layer mode. Most often you will use Darken or Multiply to darken the result, and Lighten or Screen to brighten the result.

Layer modes and their functions become very important to Calculations and Mixing, so having a list of what the modes do is imperative to getting good results. There is a listing in the Appendix and in the Hidden Power Tables for your reference.

4. Change the mode of the upper layer to the desired calculation and adjust opacity.

5. Flatten or merge the result.

That is pretty much all there is to it, but this simple set of steps opens numerous possibilities. Calculations can be corrected with curves or other correction options all at the same time. You can add masks to the layers in the calculations as well as making other tonal adjustments. For example, inverting can often be handy in subtracting one area from another. Because of the staggering number of variations this procedure opens up, you might see how this could quickly

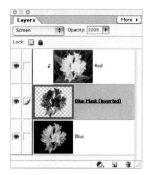

Figure 5.28

This layer setup shows how you can use reversed masking in layers.

amount to a book of its own. This method can be used for masking and selection techniques as well as for making complicated blends for spot colors and other separations (as we'll see in the next section on CMYK separation).

To use masking in calculations, you can use selection or create (or copy) masking channel(s) to the new image. Apply your masks by putting the mask layer below the layer you want to mask, then group the two layers. If you want to apply a reverse masking, just invert the layer content, as in Figure 5.28.

When you have achieved the results you want, you'll have to copy it back to your image. You can use various Hidden Power masking tools to make quick work of applying any masks that you've created.

Channel Mixing Setup and Application

Channel mixing is a little more concrete than Calculations, and offers more opportunity for straight color correction and color modification. The setup is similar to Calculations, but you will duplicate the layers and keep them in the same image, because you are trying to affect a color change with these as an adjustment. The idea is that there is no better means to adjust select areas of an image than by using the image itself. Rather than creating complex areas of tone and color, all you have to do is manipulate what is already there, using other channel information.

1. Separate your image into RGB using Split RGB w/Preview on the Separations tab of Hidden Power Tools.

2. Choose a target channel you want to influence the mix of and create a black Screen mode layer below, then group them. Do not change the modes of the black layers during the mixing. You can change the opacity of the target channel to lessen its influence.

3. Duplicate the other color channels and stack them directly above and grouped to the layer you want to make the change in. (It will be easier to drag the original into place rather than the duplicate). Set the Opacity of the duplicate layers to 0% to start. See Figure 5.29.

4. Change the mode of the upper layers to the desired calculations, and change Opacity as necessary to make the layers blend.

The mode and Opacity you use depends on what you are trying to accomplish. Like calculations you will often just use Screen or Lighten to brighten the mixed result and Multiply or Darken to darken it. Use the Opacity of each layer to control the strength that the layer is applied. To view the color result, leave the color and visibility for all layers turned on. To view the change in black-and-white, turn off the visibility for the color layer for the mixing set, and turn off the visibility for the other channels (see Figure 5.30).

You can switch back and forth between viewing the color composite and viewing in black-and-white without effecting the result. Other options, including inverting channels and using multiple channels with different Modes, give you ultimate control over mixing in a way that can't be matched by even the Channel Mixer interface in the full version of Photoshop.

Mixing can be used to make many different kinds of corrections, but it is often most useful in replacing image tone or qualities in image areas that have been ravaged by saturation, or exposure extremes that distorted or clipped image information. A very practical application of calculations and mixing can be seen in making custom CMYK separations, as we'll do in the next few sections. A great example of the power of channels and mixing is creating a manual unsharp mask.

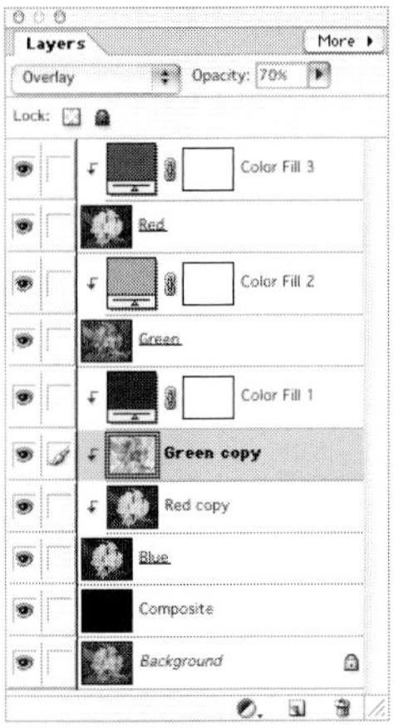

Manual Unsharp Masking: Calculations in Action

There are many things you can do with calculations and channel mixing, and not all of them will be obvious immediately. One of my favorites is creating unsharp masking manually. Unsharp masking, as mentioned earlier, was actually a darkroom process where the person doing the developing would sandwich a blurred film negative copy of the image with the original to burn in (increase exposure of) the image shadows. The blur would target the contrasty edges, and the result after the application would be increased shadow detail and a sharper look to the image.

Figure 5.29

Layer palette on the left shows mixing with just the separated channels and no color preview; the result on screen will be grayscale. Palette on the right shows how to set up if you want a full-color preview.

You can imitate this darkroom effect using the following steps:

1. Open a flattened image that you'd like to apply unsharp mask to.

2. Duplicate the background layer.

3. Invert the Background copy layer.

4. Blur the layer. The size of the blur will depend on the resolution of the image and the amount of detail. The more detailed the image, the less blur; the higher the resolution, the greater the blur. Start with 5 pixels for a 3x5 image at 300 ppi.

5. Change the Layer mode to Overlay.

6. Reduce the opacity of the duplicate layer to 50%; adjust the opacity as desired.

7. Apply a curve to adjust for contrast changes in the image.

Figure 5.30

To view the black-and-white result of the channel mixing if you are using color previews, turn off the visibility for all but the target and copied layers.

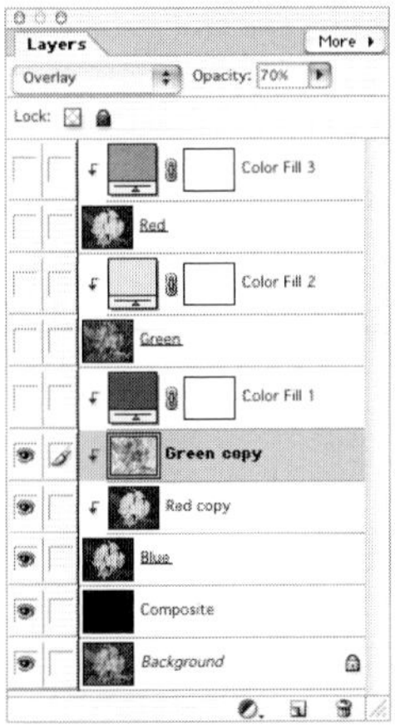

Unlike the Unsharp Mask filter provided with Photoshop Elements, this sharpening filter has less of a tendency to produce halos. It also has the interesting side effect of decreasing contrast. Because the effect is the opposite of the Unsharp Mask filter, the two can often be used together to greatly intensify image sharpness. The result you get is brought about by a masked calculation: the inverted 'negative' acts to mask the highlights and applies the Overlay calculation more intensely over the dark portion of the image, resulting in contrast edge enhancement.

The best results for the unsharp masking calculation will be had by applying the change to the image luminosity. If you split RGBL or use Split Luminosity, you can then apply the sharpening to the Luminosity layer. Color won't be altered, and you may achieve even better results.

Two tools called Sharpen and Sharpen Plus are provided with the Hidden Power Tools. Sharpen will run through the basic process described in the steps above, allowing you to select the intensity of the blur. Sharpen Plus will allow you to run through the sharpening process and adds an Unsharp Mask filter application as well that you can control. To use these tools, click on the layer you want to sharpen (this may be the image background of any layer, but using a luminosity layer is suggested) and click on the Hidden Power Tool. You will be able to adjust the intensity of the application using layer opacity after the tool runs you through the process.

Separating CMYK Color

One thing that Photoshop Elements supposedly does not handle at all is CMYK color. However, there are ways to extract CMYK, just as there are ways to extract RGB. CMYK is just a little more complicated. The procedure for separating CMYK color is probably not something you will need to use every day. You will use this only in situations where CMYK is a must, or when you want control over the separations you make on a printer that will not allow you to make your own separations.

Many home printers would take an image you created in CMYK and print it without directly using the CMYK data. In effect, what happens is that you don't really get from the printer output the CMYK that you put in. We'll take a look at how to get around that potential problem.

In order to fully understand what's going on here, you need to have a decent understanding of just about everything that we've discussed up to this point in the book. Because CMYK separation can be a very complicated topic, we'll first look at the process of how to separate, and then discuss some additional theory. This topic could fill a book on its own, so we'll just give you enough to get started with here. You can learn more from experimentation and discussions on the Hidden Power website and in the Hidden Power newsletter.

With the following techniques, you can create your own separations and not only use them in four-color print jobs, but force your printer to make a CMYK print to your specifications.

Making the Basic Separation

The easy part of this separation is filtering out the CMY. Although it isn't as straightforward and easy as making an RGB separation, the process for separating is somewhat similar.

In the RGB additive color scheme, cyan is a combination of pure blue and pure green; magenta is a combination of pure red and pure blue; and yellow is a combination of pure red and pure green. It just happens that screening an image for blue and green will reveal cyan, screening for red and blue will reveal magenta and screening for red and green reveals yellow. Completing the separation will give you a very basic CMY separation that works on screen, and in a perfect world.

Preparation Set up the colors for separation by duplicating the original image. Once the image is duplicated, you are ready to start making the real separations based on existing color.

CMY Separation Screen each layer by the color components to reveal the color separation and simultaneously create the preview for the color. This state is temporary, because to make this a really useful separation you'll have to convert each channel to grayscale. That statement may sound odd, but there is no way to represent the intensity of component color other than by using its tone.

Convert Colors to Tone Adjust each color to display tone. The leap here is that you have to remove the color that it seems you have already separated, and then create it all over again.

Preparation

1. Open gorskii.psd (found on the CD), and duplicate the flattened image and name the new layer Cyan.

2. Change the Mode of the duplicate layer to Multiply.

3. Duplicate the Cyan layer and name the new layer Magenta.

4. Duplicate the Magenta layer and name the new layer Yellow.

5. Select the background layer.

6. Create a new layer and name it Composite.

7. Fill the Composite layer with white.

The image will look awful at this point, but that doesn't matter. These are only the initial steps and you'll be taking quite a few more before you are done. The layers should look as they do in Figure 5.31. Steps 1 thru 7 can be completed by clicking CMY Setup in the Hidden Power Tools.

CMY Separation

Just like separating the RGB components, we'll add some screening layers to filter out CMY color from the image.

8. Activate the Yellow layer by clicking on it or by pressing Option+Shift+]/Alt+Shift+].

9. Create a new layer, checking Group With Previous. You can name the layer Red Screen if you want, but it is only a temporary layer, so naming is unnecessary.

10. Fill the layer with pure red (255,0,0 in RGB) and change the mode of the layer to Screen.

11. Duplicate the Red Screen layer. Fill the layer with pure green (0,255,0 in RGB). Again, this is a temporary layer, but you can name it Green Screen. This completes separation of the yellow.

12. Select the Magenta layer.

13. Create a new layer, checking Group With Previous.

Figure 5.31

With this setup, you are all ready to separate the CMY colors.

Figure 5.32

The basic RGB-CMY separation setup

14. Fill the layer with pure red (255,0,0 in RGB), and change the mode of the layer to Screen. Rename the layer Red Screen if desired.

15. Duplicate the Red Screen layer from the previous step. Name the layer Blue Screen.

16. Fill the layer with pure blue (0,0,255 in RGB). This completes separation of the magenta.

17. Select the Cyan layer.

18. Create a new layer, checking Group With Previous.

19. Fill the layer with pure green (0,255,0 in RGB), and change the mode of the layer to Screen. Rename the layer Green Screen if desired.

20. Duplicate the Green Screen layer created in the previous step.

21. Fill the layer with pure blue (0,0,255 in RGB). Change the layer name to Blue Screen if desired. This completes separation of the cyan.

If you have completed these 21 short steps without a hitch, you'll be looking at the same image you started with and the layers will look like Figure 5.32. If you turn off the visibility for any two of the three color layers, you'll see the separation named in the remaining layer. Hidden Power Tools will take care of these steps if you click CMY Color.

While it would be possible to work with this image to some extent at this stage of the separation, it is still a color representation rather than tone. You really have to have grayscale representations of a color as tone for it to be useful as a separation. In the next segment we'll convert the color to tone.

Converting Color to Tone

22. Select the Cyan layer.

23. Link the screen layers (blue and green) to the Cyan layer by clicking and dragging your cursor over the link boxes.

24. Merge the linked layers by pressing Command+E/Ctrl+E. This merges the three layers into a single Cyan layer.

25. Select the Magenta layer.

26. Link the screen layers (blue and red) to the Magenta layer by clicking and dragging your cursor over the link boxes.

27. Merge the linked layers by pressing Command+E/Ctrl+E. This merges the three layers into a single Magenta layer.

28. Select the Yellow layer.

29. Link the screen layers (red and green) to the Yellow layer by clicking and dragging your cursor over the link boxes.

30. Merge the linked layers by pressing Command+E/Ctrl+E. This merges the three layers into a single Yellow layer.

31. Open Hue/Saturation by choosing Layer → New Adjustment Layer → Hue/Saturation. When the New Layer dialogue opens, be sure the Group with Previous box is checked.

32. Change the Edit selection from Master to Yellows.

33. Move the Saturation and Lightness sliders all the way to the left (see Figure 5.33). This will remove the color from the Yellow and enhance the tonality to make a full yellow plate.

34. Click OK to close the Hue/Saturation dialog box.

35. Shut off the view for the Yellow layer and activate the Magenta layer.

36. Open Hue/Saturation by choosing Hue/Saturation from the New Adjustment Layer submenu under Layers.

37. Change the Edit selection from Master to Magentas.

38. Move the Saturation and Lightness slider all the way to the left. This will remove the color from the Magenta and enhance the tonality to make a full magenta plate.

39. Click OK to close the Hue/Saturation dialog box.

40. Shut off the view for the Magenta layer and activate the Cyan layer.

41. Open Hue/Saturation by choosing Hue/Saturation from the New Adjustment Layer submenu under Layers.

42. Change the Edit selection from Master to Cyans.

43. Move the Saturation and Lightness slider all the way to the left. This will remove the color from the Cyan and enhance the tonality to make a full cyan plate. See Figure 5.34 for the result of the steps to this point.

The result of these steps creates the color channels as tone but it also removes the color so that there is no preview. The preview can be added back by repeating the steps for CMY Separation. The only difference in those steps is that instead of choosing the color plate to add the screens to, you select its grouped Hue/Adjustment layer instead. You can merge the Hue/Saturation layers back into the plates, and you'll end up with layers that look like Figure 5.35.

Hidden Power Tools will do all of the steps in this section as well as adding back the color if you click CMY Separation in the Hidden Power Tools.

Of course, this is only part of the separation. The next part of the separation is adding black.

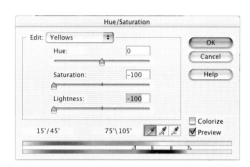

Figure 5.33

The Hue/Saturation settings for changing the yellow separation to a grayscale yellow plate

Figure 5.34

The Hue/Saturation layer for each plate should be positioned directly above the color plate.

Figure 5.35

A complete CMY color separation should look like this with all the layers.

Handling Black Separation

CMYK separation from RGB requires separation into CMY, and then generation of elements and masks to implement black (K). Black implementation can vary depending on preferences. We'll look at one style, and that should give you the information you need to make variations that you find pleasing. Now that you have the base plates, the rest of the separation is based on saturation and luminosity. We'll be continuing the separation into CMYK using the CMY separation and preview you have created from the gorskii.psd image.

You'll have to know how to create saturation and luminosity masks. The following procedures give you the basics for completing the black separation:

1. Make the saturation mask.

2. Make the luminosity mask.

3. Apply the Black in the separation.

4. Remove color under the black.

Making the Saturation Mask

Making a saturation mask similar to the one used in the saturation masking example will allow you to target gray and nearly gray areas of the image. With these areas targeted, you can replace RGB combinations with black to be sure ink does not oversaturate, which can cause problems in printing:

1. Duplicate the image background by choosing Duplicate Layer from the Layers palette pop-up menu. Choose New as the Destination Document in the Duplicate Layer dialog box. This will open the duplicate in a new image.

2. Split the Luminosity by clicking Split Luminosity in the Hidden Power Tools.

3. Turn off the visibility for the Luminosity layer and move it to the top of the layer stack.

4. Duplicate the Composite layer.

5. Merge the Composite Copy and Color layers.

6. Set the result to Difference mode.

7. Merge the layer with the Composite.

8. Create a Hue/Saturation adjustment layer (Layer → New Adjustment Layer → Hue/Saturation). Move the Saturation slider all the way to the left to set the Saturation to −100%. Click OK.

9. Create a Levels adjustment layer (Layer → New Adjustment Layer → Levels). Set the sliders to adjust tonality by moving the white slider to 128. This adjustment can vary depending on the image and what you want to accomplish, as well as how you want to affect the separation. Making a stronger change will confine black generation to more saturated areas.

Figure 5.36

The saturation mask shows lighter in areas where the color is most pure (has the least gray).

Figure 5.37

The dark portion represents the darkest half of the image (50%–100% black).

10. Merge the Composite, Hue/Saturation, and Levels layers. This will give you your saturation mask and it should look something like Figure 5.36. It represents a mapping of color in the image from the most saturated (lightest) area to the least saturated (darkest) area. Rename this layer Saturation.

Making the Luminosity Mask

The luminosity mask will help you target the darkest colors where the black can influence the color range:

1. Add a new layer above the Saturation layer. Name the new layer Black and fill it with 50% gray (128,128,128).

2. Activate the Luminosity layer.

3. Make a levels correction by opening Levels (press Command/Ctrl+L) and moving the white slider to 128. This will change the mask so only 50% grays or darker will appear as gray. It should look like Figure 5.37.

4. Select the Saturation layer, change its mode to Lighten, and move it above the Black layer.

5. Merge the Saturation layer with the Black layer. The result will be your black plate.

Applying the Black in the Separation

Once the separation is complete, you have to apply the black and adjust the other color plates:

1. Duplicate the Black layer completed in Making the Luminosity Mask back to the original image using the Duplicate Layer function and selecting the original image as the target. The layer name should remain Black.

2. Move the Black layer to the top of the layer stack in the original image. Change its mode to Multiply.

Up to this point, the steps of the black separation will be taken care of by Hidden Power Tools if you click CMYK Black. That tool will make the saturation mask and the luminosity mask and apply the separation to the original image. The result will look a little dark. This result can be adjusted if necessary after testing to be sure adjustment is needed. Another influence will be removing color under the black.

Remove Color Under Black

To keep ink use lower and to get better results on a press and in your printer, you will want to reduce the amount of ink printed in the darkest areas of the image. This reduction can keep the ink from over-saturating, streaking, and drying poorly:

1. Copy the Black layer and Invert it.

2. Open Levels and change the white Output slider to somewhere between 128 and 191 levels. This change will determine how much of the color below the black you will be taking out. The layer will look like Figure 5.38. I used 128 for the example.

> Using 128 will remove 50% of the color under the black ink, and 64 will remove 25% of the color. At 25% removal, your maximum ink outlay in blacks will be 325% (C75+M75+Y75+K100), which is a little higher than what is usually suggested for press work. We are just making a flat change here, because this can get really intricate. For example, you may choose to use Curves, and adjust those separately for each ink.

3. Select the Black copy layer and move it to just above the Yellow layer.

4. Change the Black copy layer's mode to Screen. This will reduce the gray values in the Yellow layer by the intensity/density of the black ink.

5. Duplicate the Black copy layer and drag the copy to just above the Magenta plate.

6. Duplicate the Black copy layer grouped with the Magenta plate and drag the copy to just above the Cyan plate. Your layers should look like Figure 5.39.

That's it. What you have now is a complete separation that shows the cyan, magenta, yellow, and black with color removed under the black to reduce the density of inks so there won't be over inking on press. The results appear here in Figure 5.40 as gray components, and the printed result is shown in the color section. The steps in Remove Color Under Black can be taken care of by clicking Remove Black Color.

The entire process from setup through applying color removal can be completed by clicking CMYK Process in the Hidden Elements tools. You will be required to make adjustments to levels to complete the processing. You may see the potential here for manually adjusting the performance of your images, in that there are many other variations you can consider. For example, it is often practiced that the reduction of cyan (traditionally a weaker, less efficient ink) is less than yellow and magenta in under color. The under color is also often reduced using Curves, and this option is included in the Hidden Power Tools. All this requires is using Curves to make the alteration done here with Levels, and perhaps making separate reduction layers for each of the colors. However, all of this will require a little testing to get the best output, so these some-what generic steps will have to do.

With the separation in place, you can make adjustments and changes to the image in CMYK, just as you would adjust an RGB image. In other words, if you feel that there is a little too much or too little of any color, you can reduce this imbalance by insinuating a Curve or Levels layer just above the plate color layer and then making adjustments. The changes will be previewed directly in the image as you make them, so you can see the result right on screen.

Once you arrive at a method for arriving at the settings you use in a particular process, you can reuse that method over and over again for the same output. For example if you note your prints are all a little magenta heavy, you can add a curve to the Magenta layer as part of your process to reduce the magenta influence. At the same time, you are not subject to automatic conversions. You have the advantage of making corrections to your CMYK content that you simply can't control otherwise in Elements—or Photoshop.

Figure 5.38

This is really a mask that you will use to screen other colors.

Figure 5.39

With the Black copy layers in place, you've essentially completed the look of the separation.

Figure 5.40

Your completed CMYK separation should look something like this in order: C, M, Y, and K.

Using CMYK Color

Once you have a viable separation, you'll want to be able to use it, right? You can merge the Black copy layers with the plates to accept the changes. This will leave you with the plates and their color preview (screening) layers. To print any of the plates, you follow the same procedure you used for printing duotones. That is, you can flatten the layers individually to get C, Y, M, and K plates in color, and then run the sheet through your printer four times, once for each color. Your other option could be to throw out the color screening layers and save the plate layers as separate files, and provide these to be used to output film. While these are viable options, what you'll really want to do instead is build a real CMYK file with them.

The only problem with all this is there is no direct way to save the file as CMYK, since Photoshop Elements won't handle CMYK channels. However, using a DCS file template, it is possible to save your custom separations for use in a PostScript environment.

Printing with DCS EPS Files

All that is left to do is give you a means of using the CMYK separations you create. The method here may be a little bit of a horse-and-buggy approach in our modern digital image world, but it is the only method that Photoshop Elements allows, and it does let you at least complete the process and apply the image.

What we'll do is hijack a DCS EPS file. You will split out the individual plates from the CMYK image, and then insinuate your content into the file. You'll have to know a little about DCS files and what to do with the template, but that part is relatively easy.

DCS files can come in several types, but the one we'll be using here is a five-part file. The file has a preview, low-resolution image (that you can use for placement in layout programs that handle PostScript information), and separate grayscale files for each of the plates (cyan, magenta, yellow, and black). The placement file is essentially a resource fork that points to the other files. When the file is encountered by a PostScript device, it will reference the high-resolution information in the separately saved plates. As long as you don't change the file that is being referenced, any PostScript device will be fooled into thinking that the content in those files will be what it needs to print…and there it can reference your separations.

All you will be doing is opening the DCS EPS template parts and then replacing the content:

1. Copy a template from the **DCS** folder on the CD to a new directory/folder. The directory should have a name that describes the image. Be sure to copy all five parts of the template.

2. Open an image that is color-separated into CMYK components or open an image and create the separation by clicking CMYK Process in Hidden Power Tools.

3. Change the format of the file to Grayscale and do not flatten the layers. Be sure that you have merged the color components with their Black copy adjustments.

4. Open the Image Size dialog box to check the size of the CMYK separated image. Record the number of pixels. If the image is not already 300 ppi, change the ppi of the CMYK image to 300ppi. As you are adjusting the ppi, the content of the image should not change. Be sure Resample is not checked (see Figure 5.41). Close the dialog box and accept the changes if you have adjusted the ppi.

5. Select All, activate one of the plate layers, and select Edit → Copy .

6. Open the corresponding template file (for example, for the Cyan plate, open *[template]*.C).

7. Resize the file to the size noted in Step 4. Check the Resample. Don't worry about image distortion of the template, as the template information is unimportant.

8. Select Edit → Paste. The image of your plate should get pasted to a new layer.

9. Flatten the file or merge down (Command/Ctrl+E).

Figure 5.41

The 1200×1761 dimension is what you'll want to note in this image. Each image can be different.

Image Size		
Pixel Dimensions: 6.05M		
Width:	1200	pixels
Height:	1761	pixels
Document Size:		
Width:	4	inches
Height:	5.87	inches
Resolution:	300	pixels/inch

☑ Constrain Proportions
☑ Resample Image: Bicubic

OK
Cancel
Help

10. Save the file (Command+S/Ctrl+S). Don't use Save As, because it may change your file and make it invalid.

11. Close the template file.

12. Repeat Steps 5 through 11 for each of the color plates, selecting the appropriate template file for each.

13. Go into the folder/directory where you saved the plates, and rename the placement file (it will have an .eps extension) to whatever you want. *Do not* rename the component files. Renaming components will cause the image to fail.

Figure 5.42

The preview is meant to help place the image in an image box. The box for a 3x3 inch image (900x900 pixels) should be aligned to the 900 pixel hash. If using a 2x3 image (600x900 pixels) would be aligned to the 600 pixel hash in width and the 900 in height.

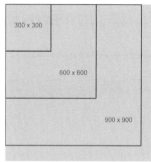

When you have completed these steps, you will have saved the CMYK components of your image so that they can be placed in layout programs like QuarkXPress or Adobe InDesign. These programs will recognize the DCS file, and will reference the high-resolution components when it is time to print. The placement file will look like Figure 5.42 as a preview. The preview is meant to help with placement of the image. Be aware that the preview will not resize automatically and shows a set 1000 pixel square for a 300 ppi image.

Be sure not to save more than one image (the five parts are one image) to a folder. Using separate folders will keep your files from overwriting one another. If there are a lot of files to work with, place the separate folders in a main folder (such as My CMYK Images, as shown in Figure 5.43).

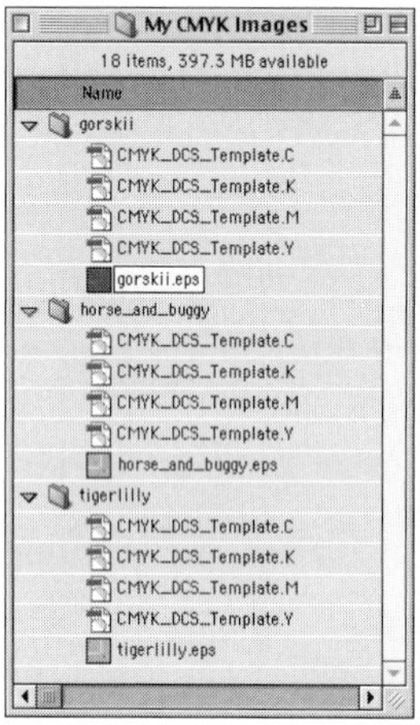

Figure 5.43

The directory inside the main directory can have generic names, but naming the directory using filenames that describe the images can help you sort them and make the images easy to find.

Templates are also provided on the CD for duotone, tritone, and quadtone images. These will have a generic name for the additional colors (i.e., Spot Color 1, Spot Color 2, and Spot Color 3). The generic colors can cause some mismatching when processing plates, but it is possible to find solutions for output. Alert your printing technician to the generic names in the spot color files before processing.

If you have digested even most of what has happened in this chapter, you are pretty much a color guru at this point. There is almost nothing you can't do with a color image coming out of Photoshop Elements. Now we can move on to working on the composition.

Part IV

Rebuilding Images

Assuming that the previous chapters have roughly tackled color possibilities, the next area of attack is the objects and shapes in your images. While the title of this part may sound like we're going to discuss image overhauls and sweeping changes, that isn't quite the point. The idea is to work with what exists in an image, and improve it as possible. Understanding a little about composition can give you a good idea (or at least a hint) as to how you might improve an image by placement of the objects. Knowing how to extract and work with objects gives you more freedom to place them however you want to in the composition. Once you're able to separate color and separate objects in a scene, you have more or less ultimate control over how an image looks. This part looks at image objects in two sections:

Chapter 6 **Altering Composition**

Chapter 7 **Shaping and Replacing Objects**

Chapter 6

Altering Composition

Before just changing things around in an image, you need a plan. An image can become infected with a lot of simple composition problems. If you treat the infection, the image will improve. Composition problems come in three types:

- Problems inherent in an image
- Problems born of careless composition
- Personal vendettas

Built-in problems are those that just couldn't be fixed when taking the image. Careless composition results when something sneaks into the frame unnoticed. The "vendetta" category is full of certain things you simply like or dislike; you might want to change a perfectly good image. There's no accounting for taste. There are guidelines to better composition, but the rules aren't rock-solid. Understanding composition can help you achieve better images both with your camera and by making better corrections.

Problems in Composition

Cropping as a Tool for Composition

Isolating Image Elements

Compositing Image Elements

Problems in Composition

Good images all have at least one thing in common: they usually flatter and enhance the subject. Chances are when you look at a good image, the subject stands out in a pleasing way. Good images also always start in the camera, but you do have opportunity to fix problems and make compositional alterations later in Photoshop Elements. The changes you make can be simplified by the understanding of color and masking that you've gained thus far, and mastered by fixing what is "broken" in the image.

You've probably seen some of the most ridiculous composition faux pas in images you shoot—regretfully this will usually happen after you've taken them and you are looking at the image result. The problems in composition will almost always have to do with placement of objects in an image, image clutter, lighting, and the perspective on the subject.

For example, say you are at an awards ceremony where the Governor comes to make an award presentation at a local lodge. You try to get a picture at the climax of the evening, just as the award is handed off to the recipient. You've never stopped to look at the background, and never considered another perspective but standing and shooting flat-footed from wherever they happened to place you in the seating lottery. Later when you look at the image, you see the massive horns. The mounted moose head on the wall in the background makes the person getting the award look more like Bullwinkle than a hero.

You could have saved the need for correction by doing a little more to anticipate the image. Such planning ahead could have included trying to position yourself for a better angle. By doing so, you could probably have avoided the moose head, and maybe you'd have found a slightly more interesting angle on the subject as well.

- Look at every object in the viewfinder when framing your images, and eliminate what you don't need or want whenever possible.

- Take advantage of different angles that may reveal interesting perspectives on your subject if it is appropriate, as shown in Figure 6.1.

Figure 6.1

This chair can be framed to fill the entire image, or moved to another position in the frame so the image includes more of the setting and potential interest.

Another common problem with composition is that it is often just boring. When you take a portrait of friends who have come to visit from overseas, you line them up like cattle and take pictures slightly more interesting than mug shots. And the only reason they are slightly more interesting is that you've again forgotten the moose head on the wall—which they probably don't happen to have in the police station's booking room.

If you take an image with an on-camera flash of three static people standing and smiling—perhaps even at the ultimate moment as they chorus the smiley phrase "cheese"—no matter what you do, you are going to have three static people smiling flatly-lit smiles. They may be washed out in the exposure and in various stages of blinking, sneezing, scratching, etc. For the next shot you could move them to the shade of a leafless tree where the branches cast a pattern of shadows that weave a complexity on their faces that you'll never remove (see Figure 6.2). It won't matter if you change the backdrop to something interesting—Egyptian tombs, the Eiffel tower, or a moose head—the result will be about the same: an unflattering image of the main subject.

Figure 6.2

The natural shadows in this image are complicated by unnatural shade. The result will be nearly impossible to save without editing heroics.

- Pay attention to sources of light and shadow—both artificial and natural. Use light to your advantage.

- Avoid the temptation to stagnate shots with posing and to always shoot with the subject at the center of the frame.

- Consider taking multiple shots from one position even if you think you got a good one; this can give you more image data to mine.

Many times composition problems—like bird droppings on a statue—are just part of the "ambiance" of an image. Images can have clutter and debris that is no more attractive than minor dust and dirt that you'd get in a scan, and there is no way to anticipate or avoid it without missing the shot. Taking an image of a play on a ball field with a $2000 lens will still capture the garbage caught in the swirling wind behind as the play unfolds—it just might get a better picture of it.

Zoom lenses, aperture, shutter speed…who needs that stuff? Just about any camera on the shelf can be set to an auto mode that will correct the exposure. The catch phrase is "point and shoot": all you've got to do is follow orders, right? The gizmo does something and the thingamajig does something else, and what-the-heck—you get a picture when it's all done.

- No equipment will always take a better picture just because it costs more.

- Don't depend on auto mode to know what you want. Know how to use shutter speed, lens length, aperture, and exposure to control movement and depth of field when you need it. See Figure 6.3.

Certain things can't happen when you edit an image. You won't ever take a picture of the back of someone's head and flip it horizontally and see their face. That may sound ridiculous, but in a similar way select objects can't often just be flipped right to left: you may be somewhat frozen in orientations because of lighting, perspective, and content. If the light falls from the left, the object will look odd if flipped the other way.

- Consider the image you are taking as the final product, even if you know you'll be editing it later.

- Be realistic in the results you expect from editing your images, and always start with the best images you can.

- When flipping the orientation of objects, be sure that the lighting, shadows, and content all make sense.

Figure 6.3

Lack of depth of field in this image isolates the subject from the background.

So if you have to do all these things, why is it that you need Photoshop Elements to fix your photos at all?

If you do advanced work with Photoshop Elements, you probably aren't taking images intending to spend a lot of time in front of the computer fixing them. While there are certain things you can do to your images in the computer that you can't in the heat of a flashbulb, you want to be going to the computer to enhance and flatter the images, just like good composition flatters a subject. Unless you are doing restoration, you will generally want to start with good images to make them even better, rather than spending a lot of time editing bad images to make them OK.

Whether you are taking an image in a camera or evaluating it for corrections, the same questions of composition can come to mind. Even with your best effort on every image, there will often be compositional elements to adjust. The trick to correcting problems is not always so much finessing the image as recognizing what you consider a problem—then calmly stalking the problem like a hunter.

Cropping as a Tool for Composition

Cropping an image entails you cut the edges to keep or eliminate image area. If done for the right reasons, you can crop to snip away image areas that don't matter or are distracting, to get the viewer's attention back to whatever it is that you want them to see. You can also use cropping to reorient images. Cropping is usually the first thing you will do in a digital edit when it comes to composition: it reduces the image area that you have to work on and helps focus the rest of your changes.

Reshaping an image by cropping can result in a significant change in composition and the feel of an image. The Crop tool can be accessed by pressing C on the keyboard, or by clicking its icon 🔲 in the Toolbox. To use it, all you have to do is click on the image and drag a cropping box. Once the box is on the image, you can reshape it using the handles. Figure 6.4 shows two examples of how cropping can improve composition.

One thing not to ignore when using the Crop tool is the option for color and opacity on the options bar (see Figure 6.5). You can change the color of the area outside the crop area to give you an idea of what the image looks like cropped. I often use a background gray at 90% opacity so I can barely see the image area I am removing and can get a very good idea of the result. Too little opacity gives you very little idea of the final result as a preview; too much, and you can't really see what you are cropping out.

The crop can be committed by clicking the OK button on the tool options bar or by pressing Enter. Once the crop is accepted, you can undo it by clicking Undo, pressing Command/Ctrl+Z, or stepping back in your history.

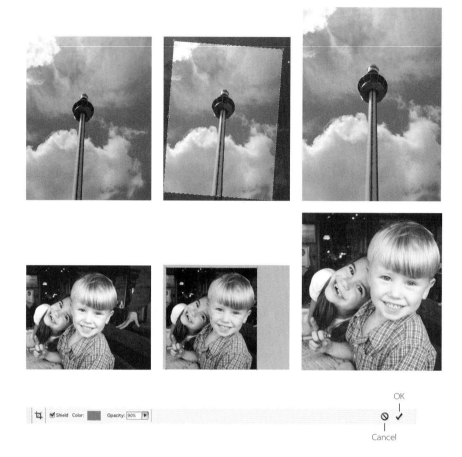

Figure 6.5

Set the color of the cropped area to contrast your image, or as a gray (or black) so it behaves as an image matte. Use the Opacity to block out any image area that you will crop, to give a good view of the result.

Isolating Image Elements

Flattering the subject can mean complementing or isolating it in some way so the object is clear in the image. Isolation is really a two-step process. First, you isolate an image area using selection and layers. This can be an involved process where you use many of the techniques that have been discussed prior to this point in the book (separations, masking, calculations, mixing, etc.). Once your elements are selected, you can cut and paste them to a new layer to isolate them from other image areas, and then apply effects to create visual isolation. The first step is technical, and the second is more probably artistic, although we'll look at a few different solutions as we jump into an example.

The `orchid.psd` file (which is included on the CD) looks like Figure 6.6. When you first open the image in Photoshop Elements, the background and foreground will show some difference, but we'll strengthen that using a drop-shadow effect and blurring. Blurring will further obscure detail in the background, and the drop shadow will serve to burn in the area around whatever selection you make.

Select the Object You have a lot of options for making selections of the orchids, from making a manual outline of them, to selecting by calculation, to making a selection with the Hidden Power Blend Mask tool. We'll look at more than one way to do this and save the selection.

Use the Selection to Isolate the Object Once the selection is made, you have the run of the house. You can manipulate the elements separately including color, tone, and any other adjustment you can think of. All you have to do is get the elements on their own layers, which we'll do in short order using the selection.

Make Separation Changes We'll blur the background to reduce the detail there and then create a drop shadow from the selection to add some separation from the background.

Making a Selection of the Object (Manual)

Here's one way to make your selection (the section that follows this one presents an alternative set of steps toward the same thing):

1. Create a new layer above the background and name it Orchid Selection. Set the opacity of the layer to 60%.

2. Change the foreground color to something that will stand out against the image. Orange would work fine for this image.

Figure 6.6

This unusual flower can be made even more distinct from the background.

3. Select the Paint Brush (or Airbrush) tool, and choose a brush that is 95% hard and 10–20 pixels in diameter.

4. Zoom in to 200%–300% (this will make sure you can see all the pixels in the image).

5. Trace the outline of the orchid (outside), staying as close as possible to the edge. If you hold down the Shift key and click, you can create short line segments that will work on all but the toughest curves. Complete the circuit of the selection, making an edge all the way around the orchids. Be sure to get the areas in between the flowers. The completed outline will look something like Figure 6.7.

6. When the outline is complete, choose the Magic Wand and Shift-click in each of the areas outside the orchids. The wand can be set to 0 tolerance, Contiguous and Use All Layers.

7. Expand the selection (Select → Modify → Expand) by half the diameter of the brush. This should make the selection fall across the center of the outline.

8. Fill with the foreground color. At this point you have completed the basic shape for the selection. Figure 6.8 shows the result.

9. Change the opacity of the layer to 0% or shut off the view. No kidding. This will hide the layer whether the visibility is on or off. It is one of two ways we'll use to hide selections in your images.

Figure 6.7

The outline is made dark here for emphasis; yours will look like an orange outline in the same shape.

Figure 6.8

The black area of this figure shows the area that should be filled when you have completed Step 8.

Making a Selection of the Object (Calculations)

You may find a number of ways to do something similar to what I am going to suggest here in using calculations. The idea is to take whatever advantages you see in the image and successfully enhance them to get the result you need. The orchids are the brightest things in the image, and that makes them a pretty easy target for this kind of selection. In a similar way, the darkest, most saturated, least saturated, or most color-defined image areas can all provide the information you need to make the calculated selection—depending on the separations you choose to make.

1. Starting with the original orchid image, make an RGB separation using the Hidden Power Tool to Split RGB Channels.

2. Look at, and then delete, the Blue channel. You won't need it for this calculation, because it offers very little practical distinction in the object you are trying to separate.

3. Duplicate the Green channel and set the duplicate to Screen mode. Doing this will take advantage of the information in the green channel and emphasize the brightness that already exists there.

4. Change the Red channel to Color Burn mode. The red is more consistently dark around the flower, and setting it to Color Burn will darken the perimeter. This should help darken the area around the flowers to black. This will result in a pretty good rough selection of the orchids on black-and-white. See Figure 6.9.

Figure 6.9

While this selection is not perfect, it uses existing image information and is much quicker than manual selection.

5. Merge the layers used in the calculation, and rename the result Orchid Selection.

6. Get a brush and touch up the rough selection made with the calculation. To touch up, fill in any areas you don't need to select by filling in those areas with the black. Use white to remove black areas to add to the selected part of the mask.

7. When you are done with the touchup, click Clear Grayscale then click Commit Transparency on the Hidden Power Tools. This will create a mask based on the black-and-white content of the Orchid Selection layer.

8. Change the opacity of the mask layer to 0%, or turn off the visibility.

Using the Selection to Isolate the Object

Whether you made your selection manually or through Calculations, you can now use the selection to manipulate elements in the image:

1. Recall the selection by holding down the Command/Ctrl button and clicking on the Selection layer.

2. Activate the Background layer.

3. Copy and paste. This will paste the orchids into a new layer. Change the layer name to Orchids.

4. Reload the selection by Command/Ctrl clicking the Orchids layer. Choose Select → Invert (Shift+Command+I/Shift+Ctrl+I) to invert the selection.

5. Activate the background layer.

6. Copy and Paste the background to create a new layer. Name the layer Orchid Background. Figure 6.10 shows a breakdown of the layers in detail and in the layer palette.

Your layers should be in the exact order shown in the figure. Isolating the background might have taken you one step further than you expected to go. However, you'll need the Orchid Background on its own layer. When you go to blur the background area, the color from the orchid would bleed into the blur if it weren't separate. Treating them separately keeps the reactions separate. You might try the blur on a copy of the background just to see the difference.

Figure 6.10

The layers you have left will be the original Background, the Orchids, and the Orchid Background neatly stacked.

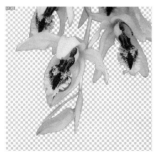

Making the Separation Changes

Now that the image elements have been manipulated into their own layers, you can edit them individually by blurring the background and creating a drop shadow:

1. Activate the Orchid Background layer.

2. Apply a Gaussian Blur (Filter → Blur → Gaussian Blur). The radius should be broad enough to significantly blur the background, but the setting is your choice.

3. Load the Orchid layer as a selection by Command/Ctrl clicking it in the Layers palette. Create a new layer and drag it below the Orchid layer. Name the layer Drop Shadow. The selection will be used to create a drop shadow on the new layer.

4. Adjust the selection. You may want to both Expand and Feather the selection (find these on the Select menu). Expanding will give you a broader base, and Feathering will blend in the effect. The stronger you want the effect to be, the broader you should make both. Try Expand and Feather settings of 10 pixels. These can be changed and redone later.

Figure 6.11

While this shows shadowing to enhance separation, using white for the shadow could add separation between a dark object and its dark background.

5. Fill the selection with black. Set the layer mode to Multiply to ensure that as areas of the image darken, you can control the intensity of the effect using layer opacity. Figure 6.11 shows the original, the drop shadow, and the result.

SELECTING FLY-AWAY HAIR?

One thing that is a common request in user forums and is really an expectation for an advanced image editing program is the ability to select fly-away hair. There is no guaranteed way to do this, and no one-size-fits-all methodology. If the hair is photographed against a distinct color, it may be a better idea to apply the content of the image using a blend mask that targets that specific color range rather than attempting to do this the other way around. Instead of trying to make an absolutely nutty selection of thin wisps of hair, build a color range mask either using Hue/Saturation or a Blend Mask. If you target the mask correctly to the color range of the background, you can use it to drop in whatever background replacement you wanted—or just use the mask to apply a targeted color change.

Placing the drop shadow increases the local contrast around the orchid and enhances the separation from the background. At this point, you may want to try painting in some highlights or working with other effects and correction, but the basic purpose has been accomplished.

Compositing Image Elements

In times of image trouble one of the greatest things to have is more than one image to work with. If you take several shots of the same scene you are really safeguarding yourself for any corrections you might have to make. For example, if you are taking one of those artificially posed group shots (we all do it at some time or another) and you take one shot, you may find that Bessy blinked, and Billy had a finger up his nose. If you pause a moment and take the same shot, Billy and Bessy might be fine while Uncle Dom is shushing a bee, and one of the twins ran off. Neither of the shots is good by itself, but since they were taken at the same time, you can use elements from each to create one good image. It is probably more time-efficient to go find the twin and try one more shot, but in a pinch, you have the information you need for the completed image. Just copy Bessy without the blink and the more flattering pose for Billy from the second shot to fix the first.

This same philosophy works to help you fix any number of other problems. Say you go out and shoot a great picture of a balloon race starting off in the early morning as they float up the hillside at the peak of fall foliage. The image is perfect, except for that one ugly balloon, or the billboard ad you can't crop out, or the electrical wires, or a water tower... If you wait a moment and snap another the balloons will have moved and you'll have a whole new set of autumn leaves to make any necessary patches with, or you can mix and match the positions of the balloons as you'd prefer. If you wait till the balloons are above the hillside, you can take a clean shot of the hill by itself and then place the balloons wherever you want. More source material in the same light, from the same angle, can be far better than just repeating information in the image. As long as the images are good, you'll have more freedom to use different parts of different images to create the image you were looking for in the first place.

This type of multi-image thinking can be turned right on its head to help you make better shots and solve creative problems. You may set up shots that you take in parts *on purpose* to get a better result.

For example, say you are taking a product shot of the teapot in Figure 6.12 to sell on a website. There is a little more than meets the eye because there are several internal parts, and you'd like to show them all in one image. Lighting multiple objects in a scene can get tricky: objects in close proximity can block lighting and cast shadows over one another. One way to rid yourself of the lighting problem is to shoot each part that you want to include and then assemble the shots into one final image. This allows you to make the best of each part and simplifies the process: you make one lighting setup, shoot each of the parts so you can easily extract it from the background—perhaps even take a picture of just the background—and then make a composite of the parts.

Figure 6.12

**This teapot opens
up into several
different pieces.**

If you take pictures of the parts of the pot separately, all you have to do is compile them in a single image. Simple, right? You may have to create a background, unless you take an image to use for that separately. You can spend a lot of time with this one depending on how meticulous you are.

Take the Image Parts I've already shot the image parts for you, and the files are included on the CD. There are five: the glass, the harness, the insert holder, the top, and the basket.

Extract the Image Parts Make a simple selection of each image part, and copy/paste the element into a new image that will be large enough to hold all of them. Use whatever method you want to use to extract the parts—you may even want to mix techniques. In some instances, calculations can prove to be pretty easy because the blue parts of the pot will provide an easy target. However, the glass and basket have highlights and a lack of color, which may prove a bit more challenging. To make this a little more interesting, I didn't color correct, so you might want to do that. You can match the color across the pieces either by making an adjustment to each image according to the background, or by correcting the background to gray. I'm not sure how it happened, but one of these darned things got shot in slightly different light. See how even the best-planned images can easily go awry?

Figure 6.13

This background was made entirely from simple gradients and should serve as a fine place to insert my objects.

Create the Background You can use a totally flat background, or you can add a little interest and make it seem more realistic with a slight gradient—perhaps multiple gradients—and a touch of noise. The background you create is up to you, but my sample is pictured in Figure 6.13. You'll have to remember only one thing: that glass stuff on the pot is transparent, so whatever you end up with as a background has to somehow make sense with what you can see through the glass. You might want to take care of that with color masking.

Arrange the Image Parts and Create Effects You can arrange the objects however you want to within the image and then apply effects to add realism or separation. A few things to do:

- Create drop shadows for each of the objects. Often just a simple, soft outlining at the base will do. This helps to blend the elements. You may want to create these shadows manually using black, a feathered brush, and a layer set to Multiply just below the object.

- Be conscious of areas where elements cross. For example if you overlap the glass onto the harness, part of that harness should probably show through the glass.

When you are all done, the image should look something like Figure 6.14.

Figure 6.14

The composite for the parts will show a clear rendering of each component without the trouble you'd otherwise have with shadows.

Alpha Channels in Elements Images

As it is the least important part of the exercise, I did leave alpha selections in the images so you can use mine (or use mine as a starting point and adjust them if you'd like). I stored them as alpha channels—one in each image. An alpha channel is just a means of storing a grayscale selection; it is stored in the same way color channels are stored, but the alphas don't affect image color. When they are loaded, they recreate the selection you stored…exactly.

One of the improvements to Photoshop Elements 2 is the ability to save, load, and delete alpha channels by choosing Save Selection, Load Selection, and Delete Selection. (For those on Photoshop Elements 1, the Hidden Power Tools include a way to work with Alphas). The only problem with that is you can't see alpha channels in Photoshop Elements, so you are working a little blind. Also, if you store a lot of selections, there isn't a quick way to purge them from your images.

I've provided two tools to help you work with selections. One will help you purge selections from your image without deleting them one at a time. The other will provide a brief preview of any of the saved selections you choose. You'll need to be able to work with alphas to save your selections so we'll look at doing that briefly first.

To load a selection, use one of the sample images:

1. Open one of the images from the example set for the teapot.

2. Choose Load Selection on the Select menu. When the dialogue appears select Alpha 1 from the Selection drop list (it should be selected for you as it is the only alpha).

This will load the alpha channel from the image. The subject of the image will be selected; that's all there is to it. You can use the Save Selection for storing your own selections as alpha channels. All you have to do is:

1. Open an image.

2. Create a selection using whatever tools you like.

3. Choose Save Selection from the Select menu.

4. Type a name for your selection/alpha channel.

5. Click OK to accept the changes and save the selection by the name you entered.

To Delete a selection, just choose Delete Selection from the Select menu. When the dialogue appears, choose the selection you want to delete and click OK to accept the change.

If you have an image where you've saved a bunch of selections and you want to purge them all, the Delete Selections and Alphas tool on the Hidden Power Tools menu can help you out. All you have to do is click Delete Selections and Alphas and Hidden Power Tools will separate all the channels, then ask you which you want to combine to recreate your image. For example, if the image was RGB, choose RGB to tell Elements what type of file it should make, then choose the color channels. In an RGB image, the RGB channels will be separated into [filename].red, [filename].green and [filename].blue (where filename stands for the name of the image before you split it; if you are splitting a file you hadn't saved, the file name will be Untitled with a number: Untitled-#).

When you have a selection, you may not know exactly what is being selected — even if you load the selection and look at the selection outline. The outline only shows where the selection is 50%+ effective. If there is grayscale in your selection, or feathering, the only way you'll know exactly is by previewing.

Hidden Power Tools provides a preview for any saved selection. Be sure you've saved the selection you want to preview and click Preview Selection on the Hidden Power Tools. This will prompt you to select a saved selection. When you have made the choice, the selection will preview automatically and fade. When the preview disappears, a message will appear telling you the preview is complete. Do not interrupt the process.

These few tools should add powerful selection storage and management features to your repertoire.

Chapter 7

Shaping and Replacing Objects

There is a whole lot to pay attention to when you are looking to "fit" an image element into a new area. You must consider light, shadow, detail, perspective, tone, and color. It becomes a balancing act where you have to make image content fit not only as part of the composition, but also as part of the color and texture of the image. In other words, at this point you need to pull together all of the bits of what you have in your toolbox. There are simple transformations, and then there are those that radically reshape an image element, in essence re-creating it in a form that didn't exist before. This kind of transformation may require isolating elements based on color, and then altering the shape of the element itself. We'll look at both reshaping and creating image elements in this chapter.

Transformations and Distortions

Shaping Image Elements with Light and Shadow

Creating Image Elements

Transformations and Distortions

Transformations and distortion are usually looked at as a means of bending an image or making something look, well, demented. However, there are reasons that you might want to distort things to make them look more natural, or simply better.

Images taken with a wide-angle lens may show some exaggeration of the size of objects at the center of the image; tall objects can sometimes show an exaggerated perspective because of the way light comes through a lens. Sometimes you will want to enhance this effect, and at other times you may want to minimize it. You may simply want to display some creativity and change the appearance of an object or reshape it to make it fit where you want to see it in an image.

Take a look at the example image in Figure 7.1. There's nothing really wrong with this image. However, there may be some things that you might want to improve or change. For example, the window seems a bit skewed, and actually the wall does, too. The horizon (where the wall meets the floor) isn't flat. The image looks as though the picture was taken with a lens that distorted the whole scene and then cropped.

Figure 7.1

An interesting image as is, it can also be a good study for perspective.

Say you are a perfectionist and just need to have that window square. One thing you can do is use the Transform feature (Image → Transform) to bend and stretch the image till the window looks right—or has the perspective that you'd prefer. All you do to use the transform tool is either make a selection around what you want to reshape and transform that selection, or have a layer active and then transform the whole layer. Click and drag the handles to reshape the bounding box. The image information inside the box changes to fit the new shape. Pressing the Enter key or clicking the OK button on the Options bar commits the changes. Pressing the Escape key will undo the transformation before it is committed. The modes for Transform are shown in Table 7.1 and are demonstrated in Figure 7.2.

Figure 7.3 shows just how much of a transformation you have to make to change the perspective of the image so that the window is square. And this change is really fine—if you want to ignore the rest of the image. The only thing it really fixes is the outside of the frame of the window, throwing everything else in the image out of whack at the same time. It also fixes only the *outside* shape of the window, not the windowpanes.

MODE	DESCRIPTION	
Free Transform	Allows you to rotate, scale, skew, distort change perspective without having to switch tool modes via the menu. Move the cursor outside the bounding box to rotate. Click any handle and move to scale the box; hold down the Shift key to scale proportionally; hold down Option+Shift/Alt+Shift to scale proportionally on center. Hold down Command+Shift/Ctrl+Shift to skew; hold down Command/Ctrl to distort; hold down Command+Option+Shift/Ctrl+Alt+Shift to change perspective.	Table 7.1 **Transform Modes**
Skew	Allows you to reshape the bounding box by moving any handle along a current axis. Hold down the Shift key to switch the tool to Perspective; hold Option/Alt to skew opposites on center.	
Distort	Allows you to reshape the bounding box by moving any point freely. Hold down the Shift key to restrict movement to a current axis (like Skew).	
Perspective	Allows you to reshape the bounding box by moving handles in sync from the center handle on a side: move a corner and the opposite corner on the same side moves in the opposite direction.	

Transformations that you make should often be slight. Larger changes will compromise sharpness in a way similar to resampling.

What you really want to do to fix things here is isolate the problems. You can make selections and move image areas to their own layer, and then work on them in isolation from the rest of the image. In fact, you can actually take the separate parts of the image and rebuild the whole thing to make the image look the way you want it to.

The image from Figure 7.1 is available on the CD (`perspectives.psd`). In the following exercise you'll see how to use what's in the image, separate it out using selection, and fix the perspective problems. The key parts of the image are the plant, the window, and the background (sidewalk and wall). You'll want to move each element to its own layer and do adjustments as necessary.

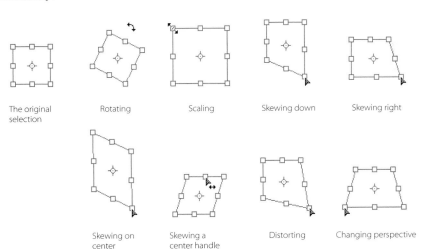

The original selection   Rotating   Scaling   Skewing down   Skewing right

Skewing on center   Skewing a center handle   Distorting   Changing perspective

Figure 7.2

The Transform options can skew, rotate, and scale your selection. Note that the cursor is different for every action.

On your way through the corrections you'll be working with two new Hidden Power Tools: Make Guide and Clear Guides. These will allow you to place non-printing guidelines on your image to help with alignment. Split RGB Channels will also be used for practical purposes in helping to create a complex masking and selection. This process is involved, be sure to allot a good chunk of time at the computer when you are ready to test it out.

Prepare the Image There is some minor cleanup to do to the image. Note the spotting and some of the inconsistent color in the paint. You can remove the bleaching effect on the windowpanes as well. What you fix will have something to do with how picky you happen to be. Once you've done minor touchups, you'll want to do general color correction. I'll be leaving all of this to your discretion and won't be including it in the steps. I hope it is enough warning to say: if you jump right into the manipulation without prepping, you will make more work for yourself rather than less. Failing to clean up may leave you spreading around attributes that you don't want in the first place. For more information, see the clean up sections in Chapters 3 and 4.

Re-create the Background Using the existing background and some patching you will create a fresh, new background to build the rest of the image on, using what exists in the image.

Add in the Sidewalk This will be a simple application of Transform on whatever part of the existing sidewalk you can salvage.

Isolate, Fix, and Position the Window The window can be selected using a variety of techniques that we've already discussed, from color and tonal techniques to manual selection. One other option is just making a rough selection that we can blend in later. This simpler technique is what I'll be using here. Once the window is selected and copied to its own layer, the perspective can be adjusted using the Transform tool. The transformation will require two separate adjustments, one to the whole window to straighten the outside of the frame, and one to adjust the windowpane. Using Guides will help keep the window in position.

Figure 7.3

To transform a flattened image, you have to first convert the background to a layer by double-clicking it in the Layers palette.

Isolate, Fix, and Position the Plant The plant will require something a little more fancy, because the selection will be used to re-create the shadow. The selection should be pretty accurate; all those tiny branches can be difficult. Although the selection can be done in several different ways, this solution uses a variety of tools, including channel calculations, Levels, Threshold, Paintbrush and Lasso in a new image.

You won't have much to do with the plant itself. The pot may need some reshaping and adjustment—the original seems to have a shadow that was generated by something off to the right of the frame.

Re-creating the Background

1. Open the image (`perspectives.psd`).

2. Make a large selection of the wall, including as much of it as you can, but excluding the window, plant, sidewalk, and shadow. This is probable easiest to do using the lasso tool. You are just looking to encompass the largest patch of unadulterated wall that you can find.

3. Copy and paste the selection to a new layer, and name it Wall.

4. Activate the background layer, then create a new layer and fill it with white. Name it Canvas. You'll be using the canvas layer to block out the background; you'll need the Background layer as source for the elements you'll be isolating. The canvas will let you see how things are progressing without constantly turning the visibility of layers on and off.

5. Use the Wall layer as source for making patches to fill the rest of the image. This is probably easiest to do using patch layers. To make a patch layer, make a feathered selection in the Wall layer, and then copy and paste the selection. This will create a new layer above the Wall layer, which can be Transformed (moved, rotated, stretched, etc.) to fill white areas. Name the additional layers Patch 1, Patch 2, etc. You can do any of the following:

   - Duplicate the whole Wall layer. This is best done by making a selection (Command/Ctrl-click the layer, then feather 10–20 pixels).

   - Make a selection over a white area as a template, move the selection to a donor area that fits the selection, copy and paste the selection, and then position the new Patch layer to fill.

   - Create patch selection shapes at random to make several Patch layers.

6. Once the wall is mostly patched, create a new layer above the other patches and make spot corrections with the Clone Stamp tool to smooth any obvious seams, holes or other obvious inconsistencies. When you are all done, the result should be a wall with no other objects, as in Figure 7.4.

7. Link all the Patch layers and then merge them using Layer → Merge Linked.

Adding in the Sidewalk

8. Turn off the visibility for the Patch and Canvas layers and then activate the Background layer.

9. Make a selection of the open part of the sidewalk using the Polygon Lasso tool. Copy and paste the selection to a new layer. Name the layer Sidewalk.

Figure 7.4

The new wall should have no other objects, and no obvious rifts and/or duplications.

Figure 7.5

The wall and sidewalk form a new background where you'll place the other image elements as you build the new image.

10. Drag the Sidewalk layer above the Wall layer. Turn on the visibility for the Wall layer.

11. Use the Transform tool (e.g., Distort) to shape the Sidewalk layer as desired. The goal would be to create a flat horizon. You may want to do this with a single copy of the sidewalk or with patches, as you did with the wall. The result should look like Figure 7.5.

Isolating, Fixing, and Positioning the Window

12. Turn off the visibility for the Wall layer.

13. Choose the Marquee selection tool (square) and make a selection around the window, leaving a fairly generous amount of wall around the edges, then copy and paste the window to a new layer and name it Window.

14. Drag the Window layer to the top of the Layer stack.

15. Place your cursor half way up the left side of the window and note the cursor position in pixels on the ruler or Info palette. Turn on the Ruler by pressing Command+R/Ctrl+R. The vertical position on the Info palette is the X value.

16. Place a vertical guide at the center position you noted in the previous step by clicking Make Guide in the Hidden Power Tools, choosing Vertical for orientation, and then entering the noted value in the Position field.

17. Make measurements and place guides for the right side of the window as well as the top and bottom edges by noting the center position for each side. Top and bottom guides will be horizontal rather than vertical orientations, and are represented by the Y value on the Info palette.

18. When the guides are all in place, adjust the window using Free Transform to fit the window as closely as possible to the guides you created. See an example in Figure 7.6. Accept the changes when you are satisfied.

19. Using a soft brush and the Eraser tool, erase the edge of the wall included with your window selection to blend it in with the Wall layer.

20. Place new center guides for the right, left, top, and bottom of the window, but this time also make a guide for the inside part of the frame.

21. Make a Rectangular Marquee selection between the inner and outer guides, then copy and paste the selection to a new layer.

22. Use Image → Transform → Free Transform (Command+T/Ctrl+T) to reshape the new layer so that the inner frame of the window aligns with the guides you created. Your results should look like Figure 7.7.

Figure 7.6

Your transformation of the original should look something like this. The actual change depends on the shape of the selection you made of the window.

Isolating, Fixing, and Positioning the Plant

23. Select the background layer and copy to a new image by selecting Duplicate Layer on the Layers palette pop-up menu. When the dialog box appears, choose New in the Document drop-down list for the Destination.

24. Split the color into RGB by choosing Split RGB Channels from the Hidden Power tools.

25. Create a new layer above the RGB layers and name it Plant Selection. Fill it with black and drag the layer below the RGB layers.

26. Delete the Blue channel layer.

27. Set the Red layer to Difference mode in the layers palette. You'll note that the plant becomes a bit darker than the shadow behind it. Choosing Difference is specific to the content of this image—other images may work better using other modes (or color separation techniques) to create masks and separation.

28. Apply a levels correction to draw out the difference by making a Levels Adjustment layer. I used Input levels of 0 / 1.00 / 115 to get the result shown in Figure 7.8. Once the difference is apparent, it can be enhanced in a number of ways.

Figure 7.7

With the frame realigned, the unnatural effects of the original perspective should be all but eliminated.

Figure 7.8

Increase the appearance of separation between the tree and the wall by making a straight Levels correction to increase the dynamic range of the tone.

Before   After

Figure 7.9

I used Threshold to measure the darkest point on the wall, and used that value as the white slider position for a Levels correction.

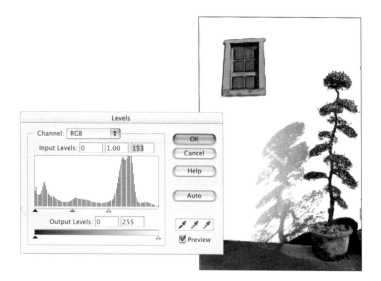

29. Make another adjustment to turn the wall (excepting the shadow) white around the tree. I used Threshold to measure the darkest point on the wall, by moving the slider until just one pixel appeared where I knew there were no branches. I used the value from the Threshold as the white slider position for a Levels correction (see Figure 7.9), and the background mostly vanished.

30. Merge the visible layers by selecting Layer → Merge Visible (Shift+Command+E/Shift+Ctrl+E).

a   b   c

Figure 7.10

I used a paintbrush and white to make a clean area around the tree and pot (a), then used the Polygonal Lasso to clear the rest of the image by making a selection (b), then filled the selected area with white (c) once the selection was made.

31. With the area around the tree mostly clear, clean up the rest of the area around the tree manually. The way I did this is shown in Figure 7.10.

32. Copy the selection made in Figure 7.10 and paste it as a new layer into the original image. Name the new layer Tree Selection.

33. Activate the Tree Selection layer, set the Magic Wand Tolerance to 1, Anti-aliased, and Contiguous, then click in the white area of the selection layer. Reverse the selection (Command+Shift+I/Ctrl+Shift+I), activate the Background, and then Copy and Paste. This will put the plant on its own layer. Name the layer Plant and drag it to the top of the layer stack.

34. Turn off the visibility of the Tree Selection layer. Don't delete the Tree Selection layer; you'll need it later.

35. Touch up the Tree. You may want to reshape the pot (copy it to its own layer and Transform), remove the shadow from the rim on the right (use color and tone adjustments), and adjust some of the branches. At this point the image should look something like Figure 7.11.

36. Save the file and name it `new_perspectives.psd`.

Figure 7.11

When you've separated the tree and window they'll look like this over the Wall and Sidewalk layers.

At this point everything has been replaced, but something still looks a little wrong. The missing piece is the shadow for the tree. You'll put that back in, in the next section, after taking a better look at light and shadow. As you've done quite a bit of work to this point and don't want to lose it (or you may need a break) the last step suggests saving the image as a PSD to retain all the work you've completed. We'll get back to it in a moment.

Shaping Image Elements with Light and Shadow

Light and shadow affect the shape of objects and how they appear relative to one another. Shading and highlighting can provide separation between objects as well. It is light and shadow that affect depth and texture in an image.

Making a raised button provides a good, simple example of how light and shadow can create shape. The following steps will create a shaped and elevated button from a flat gray square:

1. Create a new Grayscale image (File → New) that is 500×500 pixels.

2. Make a Marquee using the Fixed Size option on the Options bar. Set the size to 300×300 pixels and click the tool at 100,100 (x,y). If you click exactly on that point (use the rulers; if the rulers are set to inches, change the preferences to pixels) the selection will be centered exactly on the image. In this case it doesn't matter if you are off by a few pixels.

3. Create a new layer named Button and fill it with 50% gray.

4. Select the Background. Create a new layer named Drop Shadow and set it to Multiply. Creating the new layer here will keep the drop shadow behind/below the button.

5. Feather the current selection 20 pixels and fill it with black. Change the layer opacity to 75%.

6. Deselect by pressing Command+D/Ctrl+D.

7. Offset the shadow layer down 20 pixels and right 20 pixels. To do this, choose the Move tool, hold down the Shift key and press the right arrow and down arrow keys two times each.

8. Activate the Button layer.

9. Create a new layer and name it Highlight. Check Group with Previous set the layer mode to Screen and change the Opacity to 50%.

10. Reload the previous selection by pressing Shift+Command+D/Shift+Ctrl+D. Invert the selection (Shift+Command+I/Shift+Ctrl+I) and fill it with white.

11. Create a new layer and name it Shadow. Check Group with Previous, set the layer mode to Multiply, fill the layer with black and change the Opacity to 50%.

12. Choose Select → Deselect.

13. Choose the Move tool and offset the Highlight layer down 20 pixels and right 20 pixels. To do this, hold down the Shift key and press the right arrow and down arrow keys two times each.

This will leave you with a square button that appears to be slightly raised and is separate from the background. Figure 7.12 shows what your results should look like: the flat square will be transformed into a shaped button with apparent depth. The drop shadow between the button and the Background creates distance between those objects; the highlight and shadow create object shape by mimicking how a raised button might look if a light were coming from the upper-left corner of the image. The more extreme the effects, the greater the depth or distance appears.

Simple highlighting and shadow creation of this sort happens when using layer effects. The way you choose to handle shadows affects the shape of the object, but the final image has to show some consistency with the scene to portray the desired effect and the direction of the light. If you now move the Highlight up and left 40 pixels, and the Shadow down and right 40 pixels, it inverts the effect of the highlight and shadow on the button. The button should appear to be concave—more like a dish than raised.

A convex button   A concave button

All this is to say you can create some cool effects with light and shadow, but you can't just drop a shadow into an image willy-nilly and have it look correct. You have to take existing lighting into account and make adjustments for angle and direction. You also have to make adjustments to the landscape to make the shadow fall correctly.

Figure 7.12

A flat area of color can be both raised from the background and shaped with simple application for highlights and shadows.

When placing the shadow back in the image we were rebuilding in the previous section, you'll have to make some compensation for light direction and the interplay between objects in the scene. Depending on how you handle the shadow, you can also affect the distance between the pot and the wall. These considerations affect realism in the result. While Elements will have some very basic means of creating a drop shadow, knowing how to create your own shadow allows you to have far more control in applying realistic shadows.

Let's look at a flat application and then a more realistic one and compare the results.

The Quick Way   The quick way to make a shadow for the tree would be to make minimal adjustments for how the shadow might fall. It ignores all the possible nuances of light angle and direction and just gets the job done. The results may not be optimal.

Figure 7.13

Two shadows will be used to create one complete one.

The Better Way   A better way to make the shadow takes into account some distortion that will occur because of the angle of the light and the position of objects where the shadows fall. The result should appear more realistic.

The Quick Way to Make a Shadow

1. Open the new_perspectives.psd file created in the Transformations and Distortions section example.

2. Duplicate the Tree Selection layer two times. Set both of the new layers to 50% Opacity and Multiply mode. Drag both layers up below the Tree layer. The Layers palette should look like Figure 7.13.

3. Change the name of the copied layers to Sidewalk Shadow and Wall Shadow.

4. Activate the Wall Shadow layer and drag the Wall Shadow layer so that it looks like the shadow is falling on the wall from the tree, using the Move tool. Just look at the shadow on the wall, ignoring the portion of the shadow that falls on the sidewalk; we'll clean that up later.

Figure 7.14

With both shadows visible, get the trunk of the tree to meet at the juncture of the sidewalk and wall.

Figure 7.15

This isn't bad for a few minutes of work, but it may not be the most accurate shadow you can make.

5. Activate the Sidewalk Shadow layer. Choose Image → Transform → Distort, grab the top-center handle, and pull the handle left and down until the tree trunk matches up at the base of the wall. You may have to zoom in and out of the image (Command/Ctrl+hyphen, Command/Ctrl+plus sign) to view the changes and adjust the handle. The result of the adjustment will look something like Figure 7.14.

6. Load the Sidewalk layer as a selection by Command/Ctrl-clicking the Sidewalk layer in the layers palette. Feather the loaded selection 1 pixel.

7. Activate the Wall Shadow layer and press the Delete key. This will delete the area of this layer below the Sidewalk line.

8. Invert the selection, activate the Sidewalk Shadow layer, and press the Delete key. This will delete the area of this layer that is above the sidewalk.

9. Make manual adjustments to the shadow layers by using a painting tool (such as a slightly soft brush) with white and black. Using black will add shadow; using white will remove it. This touchup might include making the stem match up at the base of the wall and/or completing and adjusting the shadow around the base of the pot. When you are all done, the result should look something like Figure 7.15.

The Better Way to Make a Shadow

A problem with the quick way that you might have noticed is that the shadow looks nothing at all like the original shadow. There is no angle to the way the shadow falls on the wall, and the shadow on the sidewalk represents a front view of the pot. In neither case is it very accurate.

The sad fact is that it is actually impossible to render an accurate drop shadow using a single image. The shadow that you see is accurate only from the perspective of the light source. In other words, you have to take another image from the position of the light source or shoot from the position of the shadow toward the light source to have a representation of your object that matches what the shadow looks like. We don't have that luxury here, because we don't have an image shot from those angles, and considering the proximity of the plant to the wall and the angle of the sun, we may not have been able to anyway.

The next best thing we can do is be a little more creative with what we do have to work with in the image. Natural shadows will distort somewhat because of angles—how the light strikes the object and how the shadow then drapes on the wall. You can use distortions and transformations to your advantage in re-creating a more realistic shadow.

1. Jump back in the Undo History palette to the point in the image right after you completed the tree placement without the shadows.

2. Make a selection of the Sidewalk and invert it.

3. Create a new layer named Wall Shadows below the Tree layer. Set the Opacity to 50% and the layer mode to Multiply.

4. Fill the Wall Shadows layer with white. Every shadow component you create in this exercise for the wall should be grouped with this layer. All of these component layers will be set to Darken and 100% Opacity.

5. Duplicate the Tree Selection layer and arrange it in the Layers palette so that it is above and grouped with the Wall Shadows layer.

6. Move the shadow into position where you would like to see the top of the shadow fall.

7. Create a new layer and name it Light Angle. Set the Opacity to 60% and the Mode to Multiply.

8. Pick two spots that correspond between the tree and its shadow on the wall, and draw a straight line between them. To do this, choose any painting tool, and a hard brush with a diameter of 5–10 pixels. Click on the tree, then hold the Shift key and click on the exact same spot in the shadow that corresponds to the spot you clicked on the tree.

9. Transform the layer to five times its size (500%) using the numbers on the Options bar. This will just make the line you drew thicker and longer, and more useful as a guide. At this point, the image and the layers should look like they do in Figure 7.16.

Figure 7.16

The angled line will act as a guide to help make some changes in the steps that follow.

10. Make a selection of the top segment of the tree's shadow. This can be a rough selection. Copy it to a new layer in the Wall Shadow group. Set the layer mode to Darken and the Opacity to 100%.

11. Choose Image → Transform → Free Transform. Change the Skew to match the Light Angle layer by pressing Command+Option+Shift/Ctrl+Alt+Shift and moving one of the side handles.

12. Release the Skew On Center modifier keys and press Shift, then stretch the box by moving the top center handle and bottom center handle until the box is 150%–200% of the original size (watch the percentage in the H field on the options bar, and it will show you the result). The Transform box should look like Figure 7.17 as a result of the changes in Steps 11 and 12.

13. Accept the changes when the distortion seems acceptable.

14. Repeat steps 11 through 13, selecting parts of the tree in segments from the top down. In the result I used nine distinct sections. When you are done, the result should look something like Figure 7.18.

15. Duplicate the Tree Selection layer, name it Pot Top, and move it above the Tree layer. Reduce the opacity to 50% and use the Eraser tool to trim away everything but the rim of the pot (as shown in Figure 7.19).

16. Duplicate the Pot Top layer and place the copy in the Wall Shadow group, then follow Steps 11 to 13 again.

17. Load the Sidewalk layer as a selection again by pressing Command/Ctrl and clicking the layer in the layers palette.

18. Create a new, ungrouped layer named Sidewalk Shadow and fill it with white in the selected area. Set the Opacity to 50% and the layer Mode to Multiply.

19. Move the copy of the Pot Top layer above the Sidewalk Shadow layer and group them.

20. Stretch and position the pot top as desired. Be sure the edge aligns with the pot top shadow as it comes off the wall.

21. Shape and fill in manual shadows for the pot. The results should look something like Figure 7.20.

There is a comparison in the color section of the book that shows the original image, the quick way of making a shadow, and the better way. The idea is that creating drop shadows is not necessarily as simple as choosing a layer effect. Realistic work often requires custom attention, which means being able to apply custom shadows and highlights. With a little creative adjustment, it is possible to produce more realistic fixes.

With everything separate, you also have more freedom to explore different composition options. Figure 7.21 looks at two other quick ways to rearrange the objects in your image. Similar techniques can be used in other images to separate objects from their backgrounds, re-create or fill in background areas, and adjust the composition.

Figure 7.18

This shows more of a cascade of shadow and better imitates what the sun might produce as the shadow falls on the wall.

Figure 7.19

The dark area is the shape you want; use the Eraser to trim away everything else.

Figure 7.20

The completed shadow should look fairly natural, and perhaps a whole lot neater than the original.

Figure 7.21

**Being able to separate
elements can give you
ultimate freedom over
image composition.**

Creating Image Elements

At the far end of working with images is the option of creating absolutely new elements. Consider how complex the shadow for the tree was, and then multiply that complexity by all you've learned about color and tone. That's not a very concrete equation, but it is relevant in that creating something new will require creativity—and a few basic bits of understanding.

In the previous section, we looked very briefly at how highlights and shadows could shape an image. In a similar way, highlights and shadows can do far more complex things, such as create the appearance of texture. They can give shape to an environment.

But making new elements doesn't mean you'll usually want to create an image absolutely from scratch. What will more often be the case is that you'll have something specific in your image that you prefer to replace. Perhaps you need to patch what is in your image but you don't have sufficient sampling area to create a patch, or you are feeling a little creative and want to actually add an element to an image. It is much more rare that you'll absolutely create an image from scratch, unless you are doing an original illustration. We'll take a look at that illustration later in Chapter 9.

In this next section, we'll take a look at some of the nuts and bolts of what you'll need to create image elements, and leave some of the rest to your creativity. You'll need to know how to work with patterns and texture, and how to create shape using tone.

 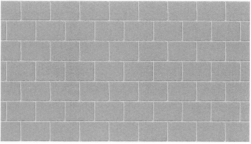

Sample area · Sample used as a pattern

Figure 7.22

Using a sample as a pattern is much easier than creating a whole wall brick by brick.

Creating Texture and Patterns

Say you have an image where the background wall was painted this sort of pastel pink color and there was this weird window and some funky-looking tree that was casting this awful shadow, and you wanted to replace the wall rather than try to repair it. Silly example, right?

While it would be easy enough to fill in color, the texture of the wall would probably be the most difficult thing to deal with. We have two solutions we'll look at, and one is a better solution for this example—but it is important to know how to do both. First we'll look at working with a little bit of what you do have to create a seamless pattern, then we'll look at creating texture by generating it completely from scratch.

Creating Seamless Patterns

A seamless pattern can be used to fill an image area. Usually this type of pattern is something that you want to replicate and repeat, rather than something you want to seem random. For example, a wallpaper pattern, plaid, or bricks might make for a fine pattern to repeat (see Fugure 7.22). Taking bricks as an example, all you'd have to do is create or copy a small portion of the pattern, be sure it can be repeated without obvious seams, and then use that pattern to fill an area.

With a little touchup, you could remove any repeating patterns by changing the color or tone of a few bricks. Just make a rough selection of four or five at random, and then create a new layer and fill it with white or black. Set the layer to Screen (white) or Multiply (black) and lower the opacity (see Figure 7.23). Depending on how you use and manipulate other patterns, you can make them seem random as well, or use them as a basis for creating less obviously contrived objects.

To create a seamless pattern you really need only a small swatch of an image area that you'd like to replicate. All you do is offset that swatch (using the Offset filter),

Figure 7.23

By randomly selecting a few bricks and changing the tone by a few levels, the pattern can appear to be random.

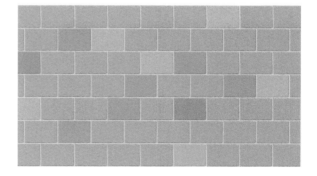

and then patch whatever seam there is. We'll use the old wall from the tree and window picture as an example.

1. Open `perspectives.psd` and make a selection of a representative area of the wall that is clear of shadows or distinct characteristics that would show in a pattern, such as the area shown in Figure 7.24.

2. Copy the selection to a new image. To do this, choose Edit → Copy, then create a new image (File → New) and choose Edit → Paste.

3. Flatten the image (Layer → Flatten Image).

4. Adjust the sample in the new image by removing notable characteristics that might be pronounced in a repeated pattern.

5. Choose Filter → Other → Offset (Figure 7.25). The offset amount you specify should be about half the height and width of the image, and be sure that Wrap Around is selected.

Figure 7.24

This area of the image has very few characteristics that would be a problem in a pattern.

6. Blend the seams of the image. You will probably want to use the Clone Stamp tool and a soft brush. The goal is not to wipe out all of the characteristics of the wall, but to smooth out the transitions.

7. Choose Select → All and create a pattern by choosing Edit → Define Pattern. Call the pattern Pink Wall.

Once you have completed these steps, you will have the portion of the wall as a seamless pattern. Go back to the original image, deselect the sample area and apply the pattern by creating a new layer and using the Fill function. Select Edit → Fill, and in the Fill dialog box, choose Pattern from the Contents drop-down list. Choose Pink Wall from the Custom Pattern drop-down list. (See Figure 7.26.)

Figure 7.25

Offsetting shifts what would be the seam of the pattern into the center of the image (a). You can then clean up the transitions to make it seamless (b).

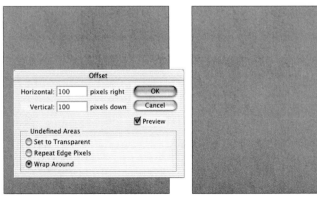

a

b

The pattern will fill the whole layer. It will look much like the wall, but it will be… a pattern. And you can pretty much see that it is (see Figure 7.27). It's a good start, but you can do better.

Creating Texture from Scratch

The limitation of making seamless patterns is obviously that they represent only a small area of what you are trying to depict. Because of that, filling with a pattern can often look like a pattern. It isn't really a surprise. It might work if you are imitating a brick wall, but something less defined or random, such as the surface of concrete or stucco, would seem to repeat when you really don't want it to.

This is where you can be creative with layer and filter application to make the filled background look unique—not at all like a pattern—or create the background entirely from scratch. In fact, every time you make the application, you can get a different (yet similar) result, if you use filters that help generate random image information. Once you have generated the information, you can apply highlights and shadows to make the noise seem textured. You can use the texture to either enhance the existing texture or create new texture where there was none.

Working with filters is almost always a process of experimentation, unless you use a filter that has a specific behavior. You rarely can just reach into the pile of filters and pull out one that will do exactly what you want without making adjustments—or using them in combination. Filters are usually best used to enhance an image rather than change it, which is why it may be wise to use what you already have and adjust it.

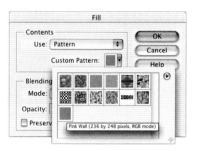

Figure 7.26

When the pattern was saved, it was stored in the pattern library. It can be selected wherever patterns are available and stays stored until deleted.

Figure 7.27

You might get away with this, but the repetition in the pattern is obvious and can detract from the image.

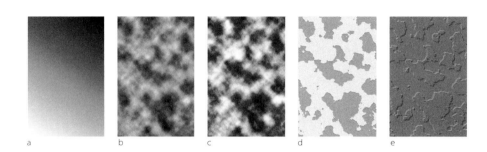

a   b   c   d   e

To work with the pattern already created, I first took a sample of the existing pink color of the wall, and then I created several layers. You can see these pictured in Figure 7.28:

A. A gradient, black to white (using the Gradient Tool, draw a line from the upper right corner to the lower left corner)

B. A Clouds filter application (Filter → Render → Clouds) on a 50% gray layer

C. A Difference Clouds filter application (Filter → Render → Difference Clouds) on a duplicate of the Clouds filtered layer, adjusted by choosing Equalize (Image → Adjustments → Equalize)

D. A Note Paper filter application (Filter → Sketch → Note Paper) on a duplicate of the Difference Clouds layer

E. An Emboss filter application (Filter → Stylize → Emboss) on a duplicate of the Note Paper filtered layer

While this may look like a hodge-podge, the results are not entirely an accident. I made a simple gradient, which I plan to use to darken the image slightly in the upper right. Next I made a series of filter changes in steps—each step based on the previous one—to try to unify the effects of the layers I'd be applying.

The trick to applying these layer results effectively is to give them each very *little* influence in the image. They are going to enhance, not take over, what is already there. The layers were applied to the background of the image by simply stacking them above it using the following settings:

LAYER	MODE	OPACITY
A	Luminosity	10%
B	Luminosity	5%
C	Color	3%
D	Normal	0%
E	Luminosity	5%

If you take a look at the layer settings, these changes affect the luminosity much more than the color—and not all that much. The idea is to randomize some information and use it to influence the tone to create texture. *Influence* is not an overhaul. My goal here was to create two things: general shading, and larger, unpredictable changes in tone and color to affect the apparent flatness of the wall.

I chose several of the filters for very specific reasons. Clouds introduces larger areas of random tones. Emboss creates highlight and shadow depth effects based on existing image content. In other words, I started with the Clouds filters to introduce randomized behaviors. I ended with the Emboss filter to create highlights and shadow that would change my tone areas into random shapes. The effect of the highlighting and shadow created by the Emboss filter acts much like the raised button we looked at earlier in this chapter.

You would probably think I was joking if I were to say it almost doesn't matter what filters you run in between generating the random information and converting that to texture by adding the highlights and shadows. You could spend hours exploring different combinations and results. Part of the fun of filters is guessing which filter might give you an interesting result. The effect of the Difference Clouds filter is to apply the Clouds filter as if to a layer above and grouped to the current layer, set to Difference mode. This filter kept my original clouds information and added some random color behaviors. Note Paper makes a threshold-based gray and white texture effect that is often good for chipped paint, rust, and similar effects.

The effect of the different layers is subtle, but a whole new wall was created by mixing random patterns with the seamless pattern. If you open up the image on the CD (`wallpattern.psd`) and zoom in, it looks pretty real. In a sense, the wall is: You retain some of the real part of the image and texture by basing the color and texture of the wall on the pattern sample, and then enhance the sample. Neither the real portion of the image (the seamless pattern) or the filter applications do it all on their own.

If you're feeling really adventurous, you might want to make a break from reality entirely and create the entire effect from scratch. The only thing you are really missing is the sort of granular cement texture. Instead of creating big random information, you'll want to create flecks and then shape those by embossing. The Noise filter will provide that. Try the following on the `wallpattern.psd`:

1. Turn off the visibility for the added layers (A through E).

2. Duplicate the Wall Pink Pattern Fill layer to a new image.

3. Resize the new image using Bilinear resampling to 10×10 pixels (uncheck Constrain Proportions). This will give you an average tone and color for the wall.

4. Make a sample of the color using the Eyedropper, and then close the image. That's all you wanted the new image for—to get the color sample.

5. Create a new layer above the Wall Pink Pattern Fill layer and fill it with the foreground that you sampled. Call it Wall Pink.

6. Duplicate the Wall Pink layer and name the new layer Cement Texture.

7. Remove the color using Enhance → Adjust Color → Remove Color (in version 1, Enhance → Color → Remove Color). Then apply Noise (Filter → Noise → Add Noise; 10%, Gaussian, Monochrome).

8. Apply a Threshold (Image → Adjustments → Threshold). I didn't change the slider from where it was (128). Changing the slider will influence the density of bumps in the cement.

9. Apply Emboss (Filter → Stylize → Emboss). I chose a 1-pixel radius, Amount 75%, and Angle 45 degrees (about the angle of the original light source). When using Emboss, you generally want to use a radius that fits with the detail you are trying to enhance: small details, small radius.

10. Apply Gaussian Blur (Filter → Blur → Gaussian Blur) to soften the embossing. Choose a smaller than 1-pixel radius, again to retain the smaller details. At this point you'll have a somewhat bumpy looking gray layer. You may want to zoom in to 100%+ to have a good look.

11. Change the opacity to about 15% and the mode to Luminosity, and look what happens. The Pink Wall becomes textured.

Add back the Cloud Filter, Difference Clouds, and Emboss layers by turning the visibility for those layers back on. If you compare the original to the result you have created entirely from filters here, you'll see that the texture is not the same but it has a similar feel. To make that comparison, drag the Wall Pink Pattern Fill layer to the top of the layer stack and toggle the visibility on and off.

You can make further improvements by adjusting the intensity of the bumps in the Cement Texture layer. Do this by adding a mask as in the following steps.

12. Duplicate the Wall Pink layer to a new image and flatten the image.

13. Run the Clouds filter.

14. Click Blend Mask in the Hidden Power Tools. When you get to the Curves dialog box, set the curve as shown in Figure 7.29.

15. Duplicate the Mask layer back to the original image.

16. Duplicate the Cement Texture layer. You can leave the name as Cement Texture copy.

17. Drag the Mask below the Cement Texture copy layer and Group the layers. To group, you can link the two layers by clicking the link box on the layers palette for the Cement Texture copy layer, and then press Command+G/Ctrl+G.

18. Change the Cement Texture copy layer to Normal mode and 100% opacity. This will allow the texture to influence the mask at 100%.

19. Change the Mask layer to 20% opacity and Luminosity mode. You want to use the mask to apply the effect. Here again you are influencing the result, not trying to overpower it. This adds 20% more intense bumps over 50% of the image. Experiment with the settings by adjusting the Mask layer Opacity only.

This series of steps (12–19) effectively masks the texture with some randomized behavior, again using the Clouds filter. As a result, some of the texture is softer and some more pronounced: the filters acting together create a more randomized effect.

You can do still more with this, but you can also play with filters forever, refining and adjusting. Combinations of filters will allow you to create innumerable textures that can be helpful in patching missing image areas or creating entirely new objects.

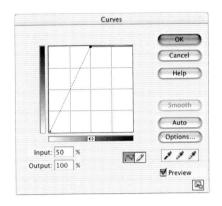

Figure 7.29

This setting will make sure the cloud layer has no tone brighter than 50% gray (128 levels).

Making an Object

Creating an object from scratch is the extreme test of everything we've been through thus far. You would have to make the basic shape of the object using tone and color, then give it depth and fit it into an image. The exercise is tricky and challenging, with varying levels of difficulty. Really, if you did the last part of the previous section and created those little cement bumps, then you created a simple, photo-realistic element. There should be nothing to stop you from going farther.

Say you took a look at that picture of the tree and window and decided that the window was the wrong one for your wall. You wanted something a little cuter…a double-hung window, and maybe some blue curtains rather than that black empty space. You could take a picture of another window and manipulate it so it fits in the space. This might require hours, hunting something down similar to what you were looking for, so that you could take a picture of it. Or you could make a window from scratch.

It may sound really easy to make a window. It's just a rectangle, maybe with a few little crisscrossed do-dads (muntins, they're called). To some extent, it is simple. But to do it you will have to use just about every darned process you've gone through thus far in the book, and learn a few more little tricks.

Making the window will require a couple of Hidden Power Tools and a lot of small adjustments, from shaping the molded look of the muntins to dropping the muntin shadows on the wavy curtains. We'll look at those changes in detail here, using a lot of images to keep you in step. There are a lot of steps to this exercise—so allow yourself plenty of time to complete it.

Make the Window Creating the box shape for the window sash is just the beginning. We'll look at adding detail to the woodwork of the sash and muntins, using curves to alter gradients. When the first sash is done, it can be duplicated to save some work, then shaded to create depth.

Make the Curtain Curves can be employed again to create wavy curtain pleats, then employing a little transformation can make the way they fall seem unique. After the curtain is created and colored, it will be placed behind the window.

Make Shadows for the Window and Curtain Once the curtain is where it belongs, the image will look a little flat. Adding a shadow from the window falling on the curtain will give it some depth. The angle of the shadow will have to approximate the source in the destination image. The real kick is trying to weave that shadow in and out of the pleats. We'll do that using the Displacement filter.

Place and Fit the Window with the Wall With the double-hung window complete, it will have to be fit into place where the current window is. This will require more transformation, some feathering, and the incorporation of still more shadows.

Making the Window

1. Open a new RGB image at 10×10 pixels with a white background. The resolution really doesn't matter, so 72 ppi will work fine.

2. Press D to restore the default color for foreground and background, and then press X to switch black to the background.

3. Change the canvas size to 12×12 pixels (Image → Resize → Canvas Size). This will create a black frame around the image.

4. Resize the image to 400×400 pixels (Image → Resize → Image Size) using Bilinear resampling. This will increase the size of the image and add an evenly stepped gradient to the edge of the frame.

5. Open a Curves dialog by clicking Curves on the Hidden Power Tools, and shape the tone of the gradient area by adjusting the curve as shown in Figure 7.30. Choose Layer → Merge Down (Command+E/Ctrl+E).

6. Copy/Paste or Duplicate the background to a new layer and name it Frame.

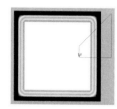

7. Turn off visibility for the background, and then clear the center of the image (click the center with the Magic Wand tool and press the Delete key).

8. Deselect, then make a selection of a segment on one of the sides of the frame using the Polygonal Lasso. Miter one of the ends to a 45-degree angle (hold the Shift key while making the angle).

9. Copy/Paste the segment to a new layer and name the new layer Miter.

10. Turn off the visibility for the Frame layer.

11. Using the Move tool, position the segment in the Miter layer so that the point of the shape falls exactly in the upper right corner.

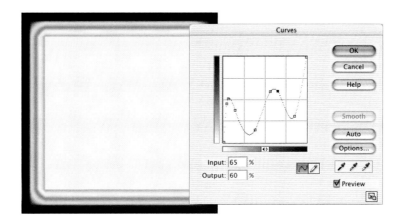

Figure 7.30

The frame is going to give you a rough look at the final bevel. We'll reshape this in the coming steps to sharpen up the corners.

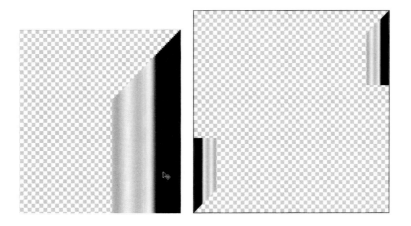

Figure 7.31

The identical segments should be 180° different and in opposite corners, tucked neatly so the point is right in the corner.

12. Duplicate the Miter layer. Rotate the duplicate layer (not the canvas) 180°, use the Move tool to position the new segment in the lower left corner, and Merge Down. The result should look like Figure 7.31.

13. Duplicate the Miter layer, Rotate the duplicate 90° either direction, and Merge Down.

14. Duplicate the Miter layer, Flip Horizontal, Merge Down. At this point, you see just the corners. Turn on the visibility for the Frame layer to see the whole frame.

15. Make a new layer, check Group With Previous, and fill the layer with yellow (255,255,0).

16. Make a new layer (not grouped), then make a selection of the black part of the frame (use the Magic Wand with Use All Layers and Contiguous checked). Expand the selection by 2 or 3 pixels, and fill the selection with yellow. Name the layer Sash Frame.

17. Duplicate the Sash Frame layer three times and call the layers Drop Shadow, Bevel 1, and Bevel 2, bottom to top.

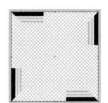

We'll need to add some effects to the frame to give it some shape. For more control you can create the effects manually, but we'll do it using Layer Styles. There are not a lot of controls for Layer Styles, so we'll use them a little creatively by using layer modes and opacity to mix the effects.

You'll need to change some effect settings. To open the Styles Settings dialog box, you have to apply the Layer Style and then double-click the layer styles indicator 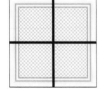 in the Layers palette. Steps 17 to 19 demonstrate some of what you might do in applying styles.

18. Add a Soft Edge drop shadow to the Drop Shadow layer using Layer Styles. Be sure the Global Angle box is checked and adjust the style to a 45° angle and 5 pixels. Adjust the strength by changing the Opacity of the layer. I used 30%.

19. Add a Simple Inner Bevel to the Bevel 1 layer. Reduce the Bevel Size to 2 or 3 pixels using the Style Settings dialog box (see Figure 7.32), and then change the layer Opacity to 30% on the Layers palette. Check the Use Global Light box on the Style Settings dialog box.

20. Add a Simple Inner Bevel to the Bevel 2 layer using Layer Styles. Reduce the Bevel Size to 2 or 3 pixels, uncheck the Use Global Light box, change the Angle to 135°, group the layer with Bevel 1, and change the mode to Darken. This will put the bevel edge all around the frame. At this point the result should look like Figure 7.33 in the image and in the Layers palette.

There are a lot of other things you can still do if you'd like, such as add effects to the frame to give it texture. The next series of steps moves on to creating the muntins.

21. Make a selection down the center of the image, create a new layer, and fill it with black. Copy the layer.

22. Rotate the layer 90°, then Paste and Merge Down. You'll end up with a cross over the image.

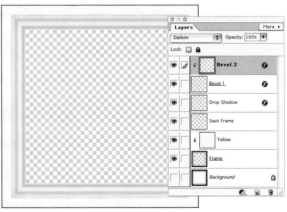

Figure 7.32

Limited controls in styles leave most manipulations to layer properties.

Figure 7.33

By unchecking the Use Global Light box, the user can choose a new angle. Using an angle that is 180° different completes a 360° effect.

23. Duplicate the layer, and then blur the new layer (I used 3 pixels).

24. Create a new layer below the duplicate and name it Muntins. Fill it with white and merge the layers.

25. Use Curves to shape the beveling on the Muntins layer. I used the curve shown in Figure 7.34. Merge the curve with the Muntins layer when you have it as you want it.

26. Load the original cross layer as a selection by Command/Ctrl clicking it in the Layers palette, then expand the selection by three to five pixels. Invert it to trim the Muntins layer. When you are done, delete the original cross layer.

27. Create a new Hue/Saturation adjustment layer and group it above the Muntins layer. Check the Colorize box and make adjustments to match the color of the bevel on the frame.

28. Place guides at 200 px horizontally and 200 px vertically using Make Guides on the Hidden Power Tools.

29. Choose the Rectangular Marquee and make a square selection from the exact center of the image (use the rulers to locate the exact center; hold down Shift+Option+Alt when dragging the cursor to make a square). Then select Transform and rotate 45° using the options bar. Figure 7.35 shows the selection and the rotation.

30. Hold down the Shift key and use the keyboard arrows to move the selection about 80 pixels to the left.

31. Activate the Muntins layer, then Copy and Paste three times. You'll use these segments to fix the bevel where the Muntins cross.

32. Activate the bottom copy layer, rotate it 90°, and center the segment in the image using the guides. This segment should align perfectly with the vertical muntin, and should overlay the intersection.

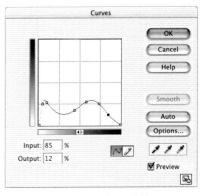

Figure 7.34

You can create far more subtle effects with a little patience and a few more curve points.

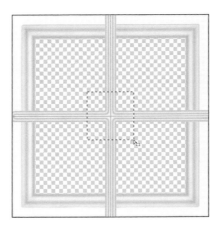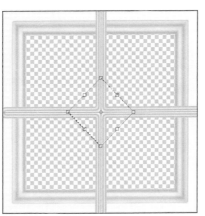

Figure 7.35

When making this change, the Hue/Saturation layer should be activated. It will keep you from making unexpected changes in any of the image layers.

33. Use the other two copies to adjust the bevel to the right and left of the vertical. The bevel may not be exact, but since reality isn't always exact, a little imperfection might look more realistic.

34. Remove the guides using the Clear Guides Hidden Power Tool.

35. Merge the Muntins Copy layers with the Hue/Saturation layer.

36. Select the Eraser Tool and use a hard, round brush to miter the muntins to the frame. See Figure 7.36.

37. Activate the Sash Frame layer and Merge Visible.

You now have a complete sash. You could run through those steps a second time to create a second sash, but duplicating should be good enough. You will paste the duplicate in a new layer above. The upper portion of a double-hung window runs on the outside, and such a detail is important to remember in imitating real objects.

38. Change the height of the canvas from 400 to 800, anchoring the bottom of the image, as shown in Figure 7.37.

39. Duplicate the Sash Frame layer and name the new layer Upper Sash. Change the name of the Sash Frame layer to Lower Sash.

40. Choose the Move tool, hold the Shift key, click the image, and slide the upper sash into place.

41. Duplicate the Upper Sash layer and group the duplicate layer above the Lower Sash.

42. Create a Soft Edge drop shadow for the Upper Sash Copy layer, using layer styles at 90° and 20 pixels. Change the Opacity to lighten the effect.

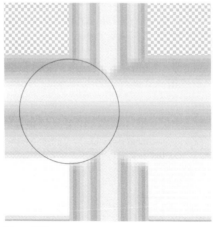

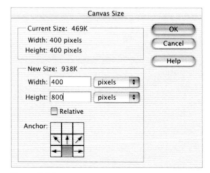

Figure 7.36

A round brush at the right size for the Eraser Tool can create a miter that follows the curve of the frame quickly and convincingly.

Figure 7.37

Anchor the canvas at the bottom.

43. Trim the image down to just the window (use the Marquee tool to select the whole window, and then choose Crop from the Image menu). Your result should look like Figure 7.38.

Although you might want to do more than this at this point, you can consider yourself finished with the window framing. If nothing else, this procedure may have given you a better appreciation for carpentry. You can still do a number of things to this image, but the techniques you have seen here should give you a pretty good idea of how to shape objects and details. Additional details are up to you.

Making the Curtain

1. Duplicate the background of the window to another image.

2. In the new image, create a new layer and name it Curtain. Fill the layer with a black to white gradient from right to left.

3. Shape the gradient using a curve that looks something like the curve in Figure 7.39.

4. Accept the changes made by the curve by selecting Layer → Merge Down, and then resize the layer to 50% width.

5. Move the resized layer to the left. If you have Snap on (View → Snap should be checked), the content should snap to (align) with the edge of the image.

6. Duplicate the resized layer, then Flip the new layer horizontally and move the content to the right until it snaps to the right edge of the image, and then Merge Down. The result of steps 5 and 6 should look like Figure 7.40.

Figure 7.38

The complete double-hung window as seen from the outside of the house.

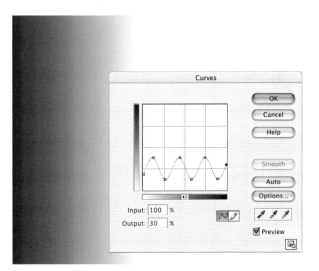

Figure 7.39

The shape of the curve will be similar to the shape that you could trace with a pencil on the floor where the pleats fall—an even, wavey line.

Figure 7.40

The basic cascade of the curtain takes shape.

7. Activate the Curtain layer and choose the Perspective Transform tool. Use it to alter the fall of the curtain somewhat, as in Figure 7.41.

8. Add a Hue/Saturation Adjustment layer. In the Hue/Saturation dialog box, check the Colorize box, and adjust the curtain to an interesting color. I chose blue, but you can use whatever you like (remember, it will be combined with a yellow window, a pink wall and a green window frame).

9. Turn off the visibility for the Hue/Saturation layer, Flatten the image, and save it somewhere as curtainmap.psd (don't worry what that means, we'll get back to the curtainmap.psd in the next section). Don't close the current file.

10. Step back in the History by clicking Hue/Saturation Layer 1 on the Undo History palette (Figure 7.42). This will bring you back to just before the save so you can keep working.

11. Merge the Hue/Saturation layer with the Curtain layer and then duplicate the Curtain layer back to the Window image.

12. Position the Curtain layer below the Sash layers if necessary. The result should look like the image and Layers palette in Figure 7.43.

Making Shadows for the Window and Curtain

1. Turn off the visibility of all layers but the Sash layers, and Merge Visible. Change the name of the merged layer to Window.

2. Load the Window layer as a selection by Command/Ctrl-clicking the layer in the Layers palette, and then invert the selection.

3. Create a new layer and name it Inner Shadow. Group this layer above the Window layer, set the Mode to Multiply, and fill the selection with black.

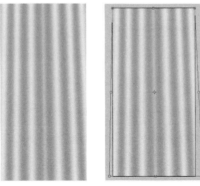

Figure 7.41

This is a simple distortion. Other filters and more complex behaviors (as we'll see with Displace in a moment) can add other touches of realism.

Figure 7.42

Stepping back in the History restores the layers that you flattened.

4. Deselect, blur the layer a little (5-pixel radius using Gaussian Blur), and offset it up and right (5 pixels up, 5 pixels right).

5. Change the opacity until it looks pleasing. The idea is to give a little depth to the inner portion of the window. You may want to turn on the visibility for the curtain layer while making this adjustment. Your Opacity will probably be between 30 and 50%.

6. Load the Window layer as a selection again.

7. Create a new layer between the Curtain and the Window and name it Curtain Shadow. Fill this layer with black.

8. Offset the Curtain Shadow layer 35 pixels down and left. Your result will look something like Figure 7.44.

9. Turn off the visibility for the Window layer and fill the area outside the window shadow frame with black. See Figure 7.45.

10. Choose the Displace filter (Filter → Distort → Displace). Set the Offset to 0% Horizontal and 30% Vertical; choose Stretch To Fit and Repeat Edge Pixels. (The vertical setting tells Elements you want the effect to be adjusted up and down only. Stretch To Fit resizes the map you use—because it was created from the same size file, you could choose Tile in this instance and get the same result. Repeat Edge Pixels will use the black border you have if the shadow stretches too far; setting to Wrap Around could send pixels that go off the bottom of the screen to the top.) When the Open dialog box appears, choose the `curtainmap.psd` file you created in the previous procedure. Your result should look like Figure 7.46.

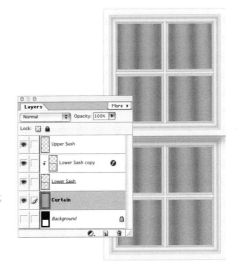

Figure 7.43

This looks a little flat, but we'll add some depth with shadows in the next section.

Figure 7.44

This is just quick positioning for the shadow; we'll soften and shape it in the coming steps.

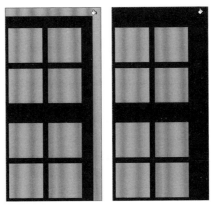

Figure 7.45

Touching up behind the scenes here makes sure that you can reshape the shadow dramatically without having to fill in later.

11. Blur the Curtain Shadow layer by about 3 pixels and set the Opacity to between 30% and 50%, and adjust the position of the layer (vertically) as desired.

12. Create one more new layer at the top of the stack. Choose a small (5 pixel), soft brush (0% Hardness), and draw a line across the bottom of the upper sash in black. Adjust the Opacity. This should appear to add some beveling or rounding to the bottom of the sash. When you are all done, the window looks like Figure 7.47.

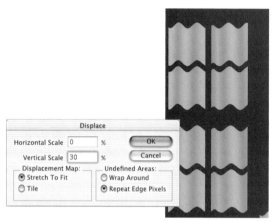

Figure 7.46

The Displace filter will use the tonality of the selected file as a map to offset the content of the layer.

Figure 7.47

With the shadow in place on the curtain, the window has some more realistic depth.

Figure 7.48

Lower the opacity temporarily to make the initial fit, and then transform to shape the space.

Placing and Fitting the Window On the Wall

At this point all that is left to do is flatten the window, copy it to the image with the wall and the tree, and shimmy it into place (see Figure 7.48). It will be the wrong size, and you will have to shape it, trim it, create a shadow for the window frame, and perhaps alter some color, sharpness, and texture.

Since you already know how to do all that other stuff, I will leave the details of fitting the window up to you. My result (complete with generated wall) can be seen in the color section and in Figure 7.49.

What I've probably been most successful in showing here is that you can spend the good part of a weekend on what is already an interesting image. But hopefully the techniques presented here for shaping and adjustment have given you tools you can use to make many creative changes.

Figure 7.49

A new wall, a new shadow, and a new window make a new, less distorted image.

Part V

Images in Print

Once you've spent a whole bunch of time making an image look just how you want it, selecting Print and sending the image to your home printer may not always achieve the results you want. But printing images to get the most out of them may require just a little bit more fancy dancing.

You may need to consider using some special tools like vectors to control the shape of your output. Understanding how your choices (and limitations) can affect printed images, and what options you have (in and out of the home) can drastically affect results.

Chapter 8

Vectors

For the most part, Photoshop Elements is a pixel-based image editor. However, vectors are another means of controlling image content. You may have seen vectors in action if you've used Shape tools. Vectors define image areas as mathematical shapes, independently of the pixels and resolution to which they are applied. They have a number of different (shall we say hidden?) uses. Vectors can be used to make shapes, sure, but they can also be used as clipping paths that redefine the actual boundaries of an image. They can be used to store hard-edged selections. They can be used as clipping layers to shape image components. They can be used to create artwork (such as logos) that can be scaled infinitely. We'll look at all these possibilities in this chapter.

Making Vectors

Creating Vector Art

Applying a Clipping Path

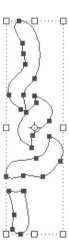

Making Vectors

The basic way to make vectors in Photoshop Elements is to select a Shape and apply it using the Shape tools. Shape tools can be accessed by clicking the shape tool in the toolbox (this will vary in look depending on which shape you used last). Once the tool is selected there are numerous options for selecting shapes on the Options bar (see Figure 8.1), including custom

⊞	Add to the current shape
⌐	Subtract from the current shape
▣	Intersect with the current shape
⊡	Exclude the intersection of the shapes

shapes ◔. You apply the shape by clicking and dragging the shape tool cursor ┼ on the image. Elements responds by creating a new layer for your shape. That's that. Slightly more complex applications allow you to combine shapes by choosing shape modes.

Using just these possibilities, you can make some interesting and complex shapes. When you have created what you want, you can combine the components into a single, complex vector shape. To do this, just click the Combine button on the Options bar.

> When you combine your shapes, you will no longer be able to adjust their positions individually. You may want to duplicate your Shape layer before combining components so you can go back and adjust positions.

Say for some reason you want to make a shape—like a fishing hook—that you can't find in the shape libraries. One thing you can't do with standard Photoshop Elements tools is to make freehand shapes. You could spend most of the day using the existing shapes that are supplied, adding, subtracting and combining, but it will probably prove a little tough. If only you could change a selection to a shape, you'd be able to make shapes based on any selection you can make. Of course, I won't leave you hanging for very long. Hidden Power Tools add some functionality that can do exactly that.

Figure 8.1

The Options bar offers possibilities for selecting different shapes and controlling how they combine.

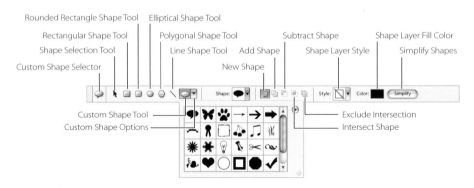

It works like this: make a selection of any shape or size using any tools you have, and then click Make Shape From Selection in the Hidden Power Tools. This will turn the selection you made into a Shape layer. Once the selection is a shape, you can copy and paste the shape to other Shape layers, and size and combine the shape with others. The difference is that the shape you make can be your own.

One of my favorite ways to create shapes is by making a rough sketch with a painting tool and then creating a refined selection using the Polygon Lasso. Figure 8.2 shows a series of images where a very rough sketch of a hook is turned into the final hook illustration.

Once a shape is created, you can store it in an image and use it in a similar way that you might one of the shapes from the shape libraries. The process is a little more manual in that you have to copy and paste the shape, but this gives you much greater flexibility with vectors than using shape libraries alone. For an example of how to store shapes in a library image, see `hiddenlibrary.psd` on the CD.

If you have shapes that you want to store, create a blank image. It can be any size, but 500x500 pixels at 72 ppi will cover most of what you will ever need the file for. Save the file with a name that reflects the shape types you expect to save there. To store a shape, choose the Shape Selection Tool and click the shape you want to store (it can be from any open image) to activate it. Copy the shape. Go to the library image, create a new shape layer and paste in the shape. Name the layer something meaningful so you will know what it is in the description. When you need to use it, you can just locate it and copy to the image you want to use it in.

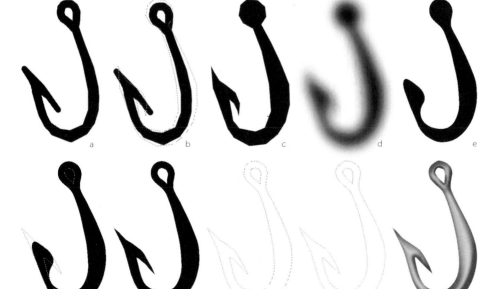

Figure 8.2

A very rough sketch (a) is used as a simple guide for creating a more refined selection (b) made with the Polygon Lasso tool. The polygon selection is refined and smoothed by filling with black (c) and using Gaussian Blur (d) and then Threshold (e). Additional selections (f) are used to make alterations (g), and the final selection (h) is converted to a shape (i). Once the shape is in a layer, layer effects can be applied (j).

Another way to store shapes in a library would be to save all the shapes as separate files in a directory (e.g., named MyShapes) and then use Photoshop Elements' Create Web Photo Gallery function (discussed in Chapter 10) to create a preview of all the shapes in the folder. This will be easy to update and will allow you to scan previews of many shapes quickly in your web browser or in the Elements file browser.

> Shapes can be another means of storing selections—as long as you want to store the selection without anti-aliasing, feathering, or other grayscale manipulations. Such hard selections can be converted to shapes using the Hidden Power Tools and the visibility can just be turned off. To create the selection again, just Command/Ctrl+click the layer where the shape is stored to convert it back to a selection.

Another handy tool provided with the Hidden Power Tools is one that will make a shape from any text you've created. This may not seem to be too much of an advantage when I tell you that you won't be able to edit the type anymore. However, it can save you from having to worry about transferring fonts with your Elements images to get them to show up correctly on other computers that don't have the same fonts installed. Changing the fonts to vectors locks the shape of the font and makes it a graphical part of the image, while still allowing you to scale the image and not have a fuzzy result. Vectors will produce sharper type results than rasterized type when used correctly. Converting to vectors also puts to rest some potentially annoying font errors. The application of both of these conversion tools should become clearer in the following example, where we'll look at using shapes to create scalable vector art.

Creating Scalable Vector Art

While pixel images are normally trapped by their content, using vectors can help you create art that can be scaled to any size while retaining sharpness. Although you can't turn all elements of a standard photograph into vectors, you can create artwork as vectors so it can be scaled to suit your needs.

Captain Hook's Bait & Tackle is a fictitious name of an imaginary tackle shop. But let's say the owner wants a logo and comes to you to make it. He wants to use the logo on his letterhead, business card, and website, and on promotional items such as caps and T-shirts. One other thing the logo will be used for is a little 10×16 foot billboard next to the Fishingtown exit from the I-1000 freeway. The only answer you get when you ask how big the logo will be on the billboard is: "Big." So it's safe to assume that the logo will run about 9 feet tall.

A 9-foot tall image in Photoshop Elements at 100 ppi would be almost 11,000 pixels square. That's about 333 MB. It isn't a file that you'll want to transfer over the Internet even if you have a fast connection. Interestingly, if you are careful, you can probably create the file you need and do it in less than 1000 pixels square.

1. Open a new, blank 1000-pixel square image. Set the resolution to 72 ppi.

2. Click the Shape tool on the toolbar, then on the options panel choose the Ellipse Shape tool. Create a new Shape layer by drawing a circle to fill the square image. If you start drawing at 500 px, 500 px (500, 500 is the image center—you can find this spot by opening the Info palette, setting the measure to pixels and then watching the coordinates change as you move your cursor in the image window) then hold down the Shift+Option/Alt keys, the shape will constrain to a circle and draw from the point where you first clicked. Leave 100 pixels or more at the edge of the image all the way around—you may need space to maneuver.

3. Click the Subtract From Shape Area button on the option bar, locate the center of the image again, and then draw a second circle from the center about half the diameter of the first. This will give you a torus—a donut shape—using the same layer. You should not have to adjust this, but if you do, use the Shape Selection tool to click on the shape component you want to move. When the component is highlighted, you can just move it freehand using the Shape Selection tool or change to the Move tool and use the keyboard arrows to position the shape.

4. Create a hook using the technique for sketching and converting a selection to a shape as shown in the exercise in the preceding section "Making Vectors." Alternatively, you can paste in the hook you made earlier, if you'd like.

5. Create the type to go in the donut. This will be the toughest part of the exercise, because Elements does not offer a lot of type controls. All you really have to work with are the Create Warped Text function ⬚, point size, and Transform. It might be easiest to set one word at a time.

   I used the Arc setting on warped text at 100% (and –100% for the bottom text) with about 30% Vertical Distortion. I added spaces before and after the text evenly to shorten the arc and control horizontal distortion caused by the arc. To add spaces at the beginning of the text, you have to add an extra junk character (I use a period) before the spaces or the spaces will just move the text to the right—but don't forget later that the junk character is there, or it will show up in your final image. Once the type is close using Arc and spaces, use transform to fit it in place if it still needs adjustment. See Figure 8.3 for a quick approximation of these steps.

6. Convert the type to Shape layers using Text To Shape on the Hidden Elements tools.

7. Create the worm. Roughly sketch in its shape as it would appear wrapped around the hook, using a soft brush (0% hardness) on a new layer. Merge with a new white layer (below the worm), and use Threshold to tighten up the edge. Load the hook as a selection by Command/Ctrl-clicking the Hook layer (Step 4). Use the selection to erase areas of the worm that would wrap around the hook using a hard brush (100%). See Figure 8.4.

8. Convert the worm to a Shape layer by selecting the worm (Command/Ctrl+clicking the Worm layer), and then clicking the Make Shape From Selection tool on the Hidden Power Tools palette.

9. With all the elements in place, apply layer effects and color to achieve desired depth and effects. You can apply manual effects as long as you want the edges blurred in the result. If you need a tight edge on any effect (such as a hard drop shadow), then you can duplicate a Shape layer and adjust the color or effects. I used strong bevels on the worm, hook, and donut, along with inner shadows and drop shadows.

At the end of this exercise, you should have something that looks much like Figure 8.5. Keep the layered version of the image, and store it safely. Change the size of the image as necessary, and use correctly targeted file types for output. These adjustments may require changing resolution up or down. Because your image is essentially composed of all vectors, you can retain sharpness in your image at any size. You can also temporarily shrink the image for moving it from one place to another, as long as the person receiving the file has Photoshop Elements (or Photoshop), they can expand the image again. The important edges remain defined by vectors. Any blends and/or effects you used for coloring and shading will simply blur more without really damaging the result so long as you resize using Bicubic or Bilinear interpolation (there will be some difference between these two interpolation types depending on the content of the image).

If you wanted to add other details (such as define the worm segments), you would have to do so using an additional Shape layer so that the effects would not blur during resizing. When you resize, you will probably need to adjust layer effects to re-create what you had.

Figure 8.3

Make the arc on the bottom of the text match the hole of the donut, and then rotate the type into place. You may have to make other tweaks to the position.

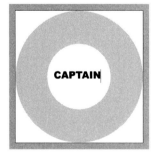

This is far easier than re-creating the entire image. And far better than just resizing an image by upsampling dramatically.

"Oh, what's the difference!" you say? The difference is a quality image rather than a soft one. Have a look at the comparison in Figure 8.6; these are depictions of the same image. Image A was created at 1000×1000 and flattened, then resized to fit our billboard. Image B was created at 1000×1000 and then resized to fit the billboard using the advantage of vectors: the image was resized with layers and vectors intact, and then flattened.

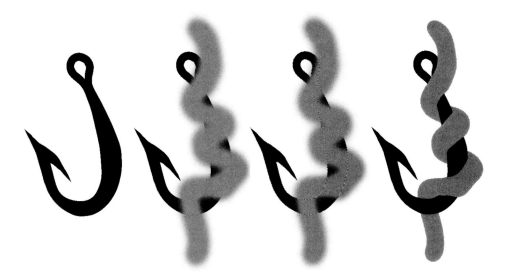

Figure 8.4

Sketch the worm roughly and remove what you don't need using the hook as a selection and guide.

Figure 8.5

Separate layers were used for each effect by duplicating the shape to which the effect was to be applied. See `captainhook.psd` on the CD and in the color section.

Figure 8.6

This small segment of the billboard was magnified. Note the softness, pixelation, and lack of definition in the upsampled image (a) compared to the vectors (b).

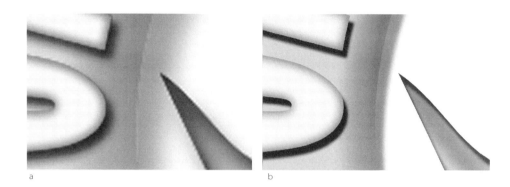

a

b

Applying a Clipping Path

Say you want to create an image that isn't constricted to a rectangular shape. The easiest way to do this is to just make a selection of what you want to keep, and then invert the selection and delete the area of the image that you don't want. As long as the background color is set to white, the image shape will appear to be a shape other than a rectangle when printed. White areas of images don't print with color (unless you are printing with a spot white ink, and you'd know if you were doing that).

This solution is okay if you don't have anything in the background below the image. If you are printing with another image or other content in the background of the digital file, using white won't work. One thing a white background will do in your rectangular image is white-wash anything behind it. If your image is like our Captain Hook logo, you might want to import just the shape of the logo rather than the whole image, if there is something in the background.

You could also just re-create the whole image in Photoshop Elements by bringing in all of the image components and reassembling them. Or you could export a compatible format so that you don't have to do the layout again (PDF or EPS). These options can work as long as there isn't any type that you didn't want to rasterize, because you'll have to rasterize the file when you open it to work in Elements. In a rasterized file, the mathematically defined lines and curves of vector art are converted into the pixels or bits of a bitmap image. Rasterizing the file will lose not only the ability to edit the type, but also the sharpness of the type, depending on the resolution you open the file with. What you really want to do to the image is clip it out of the background and paste it into the layout—as though you were making a collage.

Clipping paths do exactly what you want. These are vector shapes that redefine the boundary of your images. They allow you to "float" an image over a background in layout programs and clip the edge of the image with vector accuracy, just like you'd used scissors. This technique can work best with images that you create with shapes in mind (like the

Captain Hook's logo) and type. All you have to do is save a vector in the image as a path, and then assign that path as the image-clipping path.

Again, the problem with clipping paths in Photoshop Elements is that the program doesn't let you work with them. You can't save a path, and you can't assign a clipping path.

At least, you can't without the help of Hidden Power Tools.

To use a clipping path with our Captain Hook logo, follow these steps:

1. Prepare the image by creating the shape that you want to use for the clipping path. This involves combining the separate paths for the hook, the worm, and the donut. Use *one* of these two ways to do this:

   - Make a combined selection by holding down Command+Shift/Ctrl+Shift while clicking each Shape layer in turn on the Layers palette (Figure 8.7). This will combine the selections of each shape as you go.

   - Use the Shape Selection tool to highlight the shapes, copy them all to a single Shape layer, change the combine modes of each component to Add, and then click Combine on the options bar (Figure 8.8).

   To combine the shapes, you'll need to duplicate one of the Shape layers, choose the Shape Selection tool ![icon] (part of the shape tool set), and then click the components you want to copy. When the shapes are highlighted (you can click and drag a box to highlight the parts of the worm), you can copy, paste, and then set the component to Add by clicking that option on the options bar.

2. Assign the clipping path by choosing Make Clipping Path from the Hidden Power Tools.

At this point you'll be ready to go. Figure 8.9 shows what your Captain Hook billboard might look like.

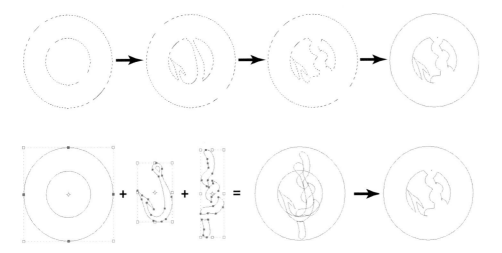

Figure 8.7

You can multiple-select your Shape layers…

Figure 8.8

…or you can copy them all to a single Shape layer and Combine.

One thing you may have noticed is that this will drop your drop shadow in the printed result as the shadow lies outside the boundary of the clipping path; even though you can still see it in the image, it won't show up in the result. If you want the shadow, you can create it using a little trick which will also allow you to place the shadow manually in the layout.

1. Copy the clipping path to a new grayscale image that is the same size and resolution as the final print file.

2. Make it a fill layer—filled with 75% black. (You may need to vary this to get the results you desire by increasing or decreasing the % black. The greater the percentage, the darker the shadow result.)

3. Change the image to a bitmap by selecting Bitmap from the Color Mode menu. When prompted, change the resolution to the output/printer dpi. Use the maximum capability of the printer.

4. Save the file as a .bmp file using Save As.

This file can be placed in your layout program below the clipped image (how you do this depends on the layout program you use). You will be able to manually move it separately from the clipped image. It may not look very pretty in the layout preview, but the result should look just fine.

The success of printing images that have clipping paths depends on two other things: you've got to save the file in a format that will respect the clipping path, and you've got to print in PostScript. The leap here is that most home printers are not PostScript. We'll take a look at a solution for testing postscript output without a postscript printer in Chapter 9.

Chapter 9

Options for Printing

You shouldn't just buy a printer and a ream of paper and assume you have every weapon you will ever need for your printing arsenal. First of all you have to know what to expect from your printer's capabilities and the type of paper you buy. Knowing about the process can help you make better decisions that lead to better results. While there are ways to get better results at home, at times you might need to print an image with a different process to get the best output. There is a reason why some printers cost thousands of dollars while standard home inkjets are much less expensive. Some of your best options for printing are just not practical for home use, but that doesn't mean you can't use them. In this chapter, we'll look at getting better color results in print.

Printers and Printer Resolution

Making Prints at Home

Printing to the Edge

Other Printing Options

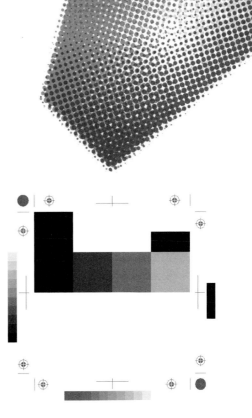

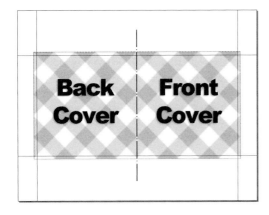

Printers and Printer Resolution

If you try hard, you can find more than two basic options for buying a printer for your home. Generally you are limited to a photo-quality inkjet printer—which is inexpensive, and not a bad choice at all—or a laser printer. The latter is often quite a bit more expensive and doesn't necessarily deliver superior results. The main advantage of a laser printer is genuine post-script printing, which you may or may not have a use for, depending on what you use printing for. Different printers handle the same image information in somewhat different ways. Understanding how each works can give clues as to how to prepare an image for output.

Both printers put tiny dots (of ink or toner) on paper that represent the absolute resolution of the printer. These dots have fixed measurements for each printer. The shape and intensity of the dots cannot be altered: they are either 100% on or off. The dots per inch (dpi) rating of a printer represents the number of these tiny dots that the printer can make in one linear inch on a page. It is essentially measured the same way whether the printer is a laser or an inkjet. The dpi of a printer can be considered its maximum resolution—the finest building block of the printer's ability to represent an image. The maximum actual resolution of a printer is the *lower* of any two numbers reported by the manufacturer. A 1200×600 dpi rating is really 600 dpi with a half-step for the rows (the half-step allows the dots to overprint). The dpi rating for a printer is always the same.

The dot pattern that laser and inkjet printers use accounts for the difference in the result. The dots used on a laser printer form larger dots in halftone screens; dots on an inkjet form an array or tonal density (as used in stochastic printing). By definition, halftone screening uses dot shapes (diamonds, circles, etc) of different sizes in halftone rows to create tone and color in halftone screens (the arrangement of halftone dots and angles); stochastic printing uses randomized printer dots (not shaped dots in halftone rows) to create arrays of tone and color. A stochastic printer can print with a lower resolution (dpi) than a laser printer and appear to create finer results because of the randomized behavior of the dots.

If you can understand halftone screening, it isn't a big leap to understand stochastic printing. We'll look at halftones first, in a little more detail. If you know some printing theory, it can help you understand how your images get put together in print and you'll better understand how to get the best results. Different image content (vectors and pixels) control printer information in different ways. Controlling that starts with understanding print theory.

Halftone Printing

Halftones are comprised of two different types of printer resolution simultaneously: *printer dots* (also known as printer elements and dpi) and *halftone dots* (known as screening frequency and lpi, or lines-per-inch). Printer dots are the smallest unit of ink the printer can print (the "dot" in "dots per inch"). Halftone dots are the screening dot (the size of the halftone dot or the "line" in "lines per inch"). The halftone dot is made up of printer dot groupings that create the halftone dot shape. See Figure 9.1.

Halftone dots are made up of smaller printer dots, with a set number of printer dots assigned to each halftone dot based on the halftone dot size. The printer dots are turned on or off in patterns on a postscript printer to represent the shape of the halftone dots. Because this is the case, halftone dots, unlike printer dots, vary in size. The greater the tone, the larger the halftone dot, and the more printer dots are turned on inside the dot grid. For example, if a halftone dot has 256 printer dots in it, a 50% gray will use half the printer dots (128) in the halftone grid.

During the process of describing the image to the printer, the shape, color, and tone of the image is converted into rows of halftone dots with the lpi and screening angles selected in the printing options (if nothing is selected, the printer will have a default). These dots are arranged in screens similar to the appearance of a window screen, one screen for each ink. The goal of applying the screening is to hopefully minimize the visibility of the individual dots and maximize ink coverage on the page so that images appear as continuous tones to the naked eye—whether you are using one ink (black) or more. The printer is then told which printer dots to print and which to keep off in order to create the halftone pattern and represent the image.

You can specify the size of the dot by the linescreen that you choose in the printer settings when going to print. The linescreen setting tells the printer how many halftone dots will be put down in an inch. The size and orientation of the halftone dots can be controlled by the halftone screen size and screening angle that you choose. The screening angle tells the printer how to offset the rows of halftone dots so they don't all land on one another, which results in a less obvious pattern. We looked at these concepts briefly when discussing duotone printing in Chapter 5. Knowing what the trade-offs are and how to optimize the use of the printer resolution can help you get the best result from printing.

Printers have a set maximum resolution (printer dots), so the more printer dots that are used to print a halftone dot, the lower the lpi. The lower the lpi, the greater the number of printer dots that are in a halftone dot, and the more tones the halftone dot can represent. A greater number of printer dots in a halftone dot leads to a greater number of possible variations. The opposite is also true: if you use fewer printer dots in a halftone dot, it will have fewer potential variations. On the other hand, if more printer dots are used to make the halftone dot, the halftone dot must get larger because the printer dots are a fixed size. As you lower lpi, the halftone dots get larger. The larger the dot, the easier it is to see and the more likely the halftone dots are to cause dot patterning (*moiré* patterns). The trick of halftone printing is to keep halftone dots large enough so that the printer can represent image tone (by being comprised of enough printer dots), but not so large that the halftone dots are easy to see.

Figure 9.1

This shows a complete printer dot grid for a 16×16 halftone dot. The black printer dots are on; the gray printer dots are off. The halftone dot uses 60% of the printer dots in the grid, so it represents a 60% tone.

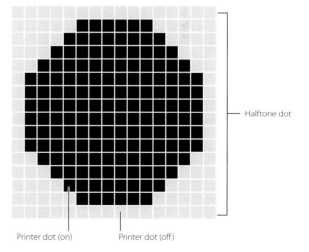

Halftone dot

Printer dot (on)   Printer dot (off)

Keeping the halftone dot as small as possible while having enough printer dots to represent full image tone requires maintaining a delicate balance. Dot size should be as small as possible while representing the maximal number of tones. In other words, you want to increase the lpi as much as possible to make the halftone dots small, yet you want to keep the dots large enough so they can represent all of the tone stored in the image.

However, just like with other types of resolution, if you have more information in the halftone dots than you can really use, you just waste it. There is no need to make a halftone dot with more information than you can extract from the image source. So, there are better and worse ways to use up the printer resolution by selecting the right lpi. You have to balance the halftone screen frequency and size of the dot to get the best result.

Screening can be optimized for printing images that you have created depending on the maximum resolution of the printer you are using. Say you have a printer that has a resolution of 600 dpi. This means it can print a maximum of 600 printer dots of information in a linear inch. At the same time, Photoshop Elements is an 8-bit program, meaning it can store 256 different tones for any pixel color. To be maximally efficient, any halftone dot would have to be able to represent 256 possible variations to present the information correctly (or at least potentially).

A 16×16 element halftone dot can actually have 256 variations (16 × 16 = 256), and can therefore represent 256 shades of tone. A 20×20 element halftone dot could represent 400 shades of gray—but it would be 25% larger—and the source image would still provide only 256 potential variations. You would be printing halftone dots that can potentially represent a lot more information (156%) than you have in your image. A 10×10 element halftone dot will be smaller and less easy to discern, but it can have only 100 variations (10 × 10 = 100), and will be less likely to be able to show the full potential of your image. The 256 variations in a 16×16 dot will allow you to fully represent all of the 256 levels of tone possible with 8-bit color. The following table shows the size of various halftone dots and the number of shades of gray they can represent.

So, if the printer has a 600 dpi resolution and you want to run a halftone dot with 256 potential tones, then your lpi will have to be set to 38 (600 / 16 = 37.5). This is actually a low linescreen frequency and a rather large halftone dot. If you step down to a lesser size halftone dot with fewer elements—say a 10×10—you can have smaller halftone dots and a higher lpi frequency, and the printed result might actually end up looking better. A 10×10 halftone dot on a 600 dpi printer would allow you to run a 60 lpi screen (600 / 10 = 60).

ELEMENTS IN HALFTONE	SHADES OF GRAY
20×20	400
16×16	256
10×10	100
7×7	49
5×5	25
3×3	9

Regrettably, a halftone dot that can represent all 256 possibilities is not always the best bet with a lower-resolution printer. Although a smaller number of elements per halftone dot means that fewer potential colors/tones can be accurately represented by a single halftone dot, this also means that there will be a less smooth transition between tones. When you step down from a 16×16 element halftone dot to a 10×10, you go from 256 levels of tone representation down to 100. If you decrease the number of elements more, the potential number of tones continues to lower. Each time you lower the number of tones you can create, you increase the potential for color and tonal banding. You have to decide which tradeoff gives you the most pleasant result.

If you have followed the discussion up to this point, you may now understand why you get noticeably better results printing to an image setter (with 2540+ dpi) than you do with even good home laser printers. With at least 2540 printer dots at your disposal, you can use line-screen values of up to 150 (158, really) and still get 256 levels of gray. Compare this result to using 38 lpi to get 256 levels of gray on a 600 dpi printer, as discussed above. Running a higher lpi will limit the gray levels in output. The only way to get the full gray-level depiction and shrink the screening dots is to have higher resolution in the printer (higher printer dpi). This is why printer dpi makes a difference in the image result. Printers with greater dpi (resolution) will be able to show a greater number of tones using the same size halftone dot.

With the halftone rows defined by the linescreen, all that is left to do is convert the image to dots that fit neatly in rows. If everything is set up correctly, colors are separated into the CMYK components and converted to halftone dots. If there is only one color (usually black), screening is fairly simple. The screen is converted to rows of dots at a specific angle. Often this angle is 45° for black in an attempt to better fool the eye into seeing tone rather than rows of dots (but it can be another angle of your choice).

Color generation is a bit more complicated because the angles of screening for each color are offset, so the result doesn't cause the inks to run in parallel. Default settings might be something like C 108°, M 162°, Y 90°, and K 45°. The colors in an area of the image are broken down into their CMYK components and then individually rendered into dot screens at the different angle settings. These screens are then placed over one another in print to create color and tone.

> If you are printing with multiple passes, you may have to adjust screening manually.

A most interesting thing about halftone dots and printer dots is that they can be controlled by the presence of vectors. Clipping paths and clipping layers, as described in Chapter 8, "Images in Print," can be used to control and reshape halftone dots. Vectors can essentially cut through halftone dot shapes and define how printer dots are assigned. Vector shapes and type can retain sharp edges in halftone screening, but might lose sharpness if portrayed as pixels alone.

Figure 9.2

The non-vector halftone edge is softer and far less defined than the vector-edged shape though both may look almost identical as digital images.

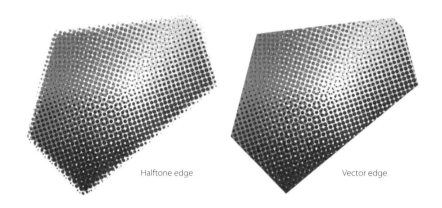

Halftone edge   Vector edge

Figure 9.2 shows an example of a shape done with four colors (CMYK) and how that would print using straight halftones or using vectors for the edge.

Stochastic Printing

If you can fathom all that is going on in printing a halftone, stochastic (inkjet) printing is comparably simple. Instead of being trapped into halftone dot shapes, stochastic printing randomizes the use of printer dots so the printing seems smoother and there is little possibility of creating moiré patterning and other potential halftone-dot related trouble. This is also why lower resolution stochastic printing can seem finer than much higher resolution halftone printing.

Figure 9.3 shows a rough approximation of how halftone and stochastic printing of the same area may compare.

While you won't have to deal with lpi settings and the trouble that halftone dots can bring, you forgo some of the refined edge sharpness you can get with postscript vector printing. Your images printed with an inkjet printer will look decidedly more like a photograph than anything you print on a laser printer. Both printing types have their advantages, and neither are truly continuous tone.

Making Prints at Home

After you've made corrections to an image, you might look at it on the screen and it will look just fine. But when you go to print it, the color might not seem as vivid as you remember from the screen. This kind of outcome really isn't unusual, as the process of printing can sap some of the strength from the color. It is a result of the necessary conversion from RGB to CMYK.

Image files created by a camera are recorded in RGB color. This is a fine way to record visible color that will be projected as light—that is, just about any color that can readily be reproduced on your camera LCD, your TV, your computer monitor, in digital projection (using a digital projector), and in creating digital film (film recording). All of these RGB processes play together fairly nicely.

Most printers you will use, on the other hand, use a straight CMYK process. By "straight" I mean plain ol' cyan, magenta, yellow and black, with no additional inks. CMYK and RGB are not very friendly to each other—CMYK can often make RGB look bad…or much worse than it has to look. Specifically, vivid red, green, and blue areas of an image can suffer in the conversion to CMYK because there are areas of RGB color that the CMYK process just can't imitate. Getting better results starts with that awareness. Adjusting an image specifically for CMYK results—working with an image that you've converted to CMYK or previewing the image as CMYK—can make a difference. We'll look at both of these options here.

 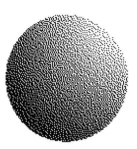

Figure 9.3

A halftone representation of an area (left) can be compared with finer printer elements in stochastic printing (right) when printers are capable of the same resolution.

What goes wrong between your image on screen and the result in print can be hard to track down. Problems can start with your monitor not being calibrated and can range to it being improperly profiled, to having problems with color management in the image, to needing adjustment to your separations, to having trouble with your printer, and even printing on the wrong thing. We've covered all of these areas but the last one. Before we get deeper into printing, we need to determine who is controlling your output.

Who Controls Your Output?

You can make a conversion to CMYK using techniques from this book, but you can't always be sure that your separation setup is going to be used for the printing—unless you test it. The reason for this is that many inkjet printers (printer drivers) like to make their own separations. Instead of just taking what you put together as a CMYK image, they might convert the information from CMYK and then back to CMYK again. It's a problem similar to what can happen behind the scenes with renegade image profiles.

> Recall that, in Chapter 1, "Essentials of Images and Image Editing," I dismissed profiles. I don't use them, I don't need them, and neither does anyone else. They can't possibly tell a printing device what I can't, and they can't see and correct to what I want as the result. Only I can do that.

You might guess that this double conversion—CMYK to RGB (or Lab) and back to CMYK—is not really desirable if you've already gone out of your way to make a CMYK separation. Printers and drivers don't do this to be naughty; they are actually trying to help you get the best results. The printer will not realize that you are a sophisticated user and have created your own separation.

The first thing you want to do is find out what your printer is doing so you'll know better how to handle your images—at least with that printer. You'll need to run a quick test to see how your printer is handling color. All you have to do is run a rich black (a black that combines black ink with cyan, magenta, and/or yellow ink rather than just using black) to the printer. Once you evaluate the results, you'll have to look at your possible options. Unfortunately, you can't print a CMYK image directly from Photoshop Elements. So that everyone can perform this test, I've provided another route using Adobe Acrobat Reader (which is available on the CD, if you don't already have it installed).

Running the Test

1. Open `CMYK.pdf` from the CD using Acrobat Reader.

    This test will not work if you open the image using Elements, because Elements will have to convert the file to RGB. You need to print the image as CMYK.

2. Print using your usual printer and the print settings you usually use.

3. Evaluate the results in a well-lit room.

To evaluate the output, you have to know what you are looking for and what this test print is supposed to be testing. The file is set up with a rich black bar (more than just black ink) across the top. The "black" bar should actually be five different colors—if your printer and driver are printing it as intended. The first three boxes are a rich black with cyan, a rich black with magenta, and a rich black with yellow, respectively. The top half of the last box will be black ink only, and the bottom half a rich black using 100% of all four inks. The next three bars in the image will be cyan, magenta, and yellow at 100%, 75%, 50%, and 25%. The separation of how that looks in color plates when separated right from the file I provided is shown in Figure 9.4.

Examining the output in the light should make apparent any differences between what you should have gotten and what you did get. If the black looks like a solid bar rather than several different blacks, your printer (or the driver) is taking liberty with your CMYK separation. Therefore, you may not be able to use the printer as a reliable proofing device to see what you will get when using another printing device or service—unless you can find a solution.

Figure 9.4

The color in your print should use cyan (a), magenta (b), yellow (c), and black (d) in exactly the patterns shown, or your printer or driver are getting in the way of your results.

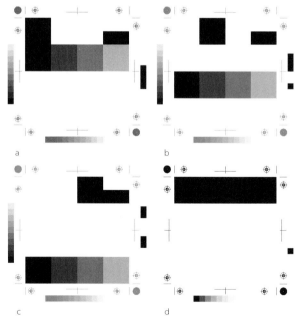

If you want to get the CMYK out that you created, you will want to get the test image to print using the original color in the image. It isn't so much that you want to be a control freak and never have image information change, you just don't want it to change without you knowing about it so that you can make proper adjustments and not waste your time.

There is more than one solution to the problem, but you have to be able to live with the result. Your solution could be as extreme as replacing your printer, but other options don't require making a decisive change in your current home setup. Your options include:

- Changing the output settings for printing
- Replacing your driver or using another method to get the right output
- Use a printing service when pre-separated output is critical
- Work in RGB and accept whatever the printer and driver give you in the conversion to CMYK
- Use a combination of the previous options

Changing Your Output Settings for Printing

Several settings that control how the printer will handle color can be hidden somewhere on the various tabs of your printer driver (and sometimes in the program you are using to do the output). These settings include the more conspicuous "Convert CMYK before printing" type to the type that vaguely mention something about color management (or profiles). There may be other options more cleverly disguised. There also may be no options at all. Unfortunately, there are few standards.

If you look through all of your printer dialog box options when you go to print and there are really no color options, then you will have to look at another potential solution. Don't give up until you actually get out the printer manual or online documentation of the driver interface and see what settings the driver has and what the settings affect. The documentation can point you in the direction of any settings that you might need to experiment with when the settings are not obvious.

There is no profile in the `CMYK.pdf`, and the result of your printing should be that the color is not manipulated by the color settings of your printer. However, some printers/drivers may either insist that you have a profile or assume a generic profile, and this can result in a conversion. Again, that will show up as a change in the black bar, and/or as influence to the pure CMYK color bars. Alternatively, you may choose to use a workaround and/or replace your driver.

Replacing Your Driver

Most printer companies will have a website for their products where you can download upgrades to system software and sometimes hardware as well (firmware). Getting new printer software from the website for your specific printer model can help give you functionality that was added after the printer was manufactured—or that enough people complained about to warrant an enhancement. When visiting such a website, don't pass up the option to complain, if necessary.

There may be third-party drivers that can do what you need. These will usually come at an additional expense. Sometimes you can use other drivers, but this can require a lot of trial and error, and is probably impractical for the most part.

One exception where you can find a free third-party driver is on the Adobe website. Adobe makes drivers that are pretty much universal in helping create PDF files, and these can be downloaded for free. There is also functionality on the site that will help you convert files to PDF. Creating PDFs to print from is often a good solution for varied applications (you'll note that I used it for the test file). Using PDFs, you can often get the equivalent of postscript output from a non-postscript printer (for example, clipping paths won't be ignored). All you do is use the driver option to Print to File. This will make a .prn (printer) or .ps (postscript) file, depending on your settings and the driver used. This file can then be turned into a PDF and you can use that to print. PDF files are also often small (depending on compression settings) and service friendly; they can be lossless, and they can embed fonts.

While it is not specifically changing your printer driver, exploring other options for programs to print from can be another solution. For example, layout programs often have capabilities that can help you get the output you want. For example, if you have Quark, PageMaker, or InDesign, printing from these programs can sometimes add options for output, or you can convert files to other formats such as EPS (encapsulated postscript).

Another clever workaround is to print your CMYK process images using multiple passes on the printer by printing one color at a time—as was outlined for making duotone prints in Chapter 5, "Color-Specific Correction Tools." While this may improve the result, it will probably not work perfectly if your driver is ignoring your separations. In other words, this only masks the problem rather than fixing it. If you can't control the settings, you still are not really controlling the result.

Using a Printing Service for Output

There are two ways to look at a printing service: 1) an expensive place that can be intimidating, inconvenient, and smells like chemicals; or 2) a resource for equipment you don't want or can't afford to keep at home. Services allow you to use sophisticated printers that you would probably never buy. Different services may have different equipment, and getting to know what is available—both locally in your area and through the internet—may give you some good options for other means of output. Options can include color laser, LED (light emitting diode), film recorders, offset printing, print-on-demand, and other processes (both high- and low-tech). For the most part, you'll know if you need a special service. Several of these options will be looked at in more detail later, in the section "Other Printing Options."

Working in RGB

You may notice that the CMYK test gives you different results than you should get if the printer is using the information you send, but another question you need to answer is whether the results are good enough. In many cases they might be, and if they are, it saves the problem of having to make and correct CMYK separations. There is nothing wrong with sending an RGB image to your printer to be separated to CMYK *if* the results are satisfactory. At other critical times (where you are making a specific separation, like I did to create the CMYK test), you may need to explore more thoroughly how you can affect CMYK output.

Using a Combination of Solutions

What the last few sections were obviously leading to is that not every image will warrant or require the same process to get the result you need. I might use all of the discussed solutions in a single day, depending on what I need to accomplish. Being aware of the options is half the battle; the other half is realizing that using the right one at the right time saves work, time, frustration, and possibly money as well. Be sensible about your choices; be honest in your image evaluations; and be ready to change the processes you use most of the time in order to get the right result in the end. The right result will vary, sometimes from image to image.

Selecting Printer Paper

When eating soup, most sophisticated soup eaters use soupspoons. In a pinch, a teaspoon or table spoon could do; if you are the chef, a ladle may be used for tasting. However, there is usually a reason why items we use every day have taken on slightly different shapes to perform their jobs.

Most people would tend not to run tissue paper through their printer in hopes of getting a good print. The same goes for toilet paper, paper towels, wax paper, litmus paper, tracing paper, shelving paper, aluminum foil, bubble wrap, plastic wrap, etc. What many people never consider is that different papers that look essentially the same have different qualities—and some of these qualities aren't a lot different than some of the sillier suggestions that you would quickly dismiss. Plain ol' typing paper may be too absorbent, acting more like a paper towel in absorbing the ink. It might have a texture or coating (such as an easy-to-erase surface) that impedes ink absorption. It might not be white. It isn't necessarily made for accepting ink from a color inkjet printer. Different inks in different printers can be…different. Because they can be different, paper that works well in one printer (such as a printer with an ink that dries quickly) may work less well on a different printer (such as a printer with ink that is slower to set).

> While differences in paper can create different results in using a laser printer, it is usually much less of an issue because absorption is not part of the equation.

Manufacturers did not put expensive photo-quality paper on the market just because they thought they could sucker in unsophisticated buyers to pay ten to twenty times more for paper they really didn't need. Photo-quality paper was made specifically to do the job of making the best quality images from your inkjet printer. It is worth the extra money to use it when printing your best quality, final images.

You don't have to use special photo-quality paper for every print, but you may need to change printer settings to adjust for the paper type. When using plain paper, it should be white. If not, the whites and lighter colors in your image will be influenced by the paper color (usually decreasing the dynamic range of the image). You will find that some brands of paper (even brands of the fancier photo-quality paper) will work better with your printer. Sometimes this will have little or nothing to do with price.

Testing Papers

If you are going to use a plain paper to proof images before printing on better photo-quality papers, or if you will be using different quality papers, be sure to "waste" a few sheets testing your output. Read the manufacturer's suggestions for the settings to choose for photo-quality and plain paper, and make prints on each using the same image. Make a few prints with somewhat different settings; for example, if there are settings for different grades of photo-quality paper, you might try more than one (especially if the paper you are using is not noted specifically by the manufacturer). Try several prints with the plain paper as well. As you make the prints, note the settings used for each by writing those settings directly on each print you make.

Compare the results of the photo-quality prints to the image on screen first. Choose the result that most closely resembles what you see on screen. (It may not be the best print!) Next, compare the print that looks the most like what is on screen with the prints on plain paper side-by-side. Make note of the settings that produced the best matches, and use those settings when you print to those paper types. Retest whenever you switch papers. If you like the quality of the prints you get with a certain brand of paper, you should tend to stick with it unless there is a good reason to change—and "because another brand costs slightly less on sale" is not a good reason. Using the same paper simplifies your process and assures you optimal results without having to retest.

Testing your paper and noting the settings that produce the best results can assure you that what you see on screen will most closely resemble what you will finally get in print. Once you make this test, it should be unnecessary to make plain-paper proofs for every image you print. With this test made, you have essentially completed the easier process of color management that I suggested at the beginning of the book. If you do not change the monitor settings or the paper you use, you can be assured every time of getting similar matching to what you see on screen.

CMYK Previews

It is not possible to preview CMYK printing in Photoshop Elements, so they say, because there is no CMYK to work with in the first place. If one can't create CMYK, there is, of course, no way to preview it—and no reason to. There is also no Preview option. Why should that stop you?

It is exactly because there is no CMYK that it is pretty easy to preview CMYK. That may sound contradictory. But what a preview has to do is take your CMYK information and convert it to RGB again. Because Elements won't open a CMYK image as CMYK, the preview is really automated (read: forced). As fate would have it, it is exactly the conversion from CMYK to RGB that will show you what you should be getting in print and will let you know—without printing—approximately what results you will see when you do print.

As I demonstrated in Chapter 5, you can build a CMYK image by making a custom separation and saving to an EPS template. To complete the process of previewing your CMYK images on screen, all you have to do is split out the CMYK channels from your custom separation and merge them. You can do this manually by copying each channel out of the file, creating the EPS, and then going back to open that file so it converts to RGB. Hidden Power Tools provides an easier way without having to save the image first. All that is required is that you can complete a CMYK separation and get a reasonable preview using output to plain and/or photo-quality paper. If you have accomplished this, you can preview your result before even sending the image to print by proofing on screen. This can save paper, ink, and cost.

The preview that you will create is just a preview file and nothing more. You do not ever want to save the preview. Just look at it, see if there is something you want to adjust, and then throw it out. You can experiment with creating a curve set that makes the preview look accurate, and you can then apply that to any image you are previewing. This will take some trial and error (or testing), but once you have achieved an accurate preview adjustment, you can use it over and over to preview the result of your separations.

1. Create a CMYK separation using Hidden Power Tools functionality. Clicking CMYK Process will lead you through the separation.

2. Click Make CMYK Split on the Hidden Power Tools menu. This will separate the C, M, Y, and K channels from the separation you created in step 1, leaving the original channels in the layers of the first image.

3. Click Preview CMYK on the Hidden Power Tools menu. This will attempt to combine the separated channels created by the split. Because Elements is an RGB program, it will stop you from viewing the image as CMYK, and convert to RGB. This CMYK to RGB conversion is exactly what you need to preview the CMYK result on screen.

Once you have completed this simple process, the image on screen should represent the CMYK you will probably get by printing the original CMYK separation (if your printer respects your separation). I say "probably" because there can be some variation specific to the printer, the inks, and the paper, as well as your setup for color management. The solution to getting a more accurate preview is to make some adjustments to the preview image on screen. To make adjustments to the preview, do the following:

1. Create a CMYK EPS separation using the Hidden Power Tool for making a CMYK separation and the CMYK template to create and save your EPS.

2. Open and print the EPS file using a layout program or create a PDF: any process that you have tested (using `CMYK.pdf`) that respects the separation you make is fine.

3. Open the CMYK EPS file in Photoshop Elements, and allow the conversion to RGB.

4. Compare the print to the screen and make changes to the preview image on screen using Adjustment layers (such as Curves, Levels, etc.).

5. Create a preview file to use with other images by saving the adjustments you've made as a sample.

To correct the preview of other images, all you have to do is drag the correction layers from the sample to the new preview. You can make your adjustments using separations to fine-tune the preview. (RGBL, looked at in Chapter 2, "Separating Color Into Tone" may be a good choice.)

Custom Picture Packages

Picture Packages are an easy way to fit multiple images (and more than one image) onto a printed sheet when you go to print images. Photoshop Elements provides a bunch of presets, and you might find one that meets your needs.

I don't know about you, but usually my sheets of paper are 8.5×11, and there are no presets for that size. A good thing to know is that you aren't stuck with the presets Adobe assigned. In fact, there are some shorthand instructions in the Layouts directory in the Presets folder that actually tell you what to do to make your own packages. But lets take a look at how to do that here, because the instructions don't make the idea or the process incredibly clear.

Say you want to print seven images on an 8.5×11 sheet—three images that are 4×5 and four smaller wallet shots at 2×2.5. See the layout shown in Figure 9.5.

What Elements needs is a simple text file defining the layout you want. The first row of text tells the program what measurements and paper size you are using. The second is the name that the picture package will have in the drop-down list on the Picture Package dialog box. All the remaining rows define where pictures fall on the sheet. I've provided a copy of this layout on the CD (`sevenshots.txt`), but let me walk you through how to build it so you can create various layouts of your own.

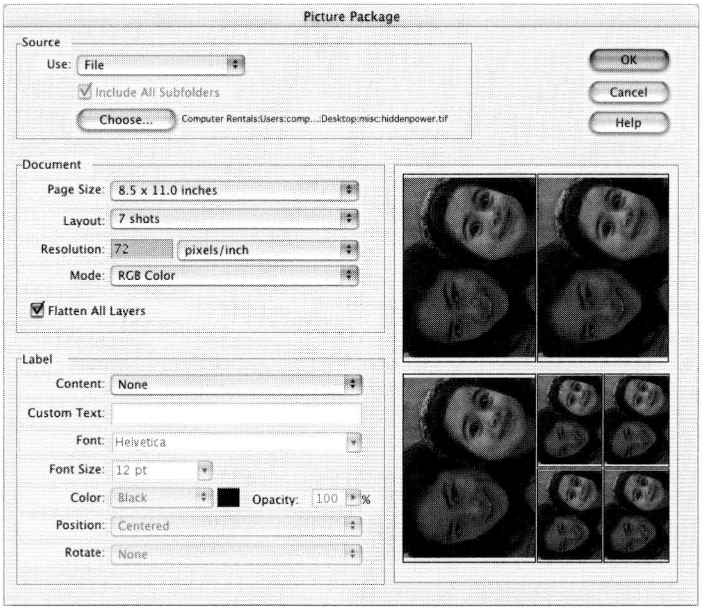

Figure 9.5

As long as you measure right, you can create a Picture Package template that will arrange images on a single sheet for you so you don't have to do it manually every time.

To create the Picture Package using the measurements from the example shown in Figure 9.5, all you have to do are the following simple steps:

1. Open a text editor (such as WordPad or Simple Text).

2. Type in the following text exactly as it is shown here:

```
I 8.5 11
7 Shots
0.25 0.25 4 5
0.25 5.5 4 5
4.25 0.25 4 5
4.25 5.5 2 2.5
4.25 8.25 2 2.5
6.25 5.5 2 2.5
6.25 8.25 2 2.5
```

3. Save the file as a text-only (`.txt`) file in the Elements `Layouts` directory. If you save it as another file type, it won't work.

> In Windows, these layout files are stored in `\Adobe\Photoshop Elements 2\Presets\Layouts`. On a Macintosh, they're in `\Adobe Photoshop Elements 2\Presets\Layouts`.

With the layout saved, you can then select it from the Layout drop-down list on the Picture Package dialog box and use it to print your images.

4. Open the Picture Package dialog box by selecting the command from the File menu (File → Print Layouts → Picture Package; in version 1, this is File → Automate → Picture Package).

5. Select the image you want to print in the Document panel of the screen, choose 7 Shots from the Layout drop-down list, and click OK.

The image will be created for you per the specifications of the layout. This may take a few moments. Elements will automatically create the best placement for the images you've specified by rotating them. You can replace individual images on the sheet if you want to by clicking the image you want to replace, and then selecting the alternate image (see Figure 9.6). Once the layout is created, you can print it.

Figure 9.6

Select the image you want to replace by clicking it and choosing an alternative in the Select An Image browser.

All those numbers you typed into the file actually do mean something. In data-speak, all you did was set up a data file that tells Photoshop Elements what to do. The first character in the first row (I) tells the program to use inches for all measurements. There are only two other options you can use: C for centimeters, and P for pixels. All the other measurements in the file will be considered as the type you specify in this first row.

The rest of the first row tells Photoshop Elements what paper size you're using. I've made these 8.5 and 11 to represent the full size of a standard sheet of paper.

The second row of the file is the name that will be used for this layout in the drop-down list on the Picture Package dialog box. Elements does not use the name of the file you are creating; it uses the name you specify here in row 2 of the file. Therefore, you will probably want to make the filename and the name you type in line 2 the same or very similar. Doing so will help you find the file quickly should you ever want to adjust it or use it as a template for creating another similar package.

The remaining rows in the file all define where pictures will be placed in the layout. These numbers indicate the distance from the top of the paper, the distance from the left edge of the paper, the width of the image, and the height of the image, respectively. All of the measurements are separated by a single space.

Printing to the Edge

Another layout problem that may confound a user is making images print to the edge of the paper. There will always be an edge area of the sheets you are printing that the printer will not print on—if you use the right paper settings. It is commonly called the *grip edge*. It is often a quarter to a half an inch broad, and may vary from edge to edge depending on how paper was designed to go through the printer. You really don't want to print right to the edge of the paper—imagine what would happen if the printer did that! You'd end up getting ink on things other than the paper, the edges would be smudged by handling, and the ink bleeding off the edges would be bound to muck up the printer, rollers, or something else eventually.

There are two solutions to this problem, which are really the same thing: buy perforated paper that you print on and then tear away in the shape of the print, or just do it the old-fashioned way and crop the paper.

For example, say you are doing a CD booklet and you want to make your image on the front and back go right to the edge of the booklet. You wouldn't start with paper that was exactly the right size and then use your printer to print the image exactly to the edge; you'd start with a larger sheet, print the cover, and then cut the paper down. Figure 9.7 shows a sample layout.

The image actually prints a bit beyond the crop edge—say, by an eighth of an inch. This provides a margin of error for the cropping. If the cut doesn't fall precisely on the crop mark, the image will still come all the way to the edge of the cropped area. Extending the image beyond the boundaries of the area you want it to occupy and then cropping the edges of the image is called *bleeding* in printing terms.

Other Printing Options

There are several other printing options for your images, and what we will focus on here are higher-end possibilities. You can turn your images into negatives or slides for use in photo printing or projection, and you can use other printing processes like offset printing and LED. You will have many more options than those mentioned here, but in dealing with digital images and photography, these will be common and useful. Check with your local services and on the Internet for more ideas.

Figure 9.7

All areas outside the crop hash are cut off and discarded.

Film Recorders

A film recorder is a means of generating film exposure using a digital image. Film recorders can be used to create slides and negatives, which can then be used for slide presentations and print exposures.

Within the film recorder, a CRT (cathode ray tube) is employed to project a thin beam of light through a filter and onto film to expose it. Film is then processed and developed using conventional photo processing, resulting in an image on traditional analog film.

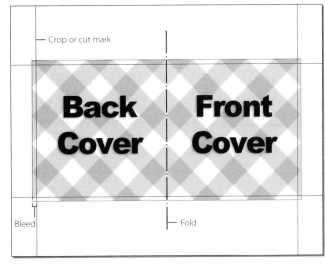

Film recorders come in varying resolution and quality based both on the number of lines of resolution possible and the quality (and size) of the CRT. Cost for processing can vary based on the quality of the film recorder and the available resolution. Usually it is not cheap, but when you need slides or film and have an image with enough resolution, the quality can be unsurpassed. Resolution of your images may have to be 650–1000 ppi at the final size.

35 mm film is generally used with 2000- and 4000-line recorders. 8000-line recorders can be used with 35 mm film, but this resolution begins to surpass the limitation of the film grain. 8000-line recorders are usually used with larger film stocks (2.25 inch), and 16000-line recorders with 4×5 inches and larger.

A list of exactly what to use as far as resolution would tend to be meaningless, because the quality of these various devices may require different sources. You'll have to contact services both to see if they have film recorders available and what they require for output.

Offset Printing

Offset printing is standard CMYK printing on printing presses. This may come in handy for producing such things as cards, business cards, books (and covers), CD inserts, calendars, posters and the like—top quality in both black-and-white and color printing. Presses can be of varying quality. The better quality presses will run upward of 133 lpi and 2540 dpi. All will use postscript and halftone approaches.

The only real reason to consider offset printing would be for multiple prints—usually numbering in the thousands rather than in the hundreds. While shorter runs may be available, this type of printing is almost exclusively effective in volume.

Light Emitting Diode (LED) Printing

Light emitting diode (LED) printers generate photographic results from RGB digital files. Somewhat like film recorders, your files can be printed without the conversion to CMYK because the process used is light-based. Exposure is created on photographic paper in sizes up to poster size, directly from digital files. Exposures are then processed (often right in the same machine).

While prints may be somewhat more expensive than traditional photo prints, the gap isn't very wide. The advantage is that you can use this process selectively with images that you have had the opportunity to correct and improve and still get photographic results. Unlike using a film recorder, which would take two steps (record to film, then print) to get results, LED printing is a single step. Because it cuts out having to pay for film and photo developing, it can end up being much less expensive to process.

Again, quality can vary, but the color results will often be superior to home printing. Files often require only about 250 ppi at final size. Check with your service to be sure, and ask to see samples of prints before you buy.

Part VI

Images on the Web

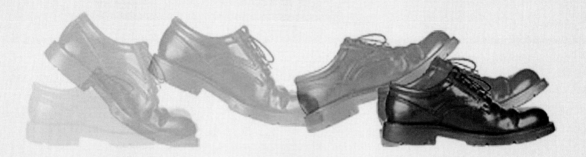

The only real difference between a web graphic and any other graphic is that the graphic result is intended for display on a monitor. This reduces some of what you need to know. For one thing, you really don't have to worry about CMYK separations or color mode conversions—unless you will be using images across print and web media and want to match business colors as closely as possible. But web image work opens up some new challenges as well as whole new arenas of image possibilities.

Chapter 10 **Creating and Using Web Graphics**

Chapter 10

Creating and Using Web Graphics

Images you create can be used on the Web as well as in print. While these can essentially be the same or similar graphics, there are some differences as to how you will apply images on the Web from how you would apply them in print. You deal with a different set of specifications as far as file type, color, and resolution are concerned. We'll look at how to apply those concepts to web images in Photoshop Elements, as well as how to insert images into web pages and how to perform image compression. A stark and challenging distinction between web graphics and the static images you use in print is the ability to make web graphics interactive and animated. We'll take a look at creating rollovers and how to go about planning, creating, and implementing animation.

Image file types for the Web

Basic guidelines for web design

Inserting images in HTML

Making a web gallery

Creating slices from a whole image

Creating rollovers

Creating animations

Looking beyond the book

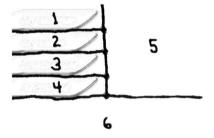

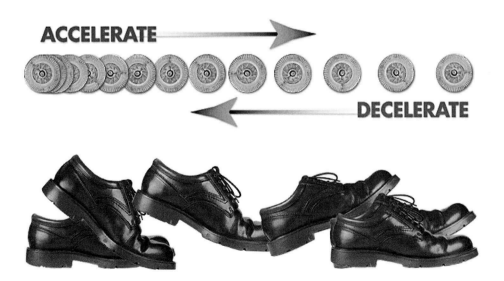

Image File Types for the Web

Although you can transfer any file type through the Internet (as an e-mail attachment or by downloading), your file type choices for web images that will be displayed is limited to those that are supported by web browsers. If the file type is not one that the browser will display, the image will just not show up. Although Elements supports many file types (see Table A.6 in the Appendix), and although you'll find many more still on the Web, generally you will want to stick with GIF and JPEG images. PNG, TIFF, EPS, PDF, and SVG images are sometimes supported with plug-ins.

> You can check to see whether an image you have saved is browser compatible by loading it directly into your browser. Simply open your browser, choose Open (this option may be called something slightly different, such as Open File or Open Page, depending on which browser you are using), and then select the file. Be aware that a plug-in you may have installed can affect the functionality of a browser: if visitors to your images or website do not have that plug-in, they may not be able to view the images. When you are unsure, view the images (and the web pages they will be included in) in different browsers to be positive they show up like you expect them to.

Be aware of the advantages each file type offers, and don't just dismiss the use of one over the other in all cases. There will be times when using each format is both sensible and desirable. The choice of which format to use is determined by the image contents of the file being saved. Generally, use the JPEG format with full-color graphics and GIF for images with limited color, such as type over a flat color background without a drop shadow. The following guidelines should give you a better idea of which format to use when saving. Choose the GIF file format for saving, if the image meets any of the following criteria; choose JPEG if the image meets none of these criteria:

- The image must have transparent properties.
- The image is a simple RGB containing 256 colors or less.
- The image is currently in Grayscale or Indexed Color mode.
- The image is intended to be an animation.

Either of these image types can be used in rollovers, tables, backgrounds, or any standard image placement on a web page. Often, you will want to use them in combination on a single page, and it might be advantageous to combine them in many circumstances. In the simplest sense, you might want to use GIF shims (blank images used as spacers) in a table to take advantage of transparency, whereas the table area itself is made up of JPEG slices to make the most of a color image you are using as a button. In a more complicated scenario, you might want to animate part of a rollover button that is a JPEG in the normal state (when it's not being rolled over or clicked). You would have to use a GIF to support the animated image of the button and a JPEG to maintain the best color quality in the static image.

JPEG

Named for its developers, the *Joint Photographic Experts Group* (*JPEG*) format is the easier of the two web images to implement, because the file type can retain full RGB color. Although there is an advantage to JPEG in its ability to retain image color, the image that results from the save can be distorted by the format's built-in compression. Compression in a JPEG file simplifies image information by making estimates as to what is actually important— based on a visual algorithm. The result of the compression can sometimes be harmless, but more often shows up in the image as distortion, known as *artifacts*—which can often be devastating to image integrity. The compression may show up only upon magnification of the image, but the potential for artifacts makes saving to JPEG an option to use only when necessary for Web display, or when space is at a premium.

Be sure to save as few times as possible—the more often you save to JPEG, the more the compression affects the distortion of your images. If you will be doing work to an image, save to a lossless file format (such as TIFF or PSD) whenever possible; use JPEG for final images only.

JPEG compression runs on a scale of 0 to 12; 0 is the most compressed with the greatest loss of image quality, and 12 is the least compressed retaining the most original image information. The higher the compression in a JPEG file, the smaller the image files, but the more the compression will damage the image information. This means that as the quality of the image goes up, so does the size of the resulting file.

GIF

CompuServe's *Graphics Interchange Format* (*GIF*), often used for web graphics, is an image compression format designed (specifically for the Web) to speed the transfer of images. GIF conversions might require finessing the color because GIF files can display only 256 colors. Mixing the 256-color palette with dithering can make it appear that there are more colors than there really are. Compression for GIF images is technically lossless, but conversion to Indexed Color is not lossless: there are a maximum of only 256 colors in a GIF color table, so the 16 million potential colors in an RGB image will be limited to fit in the palette. Conscious web design will generally keep colors simple, and this fits well with the idea of the GIF compression scheme, but mostly from the side of image creation: if you are creating a graphic image from scratch (like a logo), it is more likely that you will be able to make the color fit a GIF color table. For example, if you are running yellow text over a blue background, there will be a limited number of colors in the image. The result will probably be smaller as a GIF and may actually be represented better that way (there is no generation of artifacts that would happen with a JPEG). However, color photographs will be less likely to present well as GIF images. GIF cannot represent most of the colors in a common color photograph, so it may prove to be a bad choice for normal photographic images.

Web Image Resolution

In general, the resolution of all images saved for onscreen viewing should be set to between 72 and 96 ppi, regardless of file type. This is true for web images as well as those that are to be used in video applications. The reason for this is that 72–96 ppi matches the common range for the projection of a monitor. There may be exceptions (such as HDTV, high-definition television), but the 72–96 ppi range will cover most computer applications and will give you a good representation of the size that graphics will appear on most other computers.

On screens with higher definition web images appear smaller; the image information is used up over a smaller area, rather than projecting the existing information at a higher resolution. The result is that images fit the resolution of the display automatically, rather than being used at a fixed size as in print.

Saving for the Web

With the Save For Web command, Photoshop Elements gives you the option to compare two versions of the image, each using a different optimization method for compression and dithering. This option enables you to make a visual comparison between the original and the saved result before saving. In this way, you can select the smallest image file that still maintains the image quality you need. You can use the Save or Save As commands to create your web images, but you will have to do it without previews.

The Save For Web dialog box offers several combinations for comparing and optimizing images to be saved for Web use. Options include the following:

- File type
- Compression
- Resizing
- Animation controls
- Browser preview
- View size
- Download rates

This is a very powerful feature for making the most of your web images by making the least out of their size.

The Preview panel of the dialog box enables you to make comparisons to the original uncompressed version of the file. This will display the name and size of the original file, and the current file type, saved size, compression and approximate load time of the file that would be saved if changes were accepted. Neither image view can be edited or altered directly, but you can zoom in and move the canvas to look at different areas using Zoom and the Hand tool. The previews for the saved image will change with changes you make in the options.

The Settings panel of the dialog box enables you to select a preset optimization type from the Settings list or enter your own settings (Custom). Once the file format is selected, options appropriate to that file type will display.

The Image Size panel offers options for resizing the image being saved. The options are much like those in the Image Size dialog box (Image → Resize → Image Size), but the options are more limited, although more apropos for web-image size changes. Dimensions are changed in pixels only, and can be changed by percentage or dimension.

You can view the image directly in different browsers by clicking the Preview In Browser button. The image is opened in the selected browser, and image statistics are included in the preview. This enables you to see exactly how a specific browser displays an image.

Use the following steps to save your images for the Web using the Save For Web command:

1. Choose File → Save For Web. The Save For Web dialog box is displayed using a preview of the current image and the most recently used save options (see Figure 10.1).

2. Select optimization settings for the image, and then consider options for file type and compression. Each time you change any of the settings for optimization, look at the preview to be sure the change produces an acceptable result.

3. When the optimized version is acceptable, click the OK button. This will accept the settings and open the Save Optimized As dialog box.

4. Choose a name for the file to be saved—be sure to use a different name than the original to avoid overwriting. Choose a location and click OK to save.

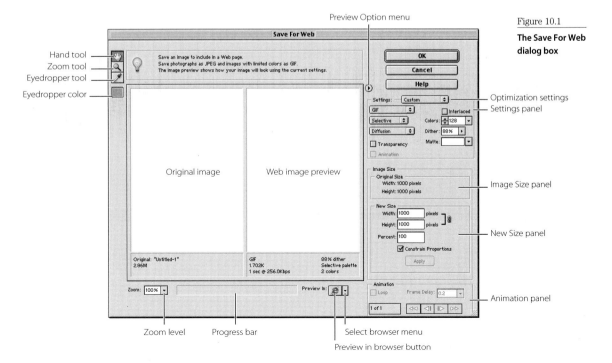

Figure 10.1

The Save For Web dialog box

Basic Guidelines for Web Design

Although there is no right or wrong, there is better or worse in web page design. Better is effective, and worse turns the visitor away. A few simple things can help limit the potential for design problems. Use these guidelines as a checklist to keep within a safety zone for your design. Of course, you can bend and break these guidelines, but they should help steer you in the right direction.

Minimize Image Size

You should strive to create the smallest possible files when creating images for the Web while still maintaining image quality. Smaller files load more quickly into a browser, and therefore allow faster browsing of your web pages. Regrettably, there is a tradeoff in consideration of quality when shrinking file size.

The size of your image file is a matter of numbers. The more information an image file has to carry, the larger the file will have to be. By reducing the pixel dimension to the minimum size (reducing the physical dimension), the image will be at its minimum effective size. By reducing the size further using compression (in the case of JPEG images), or reducing the number of colors (in the case of GIF images), images will be as small as possible and will transfer more quickly.

Following these guidelines will help keep your pages lithe and effective in design, and they will be better apt to effectively transmit your content.

- Crop images as tightly as possible to keep file sizes small. If you need extra space around the image, it is better to accomplish that with HTML code.

- Make images the exact pixel size that you want them to appear.

- Use 72 dpi for the final resolution. This will show you the effective maximum size of the image (viewed at 100%).

- In GIF images, reduce the number of colors as much as possible without distorting the image.

- Use JPEG format for images with more than 256 colors.

- Crop animation tightly to the area of motion. Keep the number of animation frames (layers) to a minimum, and use animation sparingly—or eliminate it.

- Keep rollover states to a minimum by using only the states you really need.

- Use repeating images on your pages to lower the number of elements that have to load.

Minimize Web Page Downloads

Having some general targets for code on your web pages can improve the look and speed of the pages. While you won't do this directly in Photoshop Elements, the following list is good to keep in mind while implementing your images:

Remove comments and other empty, unnecessary code from HTML. Any unnecessary code, including blank spaces, adds time to loading pages—even if it seems harmless.

Use short filenames and simple directory structures. A bulky directory structure, with extra layers and long names, can add unnecessary code because nested files must be renamed for each link. Use relative links, where possible.

Keep the total size of your entire page below 150KB. Keep it much lower if possible. Lots of people have improved their connectivity these days, but designing for the high end leaves much of the market behind.

Use a limited number of colors. Three to five colors will usually do. This helps maintain a unified look and can keep the design from becoming too busy. Another good reason to limit colors in graphics is to keep their file size tiny.

Sketch out the page before you make it. Knowing what you want will help you cut corners in creating the elements that go with it. This can keep the pages small in file size (KB) and speed the creation process.

Use simple HTML and GIF or JPG images. Don't depend on browser plug-ins to deliver effects. Standard practice should be to design with the newest standard browsers as a target. There are many cool tools available for creating amazing websites, but the simple fact is that when someone has to download a plug-in to see your page, you risk that they will miss the effect—and if so it is wasted.

Create sites offline and test your pages before and after they are live. You might get everything working fine offline and then when you set it up you might forget something or a link might be valid only within your directory structure. Always test your pages with as many different browser programs as possible, at least the two most popular ones. If possible, test your pages on different computers and different operating systems.

Create page designs at a browser-friendly size. Designing for a 21″ monitor makes assumptions that are probably unfounded about your visitors. If a page can't be viewed easily on a 17″ monitor, chances are that many visitors will have problems.

Break up pages at logical points. Don't cram so much on a page that it takes forever to scroll through. Keep pages small so loading is quick, and add links to navigate to organized information.

Make navigation simple and obvious. There is nothing worse than sitting on a page and not knowing how to get to the next step or where to go—or if there is more to get to. Good design should play a part in simplifying both the information and access to it.

Choose common fonts for the page itself and be aware of potential for reflow. Fonts used in page code (not in images) should be common, or you risk substitution. Fancy type should be set as images in Elements rather than hoping your visitors have your fonts.

Inserting Images in HTML

The following is a terribly short primer for those who have never tried to implement images on the Web. It covers the basics of what you need to understand about implementing images for display. If you have already used the Web to display your images, you might want to hop over this section and get on to rollovers.

To get your images into web pages, you have to do several things beyond simply creating the right images. Online services exist that will help you display your images, but they have simplified the way you display your images by automating the process and doing the behind-the-scenes work for you. You may want better control of what appears on your site, and for that you'll have to delve into doing it yourself—unless you've got a budget for design.

If you are going to be a do-it-yourselfer, you have to do the following:

1. Secure a web host (server) or hosting service.
2. Get a URL.
3. Create web pages to display your images.
4. Upload the web pages to the server.
5. Tell people the website is there.

The web host keeps your files at the ready so that when a visitor puts your address in their browser, the files can be accessed. This host could be anything from buying your own web server (the most serious and expensive), to renting hosting, to engaging a free service (free service usually comes at the expense of forced advertising in the form of banners or pop-up ads). Free services are excellent to practice with, and often can be all you need if you are just out to display your images casually. The more serious you get about the Web, the more serious you'll become about services.

Your URL is the web address, the infamous `http://etc.com`. Hosting services sometimes offer a web address along with the services (for example, popular services such as AOL and EarthLink offer free website space as part of their package). This URL will be the address you "advertise" by telling people where to go. Web addresses don't necessarily have to be `.com` to work, and many of the less expensive (and free) options won't be.

To display an image in a browser, you could just send people links to images (`http://www.mywebaddress.com/myimage.jpg`), but this won't allow you to put any text or description with it. To add text (and other links and descriptions) you really have to create at least one web page, and a website if there is to be more than a single page. To create a web page, you have to either write the code or get a program that will do it for you (such as Microsoft FrontPage, Adobe GoLive, or Macromedia Dreamweaver). You write the code (or it will be created) in *Hypertext Markup Language* (*HTML*), which is a series of tags that describe some parameters so the browser knows what it is supposed to do to display the page.

> One feature in Elements will take a folder of images and create a website for you to display those images. We'll look at the Web Gallery feature in a moment.

An image is inserted into a page using code that identifies the image and where it is located so that the browser knows where to look. The simplest code for inserting an image on a web page is an image tag. Here is a sample of a simple web page with an image tag:

```
<html>
    <head>
        <title>My Image</title>
    </head>
    <body>
        <img src="myimage.jpg">
    </body>
</html>
```

To create this page, you would type it in exactly as you see here using a text editor (such as WordPad, SimpleText, or Notepad), and save the file as text only with a .html extension. The file would then be uploaded to the server, along with the image file. When the URL was entered in a browser anywhere in the world, the image would display (as long as the internet connection is good and there are no limitation or restrictions to display).

The information that appears between the body tags is what displays in the browser window. The key to displaying the image is the img tag, which tells the browser to go look for an image source in the directory called myimage.jpg. If you were to type "Here's a picture of me on summer vacation" above the img line, the text would appear in the browser window along with the image.

While there is a lot more to explore as far as web controls and controlling page layout, this is not a book on web design. If the idea of using images on the Web is new to you, you may need a beginning book on web design—or feel free to ask questions on the Hidden Power of Photoshop Elements website. Another great way to explore code is to view the page source by selecting the Source or View Source option in the web browser (often on the View menu). This option will show the page code, and reading the code can give you hints as to how effects were achieved in design.

The following sections jump to more advanced implementations of images. The easiest of these to implement directly from Elements is creating a web gallery.

Making a Web Gallery

The Photoshop Elements Web Photo Gallery feature helps the user create a website to display images (a folder of images you want to share). The site will display all of the images initially as thumbnails—smaller versions of larger images. When you click a thumbnail, the larger version of that image will display. In this way, visitors to your site can "walk through" your gallery and look at the images they want. Because the thumbnails are smaller versions of the original files, they load more quickly than full versions would and they speed your visitor through loading your pages.

Elements will let you choose one of 15 predefined templates and will automatically create web pages to help you display selected images. The result is actually a reasonably sophisticated website—and the finished product can make you look like you know what you are doing, even if you have no idea.

All you do is set up the images you want to include, choose File → Create Web Photo Gallery (see Figure 10.2), select your options, and click OK. Elements takes care of the rest, automatically resizing and resaving the images from any Elements-friendly format into thumbnails and display JPEGs. When you are done, you don't have to look at a snippet of code or even know what happened; just post the content of the directory of files Elements created to your web host, and the images will be ready for everyone to see. To load the site, just enter the URL for the host in your web browser. As long as you copy all the files correctly and use the proper URL, you'll see the result. When you do, you can send the same link to anyone you want to share the images with.

You may need some details on setup and selection of options in the Web Photo Gallery feature, so here is a step-by-step procedure to follow when creating your web gallery. You'll start with some preparation outside of Elements before you jump in and make the gallery.

1. Gather the images you want to use on your photo gallery website by copying them into a single directory. Use a new directory, name the directory something distinct, and note the location. These files can be any file type that Elements will open. It may be best to use uncompressed RGB images in most cases.

2. Create a destination directory where Elements can save the processed website files. This should have a different name than the image directory. It is probably best to give this directory a name having something to do with the purpose of the thumbnail site.

3. In Elements, choose Create Web Photo Gallery from the File menu. You don't need to have any images open to kick off the process.

4. Choose the site style from the 15 choices in the Styles list. The thumbnail at the right of the dialog box shows a preview of what the site will look like.

5. Type your e-mail address in the E-mail field. This address will be used to create a link so that visitors can send e-mail to you.

6. Unless you have a preference for HTML extensions, leave that option alone.

7. Click the Choose or Browse button to locate the folder where you stored the images in Step 1 to include on the site. Check Include All Subfolders if you want to process sub-folders within the main image directory. You can use this feature to include shortcuts to other directories.

8. Click the Destination button and locate the destination directory you created in Step 2.

9. Specify options for the elements in your web gallery by selecting each element in turn from the Options drop-down list. Choose Banner to set up the display of the banner, which is a small area at the top of each page. In Site Name, enter a name for the site (this appears on the browser window bar and on the top of the web page), and then enter the Photographer's name (whoever gets credit for the images—this option does not appear on all templates) and Contact information (could be a phone number, alter-nate e-mail, physical address, etc.). There are only four font choices available because websites should use common fonts—your fonts won't necessarily display on someone else's machine. You are essentially choosing to display serif, sans serif, or monospaced type. Font size is not in points. These represent relative sizes. The larger the number, the larger the size of the display font.

10. Choose Large Images from the Options drop-down list to set up the display of images when a thumbnail is clicked. Check the Resize option if you have images of varying size that you want Elements to adjust for you, and then specify the size that you want them all to be. Note that resampling will occur for images that are not the size you select. You can choose a size from the drop-down list, or enter a custom size in pixels. Constrain will use the meas-urement you specify to control image width, height, or both according to the value selected. JPEG quality can be any value from 0 to 12. A higher number results in less compression, less damage, and a larger file size. Border will put a color frame around the images according to the number of pixels entered. For no border, enter 0. The Titles Use options allow you to select which information to use to display the name for each image. Caption, Title, and Copyright Notice are taken from the file information that was previously entered for each individual file in the File Info (File → File Info). If no file information was entered, nothing will show. Font choices here affect the type display for captions and other information that appears with the large images.

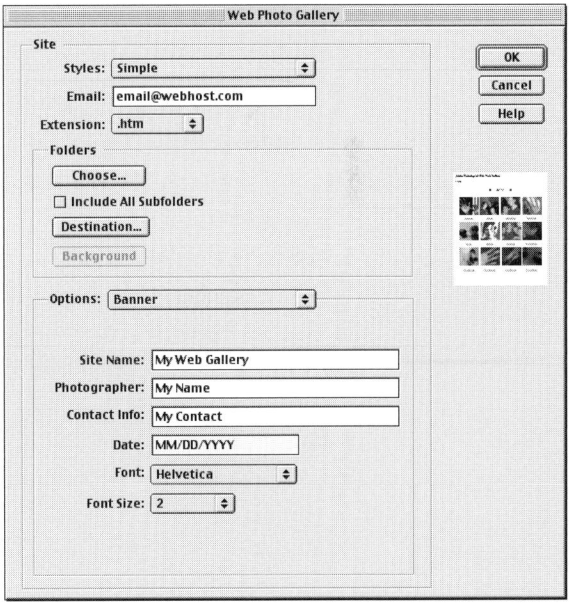

Figure 10.2

The Create Web Photo Gallery dialog

11. Choose Thumbnails from the Options drop-down list to set up the display of the smaller images used as previews for the large images. Size affects the image so that it is constrained in both directions. Columns and Rows allow you to determine how many images will be in a thumbnail row (this option is not used on all templates and may not be reflected in the preview). Border Size affects the frame around the thumbnail images. Title Use and Font specifications here work the same as those for Large Image options, but these choices affect the text that displays with the thumbnail images.

12. Choose Custom Colors from the Options drop-down list. These options affect color standards used in web pages. Click any of the swatches to call up a Color Picker dialog box to change the associated color. Background affects the color of the back of the page—the color that all the other elements are displayed on top of. Banner affects the banner area background only. The Banner color will display on top of the page Background color in the banner area only. Text is the color of the unlinked text used on the web pages. Active Link specifies the color for the frame and the name of the thumbnail that is currently displayed (for templates that show thumbnails and large images at the same time). Link shows the frame and text color for any link that has not been visited (clicked); this includes the e-mail address. Visited Link will be the frame and text color for links that have been used by the visitor.

13. Choose Security from the Options drop-down list to automatically add a simple watermark to your large images based on the selection made under Content. This requires that you have entered the appropriate information previously for each image in the File Info, unless you use the Custom Text option. Choosing Custom Text will allow you to add a single message that will be added to every large image. Font, Font Size, Color, Opacity, Position, and Rotate affect where the type ends up on the large image and how it appears.

14. Once all the options are set, click OK and wait for Elements to generate your pages.

When you have completed the process of creating your web gallery, you can preview your site by opening the `index.htm` or `index.html` file with your favorite web browser. To properly upload the files to a web host, upload all the files from the directory (do not include the directory, or you will have to adjust the URL linking).

> The resizing process is automated, so the resizing of images can cause blurring and damage to images due to resampling and compression. Be sure the target directory does not contain your original images, or you risk saving the resized images on top of the originals.

More advanced users may want to get into the templates and adjust them for their own purposes in generating websites. This will require a working understanding of, or the ability to figure out the XML used to generate the pages. You can find the templates in the Web-ContactSheet folder under Presets in the Adobe Photoshop Elements directory.

Creating Slices from a Whole Image

If you have traveled the Web at all you have probably seen examples of images that load in parts. These images are made from the original image cut up into smaller sections known as *slices*. The sliced sections of the image are held together by the HTML code. When the web page is displayed, the code tells the web browser how to display the image parts, and they are arranged when displayed so that they show up in the right order, like rearranged pieces of a very simple puzzle. When handled correctly, the image displays just as if it were whole.

There are actually some good reasons to divide an image into parts using slices. First, if an image is extremely large and takes a long time to load, the delay might cause a browser to look like it has lost a connection. The person visiting the page might wait for a long time before anything starts happening and may get the idea that the page is missing, broken, or corrupted. Using the image as arranged slices allows portions of the image to begin appearing on the screen so the visitor at least has the sense that something is happening on the page.

A better reason to cut up a graphic is so that you can make parts of the image into links and rollovers (we'll look at rollovers in the next section). Cutting an image into portions lets you work with the pieces of the web image as separate parts. You can then define any behavior each part might have separately—similar to what happens when you isolate image areas by selection, masking, or layering.

Cutting the Slices

Photoshop Elements does not provide an automated means of cutting up your image into slices. Slices can be only rectangular, and they have to be pretty accurate, so you should use the Guides tools in the Hidden Power Tools to help you along.

1. Open the image you want to slice. See Figure 10.3 for the image used in this example.

2. Decide how you want to cut the image up. Sketch a diagram of the slices (see Figure 10.4) so that reassembling the image will be easier. No slices should overlap, and all should be rectangles. Number the slices in the order that you will cut them up, from left to right and from top to bottom. The simpler you keep the pattern, the easier your job will be later. This sketch can be done right in Elements on another layer if you'd like. Be sure to shut off the view for the sketch layer when cutting up your image into slices to keep sketch lines from being included in the slices.

3. Place guides on the image to reflect your sketch. To place a guide, click Make Guide in the Hidden Power Tools and enter the pixel position for placement. Keep placing guides until the

Figure 10.3

This image shows a simple list of web page button links that might be used on your website.

slices you need to make are all outlined. Do not place any guides that you will not be using, but be sure that a guide aligns with every side of every slice. Some guides will overlay other slices, and that's okay (see Figure 10.5). Save your image with the slice guides using a different name.

If you choose the Move tool (press M on the keyboard), you can click on a guide and drag it to change its position. Guides can also be dragged off the image by pulling them over the rulers. This may come in handy when positioning the guides on your image for slicing.

4. Choose the Marquee tool and drag a selection from one corner of your first slice (for example, the upper left) to the diagonally opposite corner (for example, the lower right), making sure the selection snaps to (automatically aligns with) the guides.

5. Crop the image (Image → Crop), and save it using File → Save For Web. You will be able to choose different settings for each slice, if desired (including animation and rollover states as described in the sections that follow). Save each slice with a distinct name according to the slice number (such as slice1, slice2, etc., according to your sketch) and save them to a directory you'll use just for that set of slices. Be sure to name the files correctly, or you'll have trouble putting them together later. You may want to enter the file names for the slices on the diagram.

6. Jump back two steps in the file history by clicking the appropriate step in the Undo History palette. The step you click will be just *before* Rectangular Marquee near the bottom of the history. If you have followed these steps exactly, the step will be called New Guide. This will return the image to how it was after Step 3.

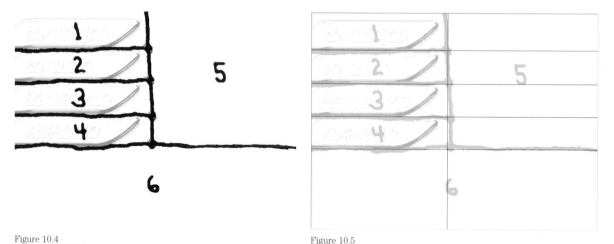

Figure 10.4

This rough sketch shows six total slices.

Figure 10.5

Guides placed over your image will create a grid that you will use to cut up the slices.

7. Repeat Steps 4, 5, and 6 until all the slices are created according to the sketch you made in Step 2.

The Save Slice Hidden Power Tool will do Steps 5 and 6 for you. Once you've marquee-selected an area, just click Save Slice to crop and save it as its own image. (You will still have to name the files appropriately.) The guides in the image will help keep your selections accurate so that the slices you create will all fit together when they are reassembled in a web browser.

Positioning the Slices

Once you finish the previous steps you will have all the slices you need, but they will be a hodge-podge of separate files and you will have to create the HTML to reassemble them properly.

Before you turn to creating the HTML, count the number of image rows (horizontals) and columns (verticals) you have created using the guides. This information will be important in helping you create the HTML easily.

The first step in assembling your images is creating an image table to place them in in HTML code. A table can create an array of rectangles to fit your images into, so you can arrange the way they appear for your visitor. To create your image table, you can open up a text processor (such as WordPad or SimpleText) and then use the sketch you made as a reference for creating the code. This table will tell the browser how to reconstruct the image in the original order and layout. The table is created by placing `table` tags in the HTML to define where the code for the table starts and ends. You insert `td` (table data) tags that represent slice columns and `tr` (table row) tags to represent slice rows.

Use the following steps to complete the code. At each stage, the code you type will be bold-faced so you can pick it out from what you've already done. The code will follow from the slice example sketched in the previous steps.

1. Type in the following code exactly as you see it. This is the basic code to use to create your table. (The `slicetext.html` file on the CD contains this starting code if you don't feel like typing it up.) This sample HTML contains a table with one row and one column (one set of `tr` and `td` tags)

```html
<html>
  <head>
    <title>My Sliced Image</title>
  </head>
  <body>
    <table border=0 cellspacing=0 cellpadding=0>
      <tr><td></td></tr>
    </table>
  </body>
</html>
```

2. Count the columns in your image and add a set of tags for each column to that line in the code (see Figure 10.6). Just count the slice columns (vertical image columns) made by the guides, and ignore the images. To add the code, highlight the column tags (`<td></td>`), copy them, and paste them so that there are as many tag sets as you have image columns. The following sample code shows what this would look like if you had two columns, as in the example image:

```
<html>
  <head>
    <title>My Sliced Image</title>
  </head>
  <body>
    <table border=0 cellspacing=0 cellpadding=0>
      <tr><td></td><td></td></tr>
    </table>
  </body>
</html>
```

3. Count the number of rows in your image and add lines to the table code to reflect that number. Just count the horizontal image rows made by the guides (see the example in Figure 10.6), and ignore the images. To add the code, highlight the row code (from `<tr>` to `</tr>`; the tags and everything inside them), copy, and then paste that code until there are as many sets of row tags as you have counted image rows. Here's what the code would look like if you had five rows (and two columns), as in the sample image:

```
<html>
  <head>
    <title>My Sliced Image</title>
  </head>
  <body>
    <table border=0 cellspacing=0 cellpadding=0>
      <tr><td></td><td></td></tr>
      <tr><td></td><td></td></tr>
      <tr><td></td><td></td></tr>
      <tr><td></td><td></td></tr>
      <tr><td></td><td></td></tr>
    </table>
  </body>
</html>
```

4. Look at the first row on your diagram, and note all the images that are partially or entirely in that row. Note the file names. Enter the image reference for the first slice (counted left to right) in the code between the sets of **td** tags. This is done with a single

img (image) tag, with the src (source) attribute providing the filename of the image. Enter the second image in the second set of tags. You would continue doing this until all the images in the row are used.

```html
<html>
  <head>
    <title>My Sliced Image</title>
  </head>
  <body>
    <table border=0 cellspacing=0 cellpadding=0>
      <tr><td><img src="slice1.jpg"></td>
          <td><img src="slice5.jpg"></td></tr>
      <tr><td></td><td></td></tr>
      <tr><td></td><td></td></tr>
      <tr><td></td><td></td></tr>
      <tr><td></td><td></td></tr>
    </table>
  </body>
</html>
```

5. On your diagram, cross out the slices that were used in the previous step (see Figure 10.7). You need to reference each image only once in the table, and this will serve as your reference that an image has been used.

6. If there are leftover td tags in the line of code that represents the slice row (`<td></td>` sets with nothing in them), delete the extra tags.

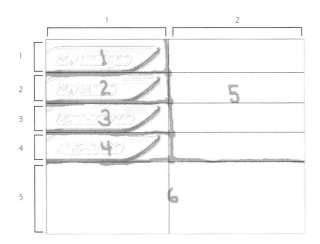

Figure 10.6

Count the rows and columns according to the number of guides you place.

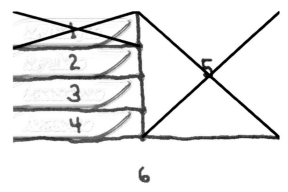

Figure 10.7

Crossing out the slices you have used will help you keep count in the rows and will make sure you use images only once in each table.

7. For each image in the current row, count the number of image rows and columns that the slice covers. If there is more than one row and/or column, go to Step 8; otherwise, go to Step 9.

8. Enter the number of rows and columns for each image by adding code that tells how many rows and columns the image belongs to. This will be done using span attributes (colspan, for spanning columns; rowspan, for spanning rows) You have to add this value to the tags only if the image covers more than one column or row:

    a. For columns, add `colspan=y` to the `td` tag, where *y* equals the number of columns that the image covers.

    b. For rows, add `rowspan=x` to the `td` tag, where *x* equals the number of rows that the image covers. Delete *y* `<td></td>` pairs in each line of code below the current line for $x - 1$ number of rows. You subtract one because the current row you are on counts as one, and you don't want to count it twice.

    For example, slice 1 from the example covers only the first row and first column, so no tags are added. Slice 5 covers the second column only, but is part of four rows (rows 1–4). For the `slice5.jpg`, you would have to add a tag for the columns it spans: `colspan=4`. The resulting code would look like this:

```
<html>
  <head>
    <title>My Sliced Image</title>
  </head>
  <body>
    <table border=0 cellspacing=0 cellpadding=0>
      <tr><td><img src="slice1.jpg"></td>
          <td rowspan=4><img src="slice5.jpg"></td></tr>
      <tr><td></td></tr>
      <tr><td></td></tr>
      <tr><td></td></tr>
      <tr><td></td><td></td></tr>
    </table>
  </body>
</html>
```

9. Repeat Steps 4 to 8 for all your slices. In Step 4, when counting the images in the row, don't include any images that you crossed out. An image should only be included in the row count if the upper-left corner of the slice is in the row.

10. When you have completed the code, save the file using a distinct file name (for example, `myslicedimage.html`) in the same directory where you saved the image slices. Your code

will vary as you cut up images in different configurations, but for this example it should look like the following:

```
<html>
  <head>
    <title>My Sliced Image</title>
  </head>
  <body>
    <table border=0 cellspacing=0 cellpadding=0>
      <tr><td><img src="slice1.jpg"></td>
          <td rowspan=4></td><img src="slice5.jpg"></tr>
      <tr><td><img src="slice2.jpg"></td></tr>
      <tr><td><img src="slice3.jpg"></td></tr>
      <tr><td><img src="slice4.jpg"></td></tr>
      <tr><td colspan=2><img src="slice6.jpg"></td></tr>
    </table>
  </body>
</html>
```

If you open your web browser and load the HTML file, your image should appear whole. If it doesn't, something has gone wrong, and you'll need to locate the problem—it will most likely be in the code.

If your image loads successfully, you can use this image table in other web pages where you want to use this sliced image. All you have to do is copy everything between and including the `table` tags and paste it into another web page. Be sure you copy the images to the same directory as the new page.

You can probably see that keeping the slices simple can help ease putting the image back together, and can simplify tracking the parts as well.

Creating Rollovers

Rollovers are often used as buttons on a web page to help the visitor realize that a section of an image is actually a web page link. Rollovers appear to change depending on action of the visitor when they view your web page. The changes depend on what the visitor does with the cursor. The term rollover comes from the idea that when you roll the mouse to move the cursor over the image, the position of the cursor can prompt the browser to change images, interactively. For example, when a cursor is rolled over a button image, the image can appear to highlight in some way, suggesting that the area of the page is live: if you click the button something else will happen. Creating a rollover requires some JavaScript which tells the browser what to do. Rollover sections of an image are often used in combination with slices so that you can create buttons, simple highlighting, or reveal additional information.

You can do more than simple highlighting with rollovers, such as creating complex interactive events that can be used for games or for more complex control in display of page information. Six different potential actions, known as *states*, exist for any rollover. These states are: Normal, Over, Click, Down, Up, and Out. They describe actions that the visitor can take with the mouse (or other input device) to affect the rollover; these states are defined in Table 10.1 and illustrated in Figure 10.8.

When creating a rollover, you don't need to use all the states. If you are trying to create a mouse-click event, it is best to use either the Down and Up combination or Click, not all three or other combinations thereof.

A rollover does not have to contain every state. In fact, a rollover could technically have only one state—although that isn't much of a rollover if it does. Usually, you will want to have at least one state in addition to Normal. Only one image state of each kind can exist in the rollover, and the fewer states you use, the better. Fewer states require less load time because they generate more code and use more images.

Not every rollover will require a click action. You can use rollovers creatively to change the page contents, and you can even develop simple puzzles and games by hiding and viewing areas of the screen depending on where the visitor's cursor is. These more-complicated rollovers are put together by using different slices to trigger different views.

There are more complex things that you can do (and perhaps we can talk about those on the website and in the newsletter where there is more opportunity for demonstration), but for now I'll show you a basic rollover. To create a rollover, you have to create the separate image states that you want to use and then insert the Java code that will exchange the two images.

Table 10.1	STATE	DESCRIPTION	JAVA COMMAND
Rollover States	Normal	The initial state of the image when the page loads.	
	Over	The state of the image when the mouse cursor is hovering over the image area.	onMouseOver
	Click	The state of the image when the mouse button is clicked while the cursor is hovering over the image area. Used instead of a Down and Up combination.	onClick
	Down	The state of the image when the mouse button is clicked and held down while the cursor is hovering over the image area. Used in combination with Up as one of two components in an option, instead of Click.	onMouseDown
	Up	The state of the image when the mouse button is released while the cursor is hovering over the image area. Used in combination with Down as one of two components in an option, instead of Click.	onMouseUp
	Out	The state of the image when the mouse exits the image area.	onMouseOut

In a simple rollover, all you need is a snippet of Java to define the rollover function, and a few basic Java commands. Open a new text file and type the following to start the page:

```
<html>
    <head>
        <title>Roll Over</title>
    </head>
    <body>
    </body>
</html>
```

Now you'll need to add the Java script code to define the swap function and use a different type of image reference. The script goes within the head tag. It defines parameters so your browser knows what to do later when it encounters the onMouse and swap commands. To enter the script, type the following:

```
<html>
    <head>
        <title>Roll Over</title>
        <script language="JavaScript1.2">
        <!--
            function swap(img, changeto)
                {document.images[img].src = changeto;}
        //-->
        </script>
    </head>
    <body>
    </body>
</html>
```

When the browser encounters the swap command attached to an action (e.g., onMouse), it knows to change an image. It can change the current image or another one on the page, as long as they are named. Here we'll make the image change once when the mouse cursor rolls over the image, and then again when it rolls off. This requires adding the onMouseOver and onMouseOut swap commands, and a named image reference.

```
<html>
    <head>
        <title>Roll Over</title>
        <script language="JavaScript1.2">
```

Normal

Over

Down

Click

Out

Up

Figure 10.8

This series shows the states as they were created in order from top to bottom. Normal and Out are the same because you usually will want to return to the original state upon moving out of the image area so that everything is as it was.

```
<!--
    function swap(img, changeto)
        {document.images[img].src = changeto;}
//-->
</script>
</head>
<body>
    <a href="#" onMouseOver="swap('imagename','2.gif');"
                onMouseOut="swap('imagename','1.gif');">
        <img src="1.gif" border=0 name="imagename">
    </a>
</body>
</html>
```

The image will start out as `1.gif` and change to `2.gif` when the mouse cursor rolls over. It will change back to `1.gif` when the mouse cursor rolls out. To add other images, add unique image names:

```
<html>
    <body>
        <a href="#" onMouseOver="swap('imagename','2.gif');"
                    onMouseOut="swap('imagename','1.gif');">
            <img src="1.gif" border=0 name="imagename">
        </a>
        <a href="#" onMouseOver="swap('imagename2','4.gif');"
                    onMouseOut="swap('imagename2','3.gif');">
            <img src="3.gif" border=0 name="imagename2">
        </a>
    </body>
</html>
```

This shows a page where there are two images, `1.gif` and `3.gif`. When you roll over `1.gif`, it will change to be `2.gif`, and when you roll out, it will switch back again to `1.gif`. Roll over `3.gif`, and it will change to `4.gif` and back to `3.gif` again when you roll out.

To make the rollover image into a link, just change the octothorp (#) in the hyperreference (`href`) to the URL you want to link to:

```
<html>
    <body>
        <a href="page1.htm" onMouseOver="swap('imagename','2.gif');"
                    onMouseOut="swap('imagename','1.gif');">
            <img src="1.gif" border=0 name="imagename">
        </a>
        <a href="page2.htm" onMouseOver="swap('imagename2','4.gif');"
                    onMouseOut="swap('imagename2','3.gif');">
```

```
            <img src="3.gif" border=0 name="imagename2">
        </a>
    </body>
</html>
```

You can improve the performance of rollovers by preloading the images. This will serve to get the images in the browser memory so that it doesn't have to go out and look for them during the behavior. If it has to go search, there can be a delay in the image change and it'll look clunky or perhaps be missed entirely if the visitor rolls away quickly before the image loads. You'll need to add a preload function in the script, and reference that preload in the body tag so the browser knows to execute it. It looks like this:

```
<html>
    <head>
        <title>Roll Over</title>
        <script language="JavaScript1.2">
        <!--
            function swap(img, changeto)
                {document.images[img].src = changeto;}

            function preload()
                {image1 = new Image();
                 image1.src = "1.gif";
                 image2 = new Image();
                 image2.src = "2.gif";
                 image3 = new Image();
                 image3.src = "3.gif";
                 image4 = new Image();
                 image4.src = "4.gif";}

        //-->
        </script>
    </head>
    <body onLoad="preload('image1','image2','image3','image4')">
        <a href="page1.htm" onMouseOver="swap('imagename','2.gif');"
                    onMouseOut="swap('imagename','1.gif');">
            <img src="1.gif" border=0 name="imagename">
        </a>
        <a href="page2.htm" onMouseOver="swap('imagename2','4.gif');"
                    onMouseOut="swap('imagename2','3.gif');">
            <img src="3.gif" border=0 name="imagename2">
        </a>
    </body>
</html>
```

To add more images to the preload, insert additional images in the Java script in the header and name them in the preload. You can substitute any name for the image variable names, but they have to match in the Java and the preload or the reference won't work. There are more complicated ways to do this.

Many websites offer free code and further instructions on this type of JavaScripting.

This is just the beginning when it comes to using HTML and JavaScript with your images on the web. These tips on using slices and rollovers are meant to start you on your way. If you have questions, feel free to bring them up on the newsletter (`hpe@yahoogroups.com`; `http://groups.yahoo.com/group/hpe`).

Creating Animations

Movement is an advantage unique to the web medium for most graphic artists not working in video or TV applications. Creating effects involves timing and consideration of space and motion that offers different challenges than still art. Animations can be created in Photoshop Elements using the GIF format, image layers, and the animation export check box in the Save For Web dialog box.

Animations work in an image by displaying a series of changes that appear one after the other to make objects seem to be moving. If you've ever seen a flip book—where you flip through the pages and an object seems to move—that is really the same idea. The same theory is used in movies. Changes in position are recorded as steps in sequence that are then displayed in frames—separate images captured on film. Usually many frames are captured per second (for animation, 12 to 16 or more). The purpose is to show the images so quickly that people can't distinguish between the separate frames, so the objects give the appearance of fluid motion. In capturing images for movies, many images are captured of objects that are already moving and the images are simply played back in a timed sequence to re-create the motion. In creating animation, images are planned to create the illusion of motion.

A specific number of frames is used to plan movement and timing. For example, if it takes a cartoon character 3 seconds to walk across the screen at 16 frames per second, 48 separate drawings would have to be created to complete the movement. These drawings would represent the sequential movement of the character in 16ths of a second. The more frames played back per second, the tighter and smoother the resulting motion appears in the sequences.

GIF animation essentially works in a similar way to cartoon animation, movies, or flip books. In creating GIF animations, you need to create a series of sequential movements that accomplish the illusion of movement. You can have control over the timing of the frames, the series of events, and the speed of the movement. The trick is to plan a smooth motion, and balance that against the number of frames you use.

Planning the motion requires deciding how long you want the motion to last, how smooth you want it to be, and what distance or space you want the movement to cover. It can also require planning for the limitations of your medium. As with most other web concerns, you need to make your images as small as possible while still getting the results you want. The more frames you use, the larger the resulting file will be, and the longer the animation will take to download. So you will want to get your animation simply and effectively. This usually means reducing the number of frames to only the frames that are essential.

Color is another limitation. Since animation is supported only in GIF files exported from Elements, you will have to export files with a maximum of 256 colors. This may lead you toward using subjects with limited color to obtain the best results, or planning which includes using a limited color scheme.

> Although animations are cool, and can be fun and challenging to do, use animations with purpose on a web page. If you just throw them up because you can or because they're "neat," you may not be doing it for the best reasons. Some animations can be distracting instead of useful and might actually encumber and defeat the purpose of your site.

Planning Your Animation

To create an animation, it is best to approach the whole thing tactically. To save time and effort, knowing what your goal is from the outset will help save steps.

Use the following steps to plan your animation and develop parts of the motion. Very simple animations like blinking eyes or flashing lights that appear to travel around a sign (often called a marquee) will go through these same steps, but the considerations will be simple, and may not require in-depth planning.

1. Decide what you want your animation to look like. It might require making sketches or taking notes to define exactly what you want the animation to do. Say you want a man to simply walk left to right on screen. You can do this many ways, and with different perspectives, such as full body, or just shoes and ankles—or shoes alone. You could build your walking man with stiffly swinging legs, but a more complicated and accurate motion will show the knee bending, the heel of the shoe lifting to bend the toe, and then the toe straightening as the leg swings forward and straightens out again. The amount of detail you want to include is important to later planning steps.

2. Roughly break down the animation into separate movements, where each change in direction or motion constitutes the end of one action and the beginning of the next. Itemize cyclical or repetitive motions that you can repeat. For example, a walking figure will take a step first with the right foot then the left, and then repeat. You may be able to save "steps" by making the right-left cycle one time, and then repeat it as needed. See Figure 10.9.

Figure 10.9

This series of motions can be used to repeat multiple steps by simply repeating the series.

3. Decide how long you want each of the movements in the animation to last, in seconds. For example, you might decide that each step should take one second. This calculation helps you determine how many frames you will be able to include for all of the details you are interested in.

4. Determine how many cycles are required to complete your motion. Make a close approximation of the distances you plan to cover using a linear or pixel measure for each movement. If the walking figure covers 100 pixels with each step, the animation is to cover your screen from left to right, and the animation is 800 pixels wide. You'll need to cover those 800 pixels. If each step takes 1 second, eight steps (four right-left cycles), will cover the distance in 8 seconds total.

5. Decide how many frames you want to use—either for each movement or for the whole animation. This should not be an arbitrary selection, but should be based on the distance of the movement, how smooth you need it to be, and the detail you need to include.

Although using a high number of frames per second makes the motion smoother, it also increases the file size. More than 32 frames per second (fps) is overkill—especially for the Web. Less than 16 fps might make the action a little blocky and rough, depending on the action. You'll want your web animation to fall in the 8 fps to 12 fps range if you are looking for smooth motion. You can use less frames, and slower frame speeds (depending on what is happening) but doing so can tend to make the animation chunky or hard to follow. Regretfully, you some-times have to accept clunky as a trade-off to file size. Table 10.2 lists some frame rates and suggested uses. These rates consider continuous motion as the desired result.

While it may make for a clunky result, using 5 frames per second for the 8 step walking animation requires 40 frames to complete. Even that will lead to a large animation. You can see where higher frame rates become unwieldy—and pretty much become a burden to deal with.

You should be able to see from the complexity of this that it is beneficial to keep animation movements simple unless you are interested in spending a lot of time animating. The other side of this is that the more frames you use and the more time you spend, the less likely that the result will be a usable GIF animation. It might end up more suited for video or other applications, but that kind of application is not supported by Photoshop Elements—at least not directly.

FRAME RATE (FRAMES PER SECOND)	FRAME DELAY (SECONDS PER FRAME)	USE
1 or fewer	1 or more	Deliberate differentiation between frames; slideshows
2	0.5	Stop-action effects
5	0.2	Very chunky web animation
8	0.13	Chunky web animation
12	0.08	Minimum smooth web animation
16	0.06	Quality web animation; TV cartoon frame rate
24	0.04	Top-quality TV/cinema cartoon animation
32	0.03	Maximum move export rate; TV/cinema film quality

Table 10.2

Typical Animation Frame Speeds

Building Your Animation

Now that you've planned out your animation, you can begin actually creating it. Create the animated parts or repetitive movements that will be part of the larger movements in the frames. Depending on the complexity of the scene you are animating, you might have to build many parts, and you might have to do it in separate images and combine them. You should animate constants or repetitive actions first, or smaller movements within larger ones; this will make it easier to combine elements into a larger movement. You might find it easiest to build a few common or frequently used elements first and then duplicate those as needed.

Once you have the image elements built, move them all into a single Photoshop Elements document and follow these steps:

1. Compile the animated image parts into corresponding frames, with each frame represented as a separate layer.

2. Stack the completed frames from the background to the front in the Layers palette. The background will be the first frame of the animation; Elements will generate each frame in succession from the bottom of the stack on up.

3. Save the layered file in Photoshop native format (PSD). This will be your backup in case you need to come back to the animation and adjust elements that are not flattened.

4. With the image still open, choose Save For Web.

5. Choose GIF as the File Type under Settings, and set the GIF options as desired.

6. Click the Animation box under Settings. This will make the Animation panel available.

7. Preview the animation by clicking the Play button to move through the successive frames. This will help you to be sure you've layered the movement correctly. If necessary, cancel out of the save and rearrange the layers.

8. Set the frame speed and looping according to the speed of motion you had planned.

9. Save the animation by clicking OK.

The animated GIF can be viewed by loading the file into a browser, or the file can be viewed as part of a web page by using HTML code for placing a GIF, just as you would place any other GIF image. The animation will be a single file.

There are numerous options for working with animation to adjust the results. You can selectively apply changes to single frames, add and delete frames by adjusting the PSD that you saved, and then regenerate the GIF.

To edit a frame individually, select the frame by clicking it in the Layers palette. If you add or delete layers to edit, be aware that these will be added to and deleted from the frames if you export the animation again. You have to merge all changes to the frame you want to include them in so that they are not exported separately.

Animating Image Elements

Animating elements requires attention to detail and an understanding of how motion is handled. For example, objects can accelerate, decelerate, move at constant speeds, turn, and so on, while you handle all the planning and execution of every movement. Here we'll look at how to make motion do what you want it to do.

Acceleration, Deceleration, and Constant Speed

When you want an image element to appear to move faster as it goes, that is called acceleration. It is the same thing that happens when you press down the gas pedal in your car to go faster. Deceleration is exactly the opposite—like putting on the brakes. A spinning top that is slowing down would be an example of deceleration. Constant speed would be exemplified by something moving that is not accelerating or decelerating but continues to move at the same pace.

Acceleration is created during an animation by increasing the movement or distance steadily between a series of frames. Decreasing movement steadily causes deceleration. It is recommended that you practice the effects of controlling speed and movement in animations.

The effects can be calculated using some plain old good sense. Say you want to give a stationary car an acceleration of 6 pixels per frame over 1 second of movement using 12 frames per second. By the 12th frame, that car would have to be moving at 72 pixels per frame (6 × 12 = 72). All you need to do is move the car 6 additional pixels with each movement: These movements would be 6, 12, 18, 24, 30, 36, 42, 48, 54, 60, 66, and 72 pixels. Figure 10.10 illustrates accelerating and decelerating movement. By the end of the 12th frame, the car will be moving at 864 pixels per second (72 × 12, or the number of pixels per frame times the frames per second). To maintain that movement at that point, you would keep the incremental movement at 72 pixels per frame.

You can certainly get more complicated and more accurate than this by applying an acceleration rate according to a bell curve if you have a target. That is, acceleration will gradually become 6 pixels per frame (say, 0.5, 1.5, 3, 4.5, 5.5, and 6, rather than immediately hitting 6). However, we are looking for only a reasonable approximation at this

Figure 10.10

The figure shows an acceleration toward the right and a deceleration to the left. The tire steadily accelerates or decelerates by moving the object more or fewer pixels between layer frames.

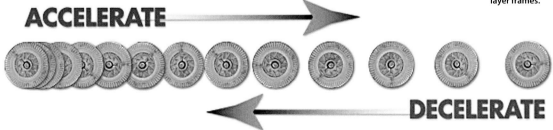

point. The main thing to remember is that to make something go more quickly, the distance between where it is and where it was will be less than where it is going to be, and vice versa for deceleration. If you want a constant speed, you are maintaining the current movement: move in even increments. If you want to stop, duplicate the frame without moving any of the elements.

> To elongate a pause in any action, you will simply duplicate a layer for the number of frames that you want the pause to occur. As long as the layers are not altered in any way, this layer addition will actually not contribute significantly to increasing the file size.

Compiling Animated Parts

As suggested in the steps earlier, you will have simple and complex movements in your animations. In addition, some motions that seem simple are actually complex. For example, a tire rolling is a simple form of a complex movement. Not only is the tire rotating, but it is also moving forward. To animate the tire correctly, you will have to show the rotation of the tire as it covers a distance, as well as moving the position of the tire.

To get the right effects from complex movements, you should attack the parts separately. This is best illustrated by an example.

The idea for this example will be to build an animated banner for a web page, including walking shoes as an example of simple motion applied in a typical animation. We'll do the animation of the shoes only, and then discuss a few possibilities at the end.

The first thing that you would normally do is create constants. Constants would be any image elements—foreground or background—that will not change. For example, a constant might be a floor for the shoes to walk on. Once the constants are created, they can be duplicated to appear in every frame of the animation. We won't be starting with any constants in this example; there will be enough to keep track of with just the shoes, as simple as they may seem initially.

For the example, the animation will have to all fit within the banner. I'm going to assume that 8 inches is a pretty safe width for display. The plan will be to use 5 frames per second, and to make each step last one second. Each frame has a duration of 0.2 seconds, and the total movement is 576 pixels (an 8-inch banner at 72 ppi). Each step will cover slightly less 2 inches, or about 120 pixels.

The motion of the shoes is actually somewhat complex: One shoe goes from being at rest to full acceleration and then stops again, then the next shoe takes over and goes through the same acceleration and deceleration. The full cycle for steps including the right and then the left shoe will cover 10 frames. To save you some time and trouble, I have included the individual shoe images on the CD. To mimic the desired motion, the images of the shoe are provided in five stages for each shoe: pushing off, swinging up, swinging down, landing, and at rest.

The motion will look like the shoes shown back in Figure 10.9, but it will be complicated by having both right and left shoes. While the right shoe is moving, the left remains still; while the left moves, the right remains still. Because of their proximity, the shoes cross in front of (right) or behind (left) one another. You'll see how this can lead to a pretty complex series of image layers.

The easiest way to attack this animation is to build the right step motion and then the left step motion, and then combine them in alternating sequences. Once you have created the simple right and left steps and combined them, the rest of the motion is actually pretty simple: the shoes travel along in a straight line horizontally, repeating the same motion three more times. The set of steps that you create can easily be duplicated (we'll see how in a minute) and then repositioned for each repetition, saving an absolute ton of work.

> Although I provided original images for each change in position for the shoes, there may be times where you will create motion by altering an original. When animation requires a transformation or resizing rather than a straight copy, you do not want to create subsequent steps from the previous one in order, as may seem natural. Always go back to the original, copy it, and then apply the change. If you don't, distortion will increase with each step. For example, if you have something rotating at 45° per frame, Elements will have to distort the image at each step in the turn: Each subsequent rotation will distort it even more. By the time the object is rotated the seventh time, distortion in detail may become apparent—just in time to cycle back to the original. This close comparison may make it evident that the images were not handled as well as they might have been. The best plan is to have originals for each position; but when that isn't possible, go with the best you can get.

To make the animation apply this planning, use these suggested steps:

1. Make a new RGB image that is the size and resolution of the animation you will be creating. In this case, the image will be 576 pixels wide and 72 ppi. Make it 2 inches (144 pixels) tall and crop it down later. Name the image Animation in the New Image dialog box.

2. Open all 10 of the shoe images and drag them into the image created in step 1. When copying the images it is probably best to use Duplicate Layer so you can name the target layer. Name the layers according to the letter and number of the file name (see Figure 10.11)

3. Arrange the layers so that they are in order, left from the bottom up. You will position the shoes in the layer after ordering the layers, so don't worry about where the shoes are.

4. Shut off the views for the left shoe and be sure all the views for the right shoe are on.

5. Duplicate the Right 5 shoe layer and call it Right 0. You want the movement to end with the shoe at rest, but you need to start the series considering the initial position of the shoe. Move the Right 0 layer to the bottom of the stack, just below Right 1.

Figure 10.11

The layers should simply be stacked in the layer palette at this point, grouped by shoe (right or left).

6. Position the shoes so they look somewhat like Figure 10.12. You may want to place a guide near the bottom to help you with the alignment of the shoes. You'll want Right 0 and Right 1 to be in just about the same horizontal position (match at the toe) and aligned on the bottom. Right 4 and Right 5 will be in the same position as each other horizontally (match at the heel) and aligned on the bottom, but about 120 pixels to the right of Right 0 and Right 1 (measured toe to toe). Right 2 will be closer to Right 1 than Right 3, suggesting acceleration between Right 2 and Right 3. Right 3 will be closer to Right 4 and 5 than Right 3, suggesting deceleration between Right 4 and Right 5.

7. Turn on views for the left layers and duplicate Left 5. Rename the duplicate Left 0 and place it below the Left 1 layer.

8. Duplicate Left 5, name the copy Left 0, and then position the left shoes. You can either repeat the steps used for positioning the right shoes or use the Right shoes as a guide. The latter is probably easiest if you turn on the view for the same number of layers and align them. Alignment does not have to be perfect, but you'll want it to be pretty close. When you are satisfied that the layers are positioned, link them.

9. Choose the Move tool, click the image, hold down the Shift key, and slide the Left shoes to the right (they should all move in unison) until Left 0 is centered between Right 0 and Right 5. You can turn on the view for Right 0 and Right 5 and Left 0 to make the image less distracting. Be sure the Left 0 image remains linked to all the other Left images— they will move even though you can't see them. This will be the basic position for the alternation of the right and left steps.

With the basic movement created for each shoe, you have to create pairings of right and left shoes and combine them in layers. If you created the animation now, you'd see the right shoe move with no left on the screen, and then the left move with no right. The shoes will have to be in pairs at all times. We'll start with the shoes in a stationary position and then take a step with the right shoe. You should save the image at this point using a name that will not be the same as the final one (such as `SeparateShoes.psd`). You may need to come back to this image for adjustments.

10. Duplicate the Left 0 layer, call the layer Right-Left 0, and then shut off the view for all layers except Right 0 and Right-Left 0.

Figure 10.12

When all the layered images are set in place for one of the shoes, the result will look something like this when all the layers are showing.

11. Drag the Right-Left 0 layer directly below Right 0, activate Right 0, and then Merge Down. Shut off the view for Right-Left 0.

12. Repeat Steps 10 and 11 five more times, naming the duplicate of Left 0 in sequence (Right-Left 1, Right-Left 2, Right-Left 3, Right-Left 4 and Right-Left 5) dragging the duplicated layer each time just below the number pairing for the Right shoe. You should end up with 6 Right-Left layers numbered 0-6 (see Figure 10.13). When you get to Right 5, duplicate it before merging with Right-Left 5 and shut off the view. You'll need the extra copy of the Right 5 layer for the Left-Right shoe series. Name the duplicate Right 0 and shut off the view.

These steps complete the right step, moving the shoe through the motion with the left shoe stationary in the scene. Next, the left shoe needs to be animated. The position of the final frame for the right and left shoes is actually the position the shoes are in at the start of the left shoe movement.

13. Be sure that all the Left layers are linked, then turn on the view for Left 0 and drag the left shoes so the Left 0 shoe is aligned with the left shoe on the Right-Left 5 layer. Then shut off the view for Right-Left 5.

14. Duplicate the Right 0 layer. The shoe should fall between Left 0 and Left 5.

15. Throw out the Left 0 layer, and shut off the views for all layers except Right 0 and Left 1.

16. Drag the Right 0 copy layer to just above Left 1 in the layer stack.

17. Merge the Right 0 copy with Left 1 and rename the layer Left-Right 1. Shut off the view for Left-Right 1.

18. Duplicate Right 0 and drag the copy above Left 2.

19. Merge the Right 0 copy with Left 2 and rename the layer Left-Right 2. Shut off the view for Left-Right 2.

20. Repeat Steps 18 and 19 by duplicating Right 0 and dragging the copy above the next Left shoe in the series (Left 3, Left 4, and Left 5), then merge and rename the resulting layer Left-Right and numbered according to the sequence (Left-Right 3, Left-Right 4, and Left-Right 5).

21. Throw out the Right 0 layer. At this point the layer stack should look like Figure 10.14.

At this point the right-left left-right series is complete. You need to duplicate it three times and then align the duplicates to complete the step series. You could spend a long time duplicating those layers and realigning, but there is a little trick that lets you duplicate multiple layers to speed the process:

22. Create a new RGB image. Make it the same size as your animation image. Name it Duplicator in the New Image dialog box.

23. Activate the original image and position it so that you can see part of the Duplicator image window.

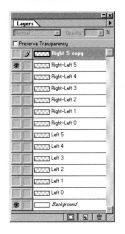

Figure 10.13

After combining the Right layers with the Right-Left layers, your layers palette should look like this.

Figure 10.14

After combining the Right 0 copy layers with the Left layers, your layers palette should look like this.

24. Link all of the Right-Left and Left-Right layers, choose the Move tool, click the Animation image, and hold the Shift key. Drag to the cursor over the Duplicator image window, and then release the mouse button. The layers will copy to the Duplicator image—they will have the same layer names, and they will be linked. The shoes will be centered on the image.

> Trying to drag from the Layers palette will not work. You need to drag from the image window to successfully copy multiple layers.

At this point, you have the step sets in the Duplicator and the Animation image. You will use the sets in the Duplicator to duplicate the sets of layers into the Animation as needed. This process saves you from having to duplicate the sets of layers one layer at a time.

25. Activate the topmost layer in the Duplicator image, and then switch to the Animation image and activate the topmost layer there. In both images this should be Left-Right 5. Activating the top layer assures that the copies you make will stack on top of the other layers in the image.

26. Activate the Duplicator image and position the window so that you can see the Animation window below.

27. Click the image, hold the Shift key, and then drag the cursor from the Duplicator image to the Animation window.

28. Repeat Steps 26 and 27 two more times.

You'll now have 44 layers in the Animation image. These will be four complete sets of the 11-step series.

29. Close the Duplicator window and don't bother saving it.

30. Turn off the visibility for all the layers.

31. Hold down the Shift key and click the Right-Left 3 layer in the Layers palette closest to the bottom of the stack. This will display the linkages in the Layers palette and you will see only Right-Left 3 in the Animation image window.

32. Using the Move tool, drag the shoes so that the left shoe just exits the left side of the screen.

33. In the Layers palette, turn on the view for the linked Left-Right 5 layer and shut off the view for Right-Left 3.

34. Hold the Shift key and click the next Right-Left 0 layer up in the layer stack. This will show all the layers linked to it in the Layers palette, and will turn on the view for the layer.

35. Drag the Right-Left 0 shoes and align them with the Left-Right 5 shoes.

36. Delete the active Right-Left 0 layer from the layers palette.

37. Repeat Steps 34 to 36 two more times.

When you are done, you will have four full right-left series, and they should be perfectly aligned. The shoes will start off the screen at the left, and then traverse the image heading toward the right. At this point, save the image (using a new name) and then run through the steps for creating an animation using the Save For Web option. This may take a few minutes to generate, but you will end up with a 41-step animated GIF. This image can be opened in a web browser and you will see the shoes appear to walk across the screen.

There is more that you can do with this. You can, of course, keep going with the animation and just walk the shoes off the other side of the screen, or you could add other elements to the image. For example, if you were doing a website banner for shoe deodorant pads, you might have the shoes walk across and stop, then have the pads fly into them, and then have flowers bloom out of the shoes. A slogan might pop up saying something like, "Leave 'em smelling like a rose." Using the same shoes, you might do a banner for a health insurance company by having the shoes walk into an open manhole and then displaying the words, "Don't get caught in a hole uncovered," then roll in a manhole cover displaying the insurance company insignia and name. You could use it for a graphic website that has tutorials by showing the shoes walking in and then displaying the slogan, "Short steps to better images"; the shoes could stop their walk in front of an image that could fill with color. In other words, these same shoes can be reused for different purposes. You will, of course, need to make adjustments to the animation to make the shoes fall in a hole or stop.

The point is that the only limitation is your creativity. By creating a series of controlled movements frame by frame, you develop the elements necessary to make objects appear to be animated. Careful attention to image placement, movement, and timing in frames per second can help you decide where image elements need to be placed and how to control them. Photoshop Elements can help do some complicated work in the compilation and creation of frames, and can save a completed animation as a single complete unit.

Looking Beyond the Book

Throughout the course of this book, we have looked at a simple set of image tools and how they have the power to do everything you need:

- You've looked at image color: how to take apart an image using three different color methods, and correct image color.
- You've extracted image elements from a scene, created new image elements, and taken static image elements and made them appear to move.
- You've taken images and implemented them on the Web and in print after adjusting them.
- You've gained control over Curves, snapshots, the History Brush, blend masks, channels, clipping paths, CMYK, and other Hidden Power Tools.

Doing all of this in the relatively short expanse of this book might have seemed, at the outset, impossible. Hopefully you now consider yourself able to do the impossible. If you do, that means I've done what I set out to do by writing this book.

While that is an achievement, there is also more to talk about, more to learn, and more image problems to tackle. In other words, this book does not end here. You can creatively combine the information, tools, and techniques described and indulged here in a myriad of different ways to make image solutions. You might occasionally need a helping hand from another program, but the entire point is that Photoshop Elements is an enormously powerful tool that can help you do anything you need to do with an image.

Please feel free to visit me at the book's website at `www.hiddenelements.com`, and sign up for the book's newsletter (send a blank e-mail to `hpe-subscribe@yahoogroups.com`). The site has additional information to specifically help readers of this book. You'll be able to ask questions, get answers, and communicate with other serious Elements users. The information provided on the site is also my way of making sure the book does not end with the last page, so that you can get help when you need it, and it also ensures that this book is a jump-off point for your creativity rather than a static tome that leaves you with no place to go. Please feel free to send me your comments and questions (`rl@hiddenelements.com`), and I'll do my best to get to as many as I can. I look forward to hearing from you and helping you grow your abilities with Photoshop Elements.

Original scene

Blue light (using a blue lens filter)

Green light (using a green lens filter)

Red light (obtained by using a red filter on the lens)

This image by Prokudin-Gorskii, titled *Man in Uniform, Seated on Chair, Outside*, was taken around 1910 by separating color into red, green, and blue components using color filters on the lenses. [Chapter 1]

Red light

Red Tone

Green light

Green Tone

The filtered light was captured on black-and-white glass plates, encoding the color information before there was ever color film. [Chapter 1]

Blue light

Blue Tone

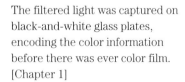

Red Tone   Green Tone   Blue Tone

Red light   Green light   Blue light

Restored original

With Photoshop Elements, you can use color properties and layer modes to turn the plates to a color image again—almost 100 years later—re-creating the scene that Prokudin-Gorskii created in full color from the black-and-white plates. [Chapter 1]

Original

Red   Green   Blue

Any image breaks down into the red, green, and blue components using the RGB separation process.
[Chapter 2]

Original

Color

Luminosity

Any image will also break down into the color and luminosity components using color and luminosity separation. [Chapter 2]

Original

Tone

Color

By separating how you work with color and tone, either or both can be optimized individually and enhanced to produce a better result. Here, color is separated from tone… [Chapter 2]

Original color

Tone

Enhanced color

Combined result

…and when the color is adjusted, color and tone are re-assembled for the final result.
[Chapter 2]

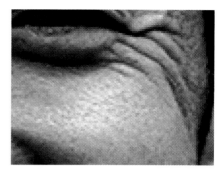

Close-up of original

Original

Close-up of blur only

Blending adjustments made with noise and blur can reduce and eliminate image problems while retaining the realistic image qualities. [Chapter 3]

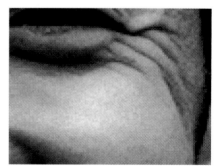

Close-up of mixed blur and noise

Before

After

Applying tonal manipulations, masking adjustments and working to mediate noise (sometimes adding, sometimes removing) can help you take images on the brink of being useless and bring them back to life. [Chapter 3]

Before

After

Simple adjustments with Levels can correct color imbalances, brighten tone, and make images more dynamic in seconds. [Chapter 4]

Before

After

Level adjustments to Luminosity can enhance tone and detail without effecting image color. [Chapter 4]

Before

After

Use Curves and separations to make fine-tuning adjustments that are accurate. [Chapter 4]

Before

After

You can enhance existing color, target color correction to color ranges, and selectively make color adjustment using masking techniques. [Chapter 5]

Reduce digital color noise in your camera shots easily by using separations to extract color from the tone of your images. [Chapter 5]

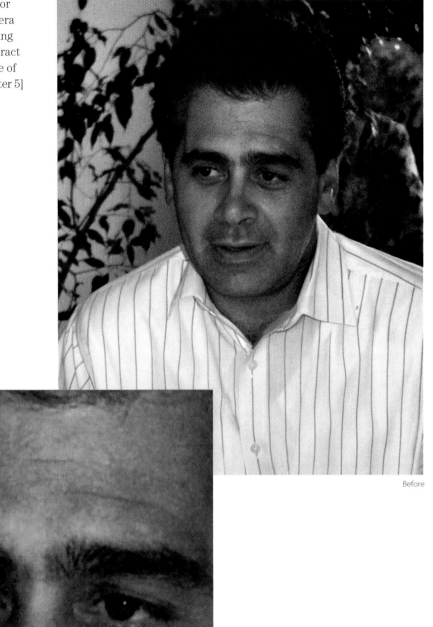

Before

Close-up

After

Close-up

Before

After

Recolor images or apply filter effects with brushes using History Brush effects. [Chapter 5]

Original tone

Spot color

Black

Duotone color result

Black-and-white images can be given some color using
duotoning techniques. [Chapter 5]

Original

Separated duotone (black)

Separated duotone (spot color)

Duotone result

Grayscale conversion from Duotone

You can color images with duotone, or you can use properties of duotoning to correct and enhance black-and-white tone. [Chapter 5]

Purple flowers

Original pink flowers

Blue flowers

Color isolation using masking, or techniques using calculations and color mixing—or both—can help you gain unique control over colors in your image. [Chapter 6]

Darkened, blurred background

Original

Recolored

Controlling the blur and brightness around a subject using selection and masking can help it stand out in the image or allow you to recolor any way you want. [Chapter 6]

A simple fill pattern

An adjusted fill pattern

You can create image patterns to rebuild image areas. Some selective work and randomizing can make a patterned fill more realistic and all but undetectable. [Chapter 7]

The original image

A simple replacement drop-shadow

A more accurate shadow replacement

You can create shadows in several different ways. These images show the original image (with a shadow distorted by the camera lens), a simple drop shadow, and a more accurate shadow created using elements from the image. [Chapter 7]

 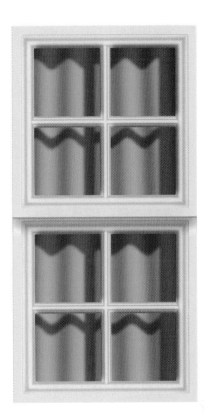

Elements such as this window can be created from scratch and given realistic dimension using shadows. [Chapter 7]

The original image

In a similar way that you can take apart color and re-arrange (or rebuild) image color, this original image can be separated and rebuilt entirely from parts to improve various aspects of the final image. [Chapter 7]

The adjusted composite

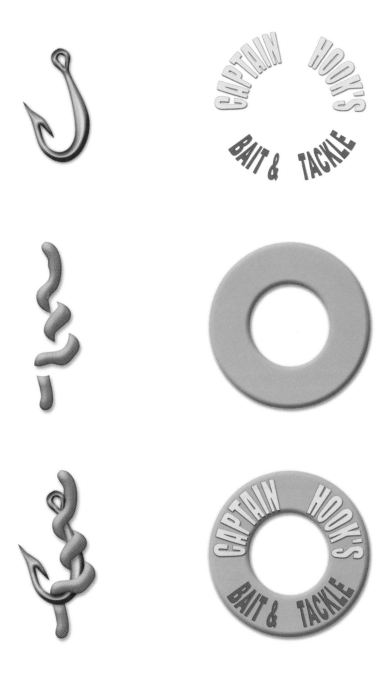

It is possible to make illustrations, logos, and other high-quality vector art with Photoshop Elements. This figure shows a breakdown of the parts of an image created entirely with vectors. The composite result appears on the facing page. [Chapter 8]

Captain Hook's logo can be scaled infinitely and re-applied to any project, from a business card to a billboard and beyond. [Chapter 8]

In CMYK color, all color is represented by cyan, magenta, yellow, and black. This figure shows a breakdown of the colors. Being able to control your CMYK output can be the key to getting better color in print. [Chapter 9]

Normal

Click

Over

Out

Down

Up

You can design up to six different rollover states to implement in your images to help you control how the page looks and what happens as the visitor navigates your website. [Chapter 10]

Employing several Hidden Power tools you can perform impossible stunts like creating custom CMYK color separations from your RGB images without leaving Photoshop Elements and creating CMYK files for print [Chapter 5].

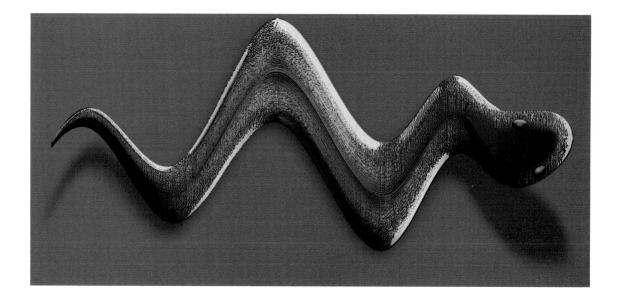

Images can be built almost entirely using Filters and Effects such as this snake and fire effect. Special effects can be discussed on the Hidden Power website and list server. [http://www.hiddenelements.com]

A lot of your work will be simplified or made possible using the Hidden Power Tools found on the CD. Access the power tools by installing them from the CD, then opening the tools menu by viewing the How To palette (the Recipes palette in Elements 1) and clicking the Hidden Power link. [Hidden Power Tools on CD]

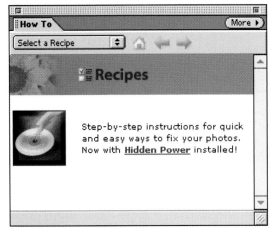

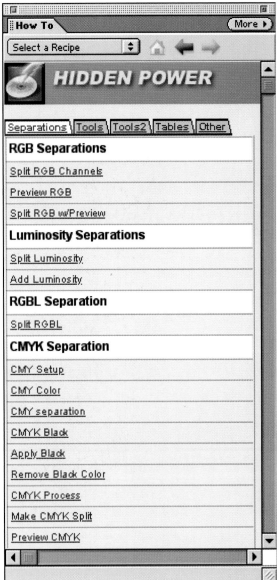

Appendix

Other Concepts and References

This appendix provides some background information that doesn't fit a particular topic in the book but that might be handy anywhere. Topics such as these are sometimes buried in obscure places, presented incorrectly on the Web, or just plain too difficult to find when you really need them.

The toolbox

Resolution

File types

Bit depth

Blending modes

The Toolbox

Table A.1 lists and describes the toolbox tools and shortcuts for selecting them. Figure A.1 maps the tools as they appear on screen. If you learn to use the shortcuts (from the map or the table), you don't have to waste time hunting for tools on the toolbar.

Figure A.1

An exploded view of the toolbar

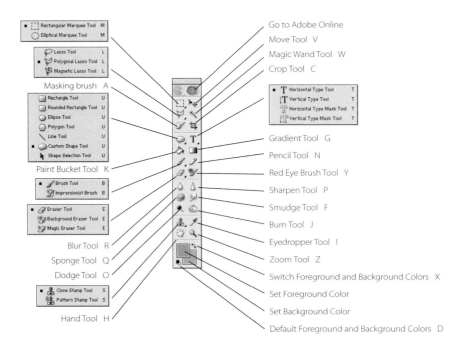

To remove the toolbox from your display, choose Windows → Tools to uncheck the option. To cycle through the toolbox from your display that have the same shortcut, press Shift and the shortcut letter.

Table A.1

Photoshop Elements Tools

TOOL NAME	SHORTCUT	DESCRIPTION
Rectangular Marquee	M	Makes a rectangular or square selection.
Elliptical Marquee	M	Makes a circular or oval selection.
Lasso	L	Makes a freeform selection formed by dragging the cursor with the mouse.
Polygonal Lasso	L	Makes a polygon-shaped selection formed by clicking the mouse to mark the endpoints of the polygon sides.
Magnetic Lasso	L	Makes a freeform selection formed by the selection lasso snapping to the edges of contrasting tones or colors.
Selection Brush	A	Paints a freeform masked area based on brush size and dynamics. The unpainted area is converted to a selection when the user selects another tool.
Move	V	Moves active (and linked) image areas
Magic Wand	W	Selects similar colors or tones based on a specified sample area and tolerance range.
Crop	C	Resizes canvas (can result in a larger or smaller image than current canvas).

TOOL NAME	SHORTCUT	DESCRIPTION
Rectangle	U	Creates a vector rectangle shape. Creates a new shape layer if a non-shape layer is currently active.
Rounded Rectangle	U	Creates a vector rectangle shape with rounded corners. Creates a new shape layer if a non-shape layer is currently active.
Ellipse	U	Creates a vector ellipse (circle or oval) shape. Creates a new shape layer if a non-shape layer is currently active.
Polygon	U	Creates a vector polygon shape with an even number of sides, based on the number of sides specified on the Options bar. Creates a new shape layer if a non-shape layer is currently active.
Line	U	Creates a vector line with a width in pixels specified by the Weight field on the Options bar. Creates a new shape layer if a non-shape layer is currently active.
Custom Shape	U	Creates a custom vector shape using the custom shape selected on the Options bar. Creates a new shape layer if a non-shape layer is currently active.
Shape Selection	U	Activates or moves shape layer components.
Paint Bucket	K	Based on the tolerance and selections specified on the Options bar, fills an area with the foreground color or a pattern. Colors the image matte if used over the matte area while the Shift key is pressed.
Brush	B	Paints with the selected brush using the foreground color and brush dynamics (click More Options on the Options bar).
Impressionist Brush	B	Paints with the selected stylized brush using sampled color and brush dynamics (click More Options on the options bar).
Eraser	E	Changes the erased area to the background color (when used on the background) or to transparent (when used on a layer).
Background Eraser	E	Changes the erased area to transparent based on the settings specified on the Options bar. Changes the background to a layer if applied to the background (using color modes that support layers).
Magic Eraser	E	Changes the erased area to transparent based on sample point and tolerance. Changes the background to a layer if applied to background (using color modes that support layers).
Horizontal Type	T	Places entered text horizontally using the font selection, point size, and other dynamics selected on the Options bar.
Vertical Type	T	Places entered text vertically using the font selection, point size, and other dynamics selected on the Options bar.
Horizontal Type Mask	T	Creates a selection based on horizontally entered text, font, point size, and other dynamics selected on the Options bar.
Vertical Type Mask	T	Creates a selection based on vertically entered text, font, point size, and other dynamics selected on the Options bar.
Gradient	G	Fills an area with a blend of one or more colors based on the gradient, applied direction, and gradient type (Linear, Radial, Angle, Reflect or Diamond), selected on the Options bar.
Pencil	N	Creates a hard-edged freehand line based on the selected brush.
Red Eye Brush	Y	Replaces the color of the brushed area with the replacement color defined on the Options bar, according to a sample area (the tool samples the initial click point).
Blur	R	Softens hard edges or areas in an image to reduce detail, based on the brush size and dynamics selected on the Options bar.
Sponge	Q	Changes the color saturation or vividness of an area defined by the brush selected on the Options bar. In Grayscale mode, the Sponge tool increases or decreases contrast by moving gray levels away from or toward neutral gray.
Dodge	O	Lightens areas where you drag the cursor based on the range (Highlight, Midtones, or Shadows), brush size, and dynamics specified on the Options bar.

continued

continues

TOOL NAME	SHORTCUT	DESCRIPTION
Sharpen	P	Applies a sharpening calculation to the area where you drag the cursor based on the brush size and dynamics specified on the Options bar.
Smudge	F	Either smudges the existing colors in your image or smears new color through your image based on the direction you drag the cursor, the brush size, and the dynamics specified on the Options bar.
Burn	J	Darkens areas where you drag the cursor based on the range (Highlight, Midtones, or Shadows), brush size, and dynamics specified on the Options bar.
Clone Stamp	S	Copies sampled pixels from one part of an image to another based on the brush size and dynamics specified on the Options bar.
Pattern Stamp	S	Paints with a selected pattern based on the brush size and dynamics specified on the Options bar.
Hand	H	Allows the user to grab the canvas and scroll to navigate a magnified image where all of the image cannot be viewed at one time.
Eyedropper	I	Samples color from the image based on a single pixel or pixel area (according to selected Options). Places the color in the foreground or background (when the Shift key is pressed). Often used with the Info palette.
Zoom	Z	Increases (zoom in) and decreases (zooms out) the magnification of image display on screen.
Switch Foreground and Background Colors	X	Exchanges the colors in the Foreground Color and Background Color boxes.
Set Foreground Color		Opens the Color Picker dialog box to allow the specification of a color to fill the Foreground Color box.
Set Background Color		Opens the Color Picker dialog box to allow the specification of a color to fill the Background Color box.
Default Foreground and Background Colors	D	Restores the Foreground Color and Background Color boxes to their default colors.

Resolution

Several resolution factors can affect your results in Photoshop Elements. These factors include input resolution, monitor resolution, and output resolution.

Input Resolution

Table A.2

Common Camera Resolutions

Digital camera resolution is weighted in dimension, total pixels, or both, but that doesn't tell you how big the resulting images will be. Table A.2 offers a brief overview using common camera abilities and maximum output size (in inches).

CAMERA RESOLUTION	TOTAL PIXELS	MAX. FINAL SIZE FOR WEB/MONITOR (96DPI)	MAX. FINAL SIZE FOR PHOTO-QUALITY (200DPI)	MAX. NEGATIVE / CHROME OUTPUT (650DPI)
320×200	64,000	3.3×2	1.6×1	0.5×0.3
640×480	307,200	6.7×5	3.2×2.4	1×0.75
1024×768	786,432	10.7×8	5×3.75	1.5×1.1
1280×960	1,228,800	13.3×10	6×4.75	1.8×1.5
1600×1200	1,920,000	16.7×12.5	8×6	2.5×1.8
2048×1536	3,145,728	21.3×16	10×7.5	3.1×2.3
2400×1800	4,320,000	25×18.75	12×9	3.7×2.8

Monitor Resolution and Settings

Monitor resolution affects how images appear on screen. Most people will just set monitor resolution to the highest setting suggested by the manufacturer and assume that it is correct—or assume that it doesn't matter. If you set your monitor resolution too high (greater than the monitor was built to handle), you can actually lose detail rather than improve it, and images can appear or present too small. If you set the resolution too low things will appear larger, and you won't take advantage of the viewing landscape on your monitor.

The maximum monitor resolution setting is dictated by the monitor's viewing size and dot pitch. Viewing size is simply the monitor area; dot pitch is, essentially, the resolution—the number of image dots that can be represented. The greater the viewing size or the lower the dot pitch, the more the monitor can show. A larger monitor will tend to have a higher dot pitch than a smaller one. Higher-dot-pitch monitors will tend to look sharper—depending on the type of display.

There are more complicated means of selecting a monitor display resolution, but in my estimation choosing the "right" resolution is choosing the resolution that makes the image appear correctly sized on screen. Choosing the right resolution has the advantage of letting you see things close to the correct size on screen, while pretty much eliminating the chance that your monitor doesn't have enough resolution. Any monitor with a dot pitch of less than .28 (about .22 horizontally) should be able to handle the range that I suggest while viewing sharply. This does not mean that having a higher-resolution monitor is wasted; finer dot pitch almost always translates into finer image display. Using a higher resolution can also have the advantage of making palettes and menus smaller, leaving more space on the screen to work.

Table A.3 is a guideline to help you create an accurately sized image on screen, and will give you a target to shoot for. It may not be exact, because there are variables in displays, but it should take you closer than just guessing at a size or choosing the maximum suggested resolution willy-nilly (or based on what you think might look good when you have the monitor control panel open). The point is that when you choose View → Print Size, your image will be close to displaying on screen at the size you intend to use it.

Monitor screen size is measured from corner to corner diagonally rather than as height or width. If you are unsure of your monitor size, a quick measure of the diagonal surface area of the screen will tell you approximately what the view size is for your monitor. Choose an available display resolution in the monitor control panel that falls between the range shown in the table (between 72 and 96 ppi) to get the most accurate sizing.

DIAGONAL VIEW SIZE	72 PPI RESOLUTION	96 PPI RESOLUTION
21"+	1600+	
21"	1280×1024	1600×1200
19"	1152×870	1280×1024
17"	1024×768	1152×870
15"	870×640	1024×768
13"	800×600	870×640

Table A.3

Common Monitor Sizes and Resolutions

If you prefer to have a very accurate view of print size on screen, you can choose your resolution roughly and make adjustments in the horizontal and vertical projection of the monitor to make the display dimensions nearly exact. To do this, you can match a display ruler (show rulers on an open image displaying at 100%) to a household one using horizontal and vertical screen controls.

Number of Colors

You may be able to change your color settings to anything between monochrome and 32-bit color in your control panel, and as with resolution, it might be tempting to always pick the maximum. These settings may be presented as bits or number of colors (depending on the operating system and the utility or control panel you are using for the setting). The more bits or colors, the more true-to-life color can be; at the same time, the more taxing the color processing can be, so this may result in potentially lower refresh rates. Optimally you will want to choose to display the most bits you can, but if you have a less powerful video card and a large monitor, or if you are offered fewer choices for refresh rates, it may be best to choose fewer bits as a tradeoff. Your images store 24-bit information (3×8 bits) in Photoshop Elements at maximum, so displaying at 32-bit is not necessarily better for viewing image color.

Refresh Rate

Refresh rate is the frequency at which an image on the screen is updated or refreshed. The rate is measured in Hertz (Hz). The higher the frequency (the more Hz), the faster the screen refreshes. The faster it refreshes, the less likely you are to detect flicker, and the more likely that your view of changes and movement on the screen (such as the cursor) will seem smooth. Quick refresh rates can also reduce eyestrain. This can be important if, like some of us, you spend a lot of time staring at your monitor.

Use only suggested refresh rates for your monitor and video card or you can run the risk of damaging your equipment. Refresh rates should be as fast as you can make them within the manufacturer's suggested range without cutting into other display properties that reduce performance in other ways.

Print Resolutions

Table A.4 shows some real-world examples of output resolution and workable ppi ranges. Calculations for the table were based on the formulas shown in the Calculation Used column; square brackets in the calculations indicate the range of values used to determine the lowest and highest resolution acceptable in that media. This table can be handy for choosing a rough estimate of file size, and you can use the equations for calculating more specific results. The table also assumes you will be printing the image at 100% of the image size; resizing the image in layout or another program will affect the calculations. Check with your printing service for their recommendations before blindly assigning these estimates.

MEDIA	MEDIA RESOLUTION BASE	APPROXIMATE FILE RESOLUTION (PPI)	CALCULATION USED
Web page	Mac/PC monitor	72–96 ppi	ppi = dpi
Poster plotter	300 dpi printer resolution	100–150 ppi	[.33 to .5] × dpi
Inkjet (stochastic) prints	720 dpi	180–234 ppi	[1 to 1.3] × (dpi / 4)
Inkjet (stochastic) prints	1440 dpi	360–468 ppi	[1 to 1.3] × (dpi / 4)
Newsprint	75–120 lpi	117–240 ppi	[1.55 to 2] dpi
Coated paper (books, magazines, etc.)	133–175 lpi	207–350 dpi	[1.55 to 2] lpi
Art publications	175–200 lpi	271–400 ppi	[1.55 to 2] lpi
Line art	Printer output resolution	600–1342ppi	$(dpi/600)^{1/} \times 600$
Film recorder	4K lines, 35mm	2731×4096 pixels	Total pixels
Film recorder	8K lines, 2.5+	5461×8192 pixels	Total pixels

Table A.4

Approximate Resolutions for Various Media

Interpolation

Say you have a pixel-based image at 5×7 and it has 300 ppi. That will print well to a variety of outputs at the original size (although there may be too little or too much resolution for some options). If you want to resize it or apply it at a different size by changing the dimension, the ppi, or both, there are many possible results. Table A.5 looks at these possibilities (all based on an original image that is 5×7 @ 300 ppi).

File Types

When saving an image, you have to select a file type. To choose the right one, it is handy to know what the available file types are and generally what they are used for. Table A.6 gives a brief overview of file types supported when saving from Photoshop Elements. Other file types are supported as "open only," meaning that you can open the files, but you will have to save them as something else.

Compression

Some file compression encoding is known as *lossy* in that it loses information from the original image information due to translation. In some instances, it is desirable to sacrifice some image quality for file size. For example, this is done with JPEG Web images to speed transfer. You might want to stick to lossless translations unless loss of information in images is okay or even desirable for your purposes.

Image-type compression (JPEG, LZW, GIF, and so on) should be considered differently than file compression. File compression (ZIP, SIT, SEA, MIME, and so on) is always lossless as it acts on the file information independent of it being an image. Image-type compressions act on image information to achieve compression.

Table A.5

Potential Resize Methods

DESIRED CHANGE	INTERPOLATION METHOD	APPLIED IMAGE SIZE (INCHES)	EFFECTIVE IMAGE PPI	RESULT	COMMENT
Increase file dimension with same ppi	Bicubic	8×10	300	Increasing the number of pixels causes image information to be added or faked.	The result will probably not be much better than applying the original image without interpolation. It will most probably be a bit soft. Image content may affect the results. Bicubic interpolation works best with blended tones (photographs).
Increase file dimension with same ppi	Nearest Neighbor	8×10	300	Increasing the number of pixels causes image information to be added or faked.	The result will be almost exactly like applying the original image without interpolation. It will most probably be a bit soft, and may be blockier than Bicubic interpolated results. Image content may affect the results. Nearest Neighbor interpolation works best with solid color and lines (screenshots).
Increase file dimension with lower ppi	Bicubic	8×10	72	Disproportional changes in ppi and dimension (in this case, decreasing the ppi dramatically while increasing the dimension) cause image information to be changed (in this case, lost).	Even though the size of the file increases in this case, the result is that there is less information in the file because of the lower ppi. While this 8×10 may display fine on screen and on the Web, the result in print will most likely be soft and undesirable.
Increase file dimension without interpolation	None	8×10	210	Proportional changes in ppi and dimension result in the same image information being distributed over a new area. There is no change in file information (or file size).	This will provide a very similar result to applying the image at increased ppi. The resolution could probably be better targeted to the desired output.
Increase (double) the ppi	Bicubic	5×7	600	Increasing the number of pixels causes image information to be added or faked.	This file will have too much resolution for just about any type of output. It can slow processing and increase file sizes unnecessarily, without improving output quality.
No change	None	5×7	300	Applied at file dimensions.	This is the targeted application of this pixel-based image.

DESIRED CHANGE	INTERPOLATION METHOD	APPLIED IMAGE SIZE (INCHES)	EFFECTIVE IMAGE PPI	RESULT	COMMENT
Decrease ppi	Bicubic	5×7	72	Decreasing ppi and keeping the dimensions the same removes information from the image.	While this can be fine for the Web, this file will have too little resolution for most types of printed output. It may look fine on screen, but that shouldn't be the determining factor.
Decrease file dimension without interpolation	None	3.5×5	429	Proportional changes in ppi and dimension result in the same image information distributed over a new area. There is no change in file information (or file size).	By decreasing the file dimension without interpolating, this file will have too much resolution for just about any type of output. It can slow processing and increase file sizes unnecessarily.
Decrease file dimension with lower ppi	Bicubic	3.5×5	72	Decreasing file dimension and ppi at the same time removes information from the image.	This image takes a double-whammy in decreasing both dimension and ppi. While it will be suited to screen display (and may not look too much different on screen than the display of the two options that follow), results in print will probably not be satisfactory.
Decrease file dimension with higher ppi	Nearest Neighbor	3.5×5	300	Disproportional changes in ppi and dimension (in this case, decreasing the dimension while retaining ppi) cause image information to be changed (in this case, discarded or lost).	Resizing an image smaller is usually less damaging to the result than attempting to add information to the image. While making images smaller shrinks the pixel base and merges and loses information, it tends to matter less than increasing image size. Nearest Neighbor interpolation, unless used with great care, is not usually your best choice in decreasing image size. Results will probably be better in most cases with Bicubic (or perhaps Bilinear) interpolation.
Decrease file dimension with higher ppi	Bicubic	3.5×5	300	Disproportional changes in ppi and dimension (in this case, decreasing the dimension while retaining ppi) cause image information to be changed (in this case, lost).	Generally it is fine to re-purpose an image by decreasing its size. Because the result will merge and blur somewhat, sharpening is recommended. Using Bicubic resizing actually invests a little sharpening for you, so that additional sharpening may not be necessary. If possible, work with images at the intended size for best results.

FILE TYPE	SAVE AS COLOR MODES	PURPOSE/USE
Photoshop document (PSD)	All	Native Photoshop Elements format. Store working/in progress Photoshop images.
Bitmap (BMP)	All	Traditionally a Windows-based file format. PC Screenshot format. Lossless compression.
CompuServe Graphics Interchange Format (GIF)	All	Web graphics. Uses an indexed-color palette (256 colors max) to achieve compression—colors are converted during save if not already indexed. Conversion to GIF from images with more than 256 color will cause image information loss.
Encapsulated PostScript (EPS)	All	Mostly used in postscript printing to retain vector, pixel, and separation information. Does not support alphas. Can use JPEG compression.
Joint Photographic Experts Group (JPEG)	Grayscale, RGB	Often used for full-color Web graphics, and digital camera image storage. Uses variable, lossy compression in storage, which can damage images over repeated saves. Better color retention than GIF.
PC Exchange (PCX)	All	Another bitmap format like PCT and BMP. Uses lossless compression.
Portable Document Format (PDF)	All	Designed by Adobe Systems to allow viewing of PostScript encoded documents (using Acrobat products such as Reader). Uses compression including lossless ZIP encoding and lossy JPEG. Compression can be controlled separately for color, grayscale and monochrome (bitmap) images. Highly portable between platforms and used broadly in print applications.
Photoshop 2.0	All	Native Photoshop format with backward compatibility to earlier versions.
PICT file (PCT)	All	The Mac equivalent of Windows BMP.
PICT resource (RSR)	All	Files used in resource forks (such as icon graphics).
Pixar Computer Image (PXR)	Grayscale, RGB	Specially designed for Pixar Image workstations, for editing rendered graphics to return to a Pixar format.
Portable Network Graphics (PNG)	All	Developed as a royalty-free replacement for GIF. Supports transparency and animation (but not via Elements). Supports both lossless and lossy compression (but not via Elements).
RAW (RAW)	Grayscale, Indexed Color, RGB	Undefined or raw image data. No compression. Can be used for custom deciphering or encoding of file formats that are otherwise unsupported by Photoshop (e.g., raw digital camera files).
Scitex CT (SCT)	Grayscale, RGB	Developed by Scitex for proprietary image-processing systems. Used with high-end scanning devices. No compression.
Targa (TGA)	Grayscale, Indexed Color, RGB	Most common in the video industry; also used by high-end paint and ray-tracing programs because of expanded bit depth. For specific application in video output. No compression via Elements.
Tagged Image File Format (TIFF)	All	A broadly used, general-purpose file type for printed output. Supports most native Photoshop Elements file features. Supports lossless compression.
Wireless BMP	BMP	For application on wireless networks.

Bit Depth

Bits and bit depth have been known to cause confusion, and understanding them may be important to shushing those ghosts from the closets in your mind. A big deal is made of 16-bit image editing, or how many bits a scanner or camera can capture. If you don't have the foggiest what bits are, that can lead right to the bus stop of confusion.

Bits represent how exactly color can be measured. They are the little encoded 1s and 0s used in computer language to describe an image. Each pixel color in your image is described by the bits. The more bits, the greater the potential accuracy of the color.

Bits themselves are just tiny chunks of information—sometimes described by the term "binary." All that term means is that each bit used in your files can be either on or off. So each bit has only two possible values: either on (1) or off (0). If an image is one-bit, each pixel in the image can be on or off. That is pretty much black and white.

The more bits per pixel, the more complex the relationship gets. If your image is a two-bit image, each bit has two potential values, and these values can be paired in any of these combinations: 00, 01, 10, or 11 to define the pixel. Each additional bit per pixel adds a multiple of two combinations, one additional set of combinations for each additional bit. Just to show how quickly this can add up, if a third bit were added to your two-bit image, this would result in the following set of possibilities for each pixel: 000, 001, 010, 011, 100, 101, 110, 111—a total of eight possible combinations. So each time another bit is added, there are twice as many possible combinations—one additional full set of possibilities for each of the two possible values of the bit.

To get the total number of bit combinations, all you have to do is multiply by two for each bit. Eight bits per channel would be $2{\times}2{\times}2{\times}2{\times}2{\times}2{\times}2{\times}2$ (or 2^8) totaling 256 combinations. In a 24-bit image, that would be 2^{24}. This is actually calculated differently, as the 24 bits in a 24-bit image are used to describe three tones: R, G, and B. A 24-bit RGB image uses only 8 bits for each of the tones: 8 bits red, 8 bits green, and 8 bits blue. These 3 groups of 8 bits describe the 256 tonal possibilities for red, green, and blue. Each of the colors has 256 possibilities that can be combined in any fashion. Whether you multiply 2^{24}, or $256 \times 256 \times 256$, you get the same number of bit combinations: 16,777,216. That is how many colors each pixel can represent in 24-bit color. If you add bits, you add potential colors: if you have an image with 30 bits, there would be 10 bits per channel, or 1024 bit combinations per pixel per color, or 1,073,741,824 different potential combinations. That is 64 times as many color combinations, with only a few more bits.

In other words, increased pixel depth exponentially increases the color possibilities, which is why increased color depth is considered potentially so valuable in color work. The negative effect of increased bit depth (for example, to 16 bits per channel from 8) is increased image size. There is also some question as to the value of increased bit depth. In fact, it seems almost useless for anything but initial corrections for two reasons:

1. If you have 16 million colors, it is not incredibly likely that having even more is going to have a lot of effect on the way you see an image.

2. Output in most cases can't reproduce more than 24-bit color.

Increased bit depth can improve the capture of detail in poorly exposed images and may be desirable for archiving. However, 8-bit is more than most people actually need.

Bit terminology can be confusing as the reference to bit depth can be referenced as bits per color/channel, or total bits. If used with care, this shouldn't pose a problem, but it can be confounding when you discover a 16 bit image actually has more image information than a 24 bit color scan. Be sure you are comparing either total bits per pixel, or bits per color/channel when looking at specifications or comparing images. Comparing bits per channel to total bits is like comparing grayscale and color images…Different representations of the same thing, but they are not equivalent.

Blending Modes

Blending modes calculate a result based on the interplay of image information. The original information is altered either physically (with direct application of the mode via a brush mode) or as a visible result (with indirect application applied via layer mode). Different modes combine the information in different ways. A blending mode used in a layer will look at the pixel qualities in the top layer and display a result based on how those combine. When a mode is used with a painting tool, Photoshop Elements looks at the quality of the color being applied (foreground color) as if the color were being applied in a layer, using the selected brush dynamics. The more significant difference is that brush application changes the content of the layer you are painting on to achieve the result.

Modes can create effects using calculations based on select color components. For example, the result might be a calculation of red, green, and blue components (tone and color together), a calculation of luminosity, a calculation of color, etc. Table A.7 describes the blending modes available in Elements.

> Adobe is pretty stingy with the exact calculations. The descriptions are actually obfuscated by the language used to describe them. To simplify: the more obscure and difficult to calculate, the less useful the mode will tend to be in normal use.

BLEND MODE	QUICK KEY	EFFECT
Normal	Shift+Option+N/ Shift+Alt+N	Plain overlay of content. The result takes on the color/tone of the pixels in the upper layer.
Dissolve	Shift+Option+I/ Shift+Alt+I	The result takes on the color/tone of the pixels in the upper layer, but the result is dithered (randomized) according to the opacity of the application. The greater the opacity, the more the selection is weighted to the upper layer. 100% opacity will produce a 0% dissolve effect; 50% opacity will produce a result where 50% of the result has the applied color.
Darken	Shift+Option+K/ Shift+Alt+K	Chooses the darker color value set for each pixel in comparing the two layers. Uses either the applied color or the original. No portion of the image gets lighter.
Multiply	Shift+Option+M/ Shift+Alt+M	Darkens the result by darkening the lower layer based on the darkness of the upper layer. Any applied tone darker than white darkens the result. No portion of the image can get lighter.
Color Burn	Shift+Option+B/ Shift+Alt+B	Burns in (darkens) the color of the underlying layer with the upper layer, darkening the result. No portion of the image gets lighter. The greater the difference between pixel colors, the greater the change.
Linear Burn	Shift+Option+A/ Shift+Alt+A	Similar to Multiply but somewhat more extreme.
Lighten	Shift+Option+G/ Shift+Alt+G	Chooses the lighter color value set for each pixel in comparing the two layers. Uses either the applied color or the original. No portion of the image gets darker.
Screen	Shift+Option+S/ Shift+Alt+S	Brightens the result by lightening the lower layer based on the lightness of the upper layer. Any color lighter than black lightens the result. No portion of the image can get darker.
Color Dodge	Shift+Option+D/ Shift+Alt+D	Dodges (lightens) the color of the underlying layer with the upper layer, lightening the result. No portion of the image gets darker. The greater the difference between pixel colors, the greater the change.
Linear Dodge	Shift+Option+W/ Shift+Alt+W	Similar to Screen but the result is more extreme.
Overlay	Shift+Option+O/ Shift+Alt+O	Multiplies (darkens) the light colors and screens (lightens) the dark ones. Colors at light and dark extremes are affected less than midtones.
Soft Light	Shift+Option+F/ Shift+Alt+F	Multiplies (darkens) the dark colors and screens (lightens) the light ones depending on the applied color. If the applied color is light, the pixel lightens; if dark, it darkens. Soft, or 50% application of the upper layer.
Hard Light	Shift+Option+H/ Shift+Alt+H	Multiplies (darkens) the dark colors and screens (lightens) the light ones. 100% application of the upper layer.
Vivid Light	Shift+Option+V/ Shift+Alt+V	Similar to Color Burn when the applied color is darker than 50% gray; similar to Color Dodge when the applied color is lighter than 50% gray.
Linear Light	Shift+Option+J/ Shift+Alt+J	Similar to Linear Burn when the applied color is darker than 50% gray; similar to Linear Dodge when the applied color is lighter than 50% gray.
Pin Light	Shift+Option+Z/ Shift+Alt+Z	Similar to Multiply when the applied color is darker than 50% gray; similar to Screen when the applied color is lighter than 50% gray.

Table A.7

Photoshop Elements Blending Modes

continued

continues

BLEND MODE	QUICK KEY	EFFECT
Difference	Shift+Option+E/ Shift+Alt+E	Reacts to the difference between pixel values: A large difference yields a bright result; a small difference yields a dark result (no difference yields black).
Exclusion	Shift+Option+X/ Shift+Alt+X	Uses the darkness of the original layer to mask the Difference effect (described previously). If the original value is dark, there is little change as the result; if the original color is black, there is no change. The lighter the original color, the more intense the Difference effect.
Hue	Shift+Option+U/ Shift+Alt+U	Changes the Hue of the original to the applied while leaving the Saturation and Luminosity unchanged.
Saturation	Shift+Option+T/ Shift+Alt+T	Changes the Saturation of the original to the applied while leaving the Hue and Luminosity unchanged.
Color	Shift+Option+C/ Shift+Alt+C	Changes the Hue and Saturation of the original to the applied while leaving the Luminosity unchanged.
Luminosity	Shift+Option+Y/ Shift+Alt+Y	Changes the Luminosity of the original to the applied while leaving the Saturation and Hue unchanged.

Reader Requests

If you think of anything you'd like to see in a chart or table that would simplify what you do, please make a request on the website or newsletter for the book. If you need it, it can probably prove useful to a lot of people. I'll make requested information available as I can—in many cases with some sort of installer so you can load the information right into Elements (for example, as part of the Tables tab in the Hidden Power tool tabs). Your input is invaluable! I can't guarantee I'll get to everything, but I may have a quick answer to help out.

Newsletter:

Subscribe: hpe-subscribe@yahoogroups.com

Send Message: hpe@yahoogroups.com

Unsubscribe: hpe-unsubscribe@yahoogroups.com

Website:

http://www.hiddenelements.com

Index

Note to the Reader: Page numbers in **bold** indicate the principle discussion of a topic or the definition of a term. Page numbers in *italic* indicate illustrations.

Q

R

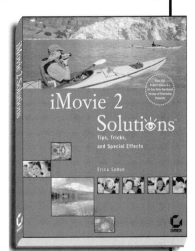
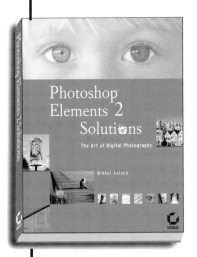

ABOUT SYBEX

Sybex has been part of the personal computer revolution from the very beginning. We were founded in 1976 by Dr. Rodnay Zaks, an early innovator of the microprocessor era and the company's president to this day. Dr. Zaks was involved in the ARPAnet and developed the first published industrial application of a microcomputer system: an urban traffic control system.

While lecturing on a variety of technical topics in the mid-1970s, Dr. Zaks realized there wasn't much available in the way of accessible documentation for engineers, programmers, and businesses. Starting with books based on his own lectures, he launched Sybex simultaneously in his adopted home of Berkeley, California, and in his original home of Paris, France.

Over the years, Sybex has been an innovator in many fields of computer publishing, documenting the first word processors in the early 1980s and the rise of the Internet in the early 1990s. In the late 1980s, Sybex began publishing our first desktop publishing and graphics books. As early adopters ourselves, we began desktop publishing our books in-house at the same time.

Now, in our third decade, we publish dozens of books each year on topics related to graphics, web design, digital photography, and digital video. We also continue to explore new technologies and over the last few years have been among the first to publish on topics like Maya and Photoshop Elements.

With each book, our goal remains the same: to provide clear, readable, skill-building information, written by the best authors in the field—experts who know their topics as well as they know their audience.